PROJECT UNLONELY

PROJECT UNLONELY

HEALING OUR CRISIS OF DISCONNECTION

───────────────○───────────────

JEREMY NOBEL, MD, MPH

AVERY

an imprint of Penguin Random House

New York

AVERY

an imprint of Penguin Random House LLC
penguinrandomhouse.com

Most Avery books are available at special quantity discounts for bulk purchase for sales promotions,
premiums, fundraising, and educational needs. Special books or book excerpts also can be
created to fit specific needs. For details, write SpecialMarkets@penguinrandomhouse.com.

LIBRARY OF CONGRESS CATALOGING-IN-PUBLICATION DATA

Names: Nobel, Jeremy, author.
Title: Project unlonely: healing our crisis of disconnection / Jeremy Nobel, MD, MPH.
Description: New York: Avery, an imprint of Penguin Random House, [2023] | Includes index.
Identifiers: LCCN 2023017185 (print) | LCCN 2023017186 (ebook) |
ISBN 9780593191941 (hardcover) | ISBN 9780593191958 (epub)
Subjects: LCSH: Loneliness. | Social isolation. | Social interaction.
Classification: LCC BF575.L7 N63 2023 (print) |
LCC BF575.L7 (ebook) | DDC 158.2—dc23/eng/20230621
LC record available at https://lccn.loc.gov/2023017185
LC ebook record available at https://lccn.loc.gov/2023017186

Printed in the United States of America
1st Printing

Book design by Laura K. Corless

Dedicated to all of us who blame ourselves for being lonely,
that we may come to see loneliness as the most human of feelings
and a call to creative self-expression and connection

CONTENTS

Contents

1

The Loneliness Crisis

This is not the book I thought I was going to write.

I had begun 2020 with excited anticipation of great things for Project UnLonely, the nonprofit initiative I'd launched in 2016 to address the growing problem of chronic loneliness. Little did we know at Project UnLonely that we were about to enter the loneliest year in modern history.

In March, I was scheduled to speak on a panel at SXSW, the annual South by Southwest conference in Austin, Texas. I'd be sharing the podium with Julianne Holt-Lunstad, one of the foremost researchers on the subject of loneliness and a fellow public health evangelist who'd become a friend in recent years. For months, together with our other panelists, we had been planning our presentations, along with other events we hoped would draw media attention to this urgent social issue. I was also excited to be visiting Austin again, to catch up with some college buddies who are part of Austin's vibrant music scene, and to perhaps find some new friends for our cause among the many thought leaders who converge at SXSW every year. Texas in March is also much warmer than suburban Boston, where I live. I was looking forward to that, too.

April would bring an exciting set of new milestones for Project UnLonely. Thanks to generous grants from the AARP Foundation and the UJA-Federation of New York, we were prepared to launch nine of our "Creativity Circle" workshops for older adults in Illinois, New York, and Maine. By partnering with a variety of community-based organizations in these states, we aimed to demonstrate for the first time at scale the healing power of arts and conversation in bringing people together and encouraging them to stay connected. Also, that month, I had a meeting set with the head of health services at Harvard to discuss the problems of on-campus belonging and connection, and I was scheduled to lead a keynote panel on loneliness at the American Society on Aging's annual conference in Atlanta.

All these plans and many more began unraveling during the pandemic's first week, in March 2020. After Washington State declared a public health emergency on February 29, major SXSW exhibitors pulled out, including Seattle-based Amazon. Our panel discussion, titled "Connecting IRL: The Antidote to Loneliness," was canceled, along with most others. Then, on March 6, the city of Austin announced it was shutting down the entire SXSW conference. No one would be connecting IRL in Austin that year.

The American Society on Aging canceled the Atlanta conference, and my meeting at Harvard was postponed. Then our whole nine-city Creativity Circle project fell apart. One by one, the various hosting organizations notified us they were terminating all in-person programs. The New York sites were first to cancel, then Maine, then Illinois. Our initial hope in April was that these were all mere temporary postponements. But as COVID outbreaks spread throughout the nation and the world, we gradually learned like everyone else to start thinking in new, unfamiliar terms—in terms of utter uncertainty.

A PANDEMIC OF LONELINESS

We are no longer facing the pandemic crisis. We are living in the pandemic era. The post-2020 world remains one of uncertainty and loneliness. The two go together. Uncertainty breeds loneliness in a fairly predictable emotional progression. Any experience of uncertainty makes us feel vulnerable, because if we don't know what's coming, we don't know if we can handle it. Feeling vulnerable in turn leads to anxiety, our biological response to threat. Anxiety tells your body to prepare to fight or flee, to breathe faster and pump more oxygenated blood to your muscles.

In that physical state, anxiety directs our mental focus toward the priority of survival. But we aren't hardwired to endure perpetual anxiety. Anxious minds stuck in survival mode are more concerned with protecting than connecting. Risk-averse minds will avoid human contact when possible. Vulnerability, driven by uncertainty, breeds anxiety, and anxiety breeds loneliness as we go into a defensive crouch and back away from those around us.

These are uncertain and lonely times. COVID-19 has created a vast landscape of trauma for millions of people from loss of work, loss of relationships, and loss of loved ones to the deadly virus. True, we are all weathering the same storm, but as the saying goes, we are not all in the same boat. We are in different boats, and some boats withstand the storm better than others. The experience of loneliness is highly personal and subjective, so the pandemic's reality has allowed some people to find safe harbors, while others are taking on water or slipping beneath the waves.

For some, the increased solitude granted time at home to invest deeply in their most intimate relationships. Many others were lonelier and unhappier than ever. The activities and social rituals that helped give meaning to their lives were gone. Millions were forced to endure agonizing months without seeing close loved ones, and without the everyday interactions that give life its social texture. The comforting hugs at family gatherings, in houses of worship, at birthdays, weddings, and funerals were suddenly unavailable.

The shared storm did not bring us together. The long-simmering grievances over police abuse of lethal force, social inequality, and the vacuum of leadership concerning issues of race exploded in the protests, marches, and riots of 2020. For a wide variety of reasons, the post-2020 world is one of expanding inequality, a terrible real-life social psychology experiment that has created mental health problems for 40 percent of the US population.

Loneliness was already a growing public health crisis before 2020. Now it has taken on a new level of gravity. In the twenty-five years I've been teaching at the Harvard T. H. Chan School of Public Health, most of the developed world has experienced loneliness as a relentlessly expanding public health calamity. It's been well publicized that medical studies show lonely people experiencing as much as a 30 percent greater risk of dying earlier than they otherwise would—the equivalent of smoking fifteen cigarettes a day. Social isolation and loneliness are increasingly recognized among the largest preventable risk factors for depression, suicide, and substance abuse. Research has linked the burden of prolonged loneliness to cancer, dementia, and diabetes and to diseases of the coronary, respiratory, and gastrointestinal systems. Studies in the US, UK, Australia, and elsewhere in Europe and Asia show similar results as loneliness metastasizes in developed societies around the world.

Among middle-aged white working-class Americans, a rising rate of "deaths of despair"—caused by suicide, drug overdoses, and alcoholism—was a major contributor to the decline in US life expectancy in 2021 to its lowest level since 1996. Psychologists studying this phenomenon have identified loneliness as one of the seven cognitive indicators of despair, along with low esteem, "feeling sorry for oneself," and feeling worried, hopeless, helpless, and unloved. Loneliness won't just make you miserable. It can kill you.

Belonging and connection are reliable ways of reducing all seven of the indicators of despair, including loneliness, but loneliness continues to accelerate, especially among certain groups of vulnerable people, including adolescents, young adults, the aged, people with illnesses, and those already marginalized by society due to gender, race, class, financial insecurity, or religious faith. A 2018 study by Cigna revealed that 46 percent of American adults report feeling lonely sometimes or always. In that same study, younger adults reported feeling lonelier than their elders, with those aged between eighteen and twenty-two the loneliest of all. In this new era of uncertainty, there is every reason to think that these groups will continue to be disproportionately impacted, including those who are burdened with the lingering effects of having had COVID or grieving the loss of loved ones due to the pandemic. Two years into the pandemic, surveys showed approximately two-thirds of the US population had experienced loneliness, with one-third experiencing sustained periods of loneliness. (Status and power, by the way, offer little relief: half of all of doctors are lonely, as are half of all CEOs.)

EVERY PANDEMIC HAS A SILVER LINING

That was the dark cloud we at Project UnLonely needed to try to find our way through when the World Health Organization declared a global pandemic on March 11, 2020. The irony wasn't lost on us that our programs for alleviating loneliness had been disrupted amid the largest wave of loneliness the nation had ever experienced.

In the process of adapting to our new circumstances, however, we learned valuable lessons about how to address loneliness in new and compelling ways. So much of our previous work had emphasized the importance of gathering in shared spaces. It wasn't at all obvious that we could meaningfully foster connection online, but for the first time we were motivated to try.

In early April 2020, we put up a website called Stuck at Home (Together), which invited people to visit, post creative work, and respond to the creative work of others, all as ways to share stories and feel connected. We also started offering free "Creative Socials," hourlong group sessions on Zoom during which guest artists and participants made art and discussed their works. These positive experiences gave us hope that we could adapt our in-person workshops for virtual, online participation.

In June, as we began revising our program designs for virtual delivery, we faced countless technical obstacles to doing things online that had been relatively simple in person. Tracking participant feedback is essential in order to measure a program's effectiveness, but achieving the same results via online tools tested the limits of everyone's technical know-how, not to mention their patience.

Then there was the question of our audience for these programs—older adults. How adept were they with computers? Could we get them on Zoom? Here is where we were pleasantly surprised. As we rolled out the first of the virtual Creativity Circles in the fall of 2020, we discovered that most participants were remarkably adept on their computers, and technical assistance for those who weren't was easily arranged. We learned that human connection is both fragile and remarkably resilient. Feelings of connection *can* be conveyed online, provided that the online exchange is a meaningful two-way, authentic, personal conversation. We also learned from the post-program evaluations that in such stressful and lonely times, our participants found the arts compelling and rewarding.

We ultimately discovered something that might have taken us years to learn were it not for the pandemic: virtual programming is ideal for many older adults who have trouble traveling to in-person events. Some can't drive. Others have disabilities that make it painful to get in and out of vehicles and then sit for hours in uncomfortable meeting-room chairs. Still others are caring for a disabled spouse and can't leave their homes. Without the pandemic, our in-person workshops would have excluded these categories of participants, all of whom are contending with difficult circumstances that can intensify feelings of isolation and loneliness.

Perhaps more important, the pandemic provided a unique opportunity to destigmatize loneliness—one of our primary goals at Project UnLonely. As the weeks and months of social distancing dragged on, we began hearing people discuss their loneliness out in the open, as never before. Stigma can make loneliness a shameful secret, increasing its intensity and, in some cases, its lethality. But there is no shame in admitting to the trauma of loneliness when it becomes a problem the entire world is struggling with. The sense of commonality made it OK to acknowledge lonely feelings and attend to them as we would any other ordinary personal need.

Unembarrassed acknowledgment of our loneliness can be a powerful force that unites us in reaching out to each other. But lonely people are often reluctant to admit they're lonely—even to themselves. Our culture idealizes autonomy and self-sufficiency. In a world of seemingly infinite opportunities for connectedness on social media, being unable to find a place for oneself in real life can be upsetting. We fear that being lonely means we are weak, deficient, unattractive, or worthless. And as remote work and virtual meetings have become more common since the pandemic's onset in 2020, our digitally enhanced modern life feeds a nagging sense of disconnection and uncertainty. It's fertile soil for loneliness, which grows wherever there is anxiety and vulnerability that makes us wary of trusting others.

Loneliness is a knotted web. The only way I know how to untangle it is to trace my own path of personal discovery, from my early years fresh out of medical school to today, where addressing the problem of loneliness and seeking solutions from a public health perspective have become a central purpose in my life.

THE PHYSICAL IMPACT OF LONELINESS

I first became aware of the damaging health effects of loneliness as a young primary care physician at Boston's Beth Israel Hospital in the 1980s. During those years, I saw many patients who at first glance seemed unwilling to take proper care of themselves. They skipped taking their prescribed medications or failed to schedule follow-up visits. They weren't "medically adherent," even after long conversations about how to manage their disease and the consequences of not doing so. People with diabetes are regularly cautioned about the grave risks of kidney disease, blindness, and amputation if they are lax in monitoring their blood sugar. Patients with high blood pressure are warned of heart attacks and strokes that can result if they don't keep a watch on it.

What was going on? Occasionally, one of my patients would give me the answer—if I had known to recognize it. I'd enter the exam room and an older man would be sitting there, looking uneasy in his paper medical gown. His chart would tell me his blood pressure was higher than it should have been, given the medications I'd prescribed.

"Are you taking your medicine regularly?" I'd ask.

"No, not always," he'd say. Then he'd make an excuse. "I'm not sure they do any good."

"Your medication is very effective," I'd tell him. "If you take it regularly, you'll feel better and you'll reduce the risk of stroke, heart disease, kidney disease. It's important."

He'd pause, then avert his eyes and look ashamed. Then would come the answer.

"I'm not sure anyone cares about me," he'd stammer. "So why should I care?" He was lonely. But it was worse than that. He was also ashamed that he was lonely. Like guilt, shame is a self-conscious emotion about having done something wrong or having failed. However, shame carries an additional component—a fear of exposure to judgment or ridicule. A lonely person may judge himself harshly for being lonely, and then avoid seeking help because he fears being judged or ridiculed by others.

It often takes connection with others to motivate us to do what's best for us. They offer their encouragement, celebrate our successes with us, and commiserate about the difficulties we face. My lonely patients felt like no one had their back. In some cases, their loneliness was so profound it was a greater threat to their health than their diagnosed illness.

During these exams, I usually asked the set of questions designed to screen for a depression diagnosis, and I prescribed some excellent antidepressant medications. I also wrote into their medical records what we call a "social history" of their responses to questions about spouses, children, relatives, and even pets. I found that many of my patients with severe chronic illnesses were living alone and lacked routine contact with other people. They were socially isolated, but it never occurred to me to ask them if they were lonely. Why? Perhaps because unlike depression, loneliness is not a disease, and there is no course of medical treatment for it. I hadn't been trained to ask if they were lonely, and if I had asked, I wouldn't have known what to do if they'd said yes. If I had even known enough to try to find it in my mental map of medicine's best practices, it would have been labeled "terra incognita."

I was also struck by how many of my patients were struggling with chronic health problems directly related to overeating, smoking, substance abuse, drinking too much, and exercising too little. My medical advice to avoid unhealthy habits was no match for the comforts of tobacco, alcohol, and high-calorie, low-nutrition processed foods. When I would talk to them about improving their diet or reducing their alcohol intake, I noted a stubborn resistance to change, even though they were clearly suffering. Yes, they wished they were healthier, but their indulgences were essential to managing anxiety and stress. Some of them disclosed their anxieties to me regarding their self-worth, often accompanied by the very uncomfortable emotions of guilt and shame.

I had entered primary care imagining I would have long, heartfelt conversations with patients, allowing them to feel a sense of trust that would assist in their treatment. Over time I realized such partnerships rarely happen. It took a number of years for me to fully accept that I was not cut out for practicing primary care medicine, in part because the healthcare system didn't encourage the type of interactions I wanted. I pursued a career in public health instead. While still working part-time in primary care, I earned a master's degree in public health and a second master's degree in epidemiology. In addition, I acquired board certification in preventive medicine with a specialty focus in occupational medicine, the discipline concerned with the maintenance of health in the workplace.

As my understanding of these fields deepened, I grew to appreciate how powerful the illness prevention and health enhancement side of healthcare could be. To help pay off my medical school loans, I took a part-time job in the 1980s analyzing very large insurance claim data sets amassed by Blue Cross Blue Shield of Michigan. By examining the payment records accumulated from millions of doctor visits, treatments, and hospitalizations for workers at Chrysler, Ford, and General Motors, we were able to identify the illnesses that were most common, the cost of treating them, and the doctors and hospitals that delivered the best care. We also had access to detailed data that shed light on the workers' health, including missed work time, disabilities, and life insurance claims that revealed causes of health impairments and death. Our analytics sifted through the data and detected opportunities in which preventive medicine strategies might have the greatest impact.

This was all considered highly innovative at the time. The newly computerized claims systems showed in hard data terms how investments in prevention such as smoking cessation and flu vaccine programs not only reduced sickness and misery for the workers but also lowered company costs, improved worker productivity, and helped carmakers remain a major source of attractive jobs in Michigan.

The experience opened my eyes to the power of using data to drive coordinated preventive health measures. Public health's potential is so great because it leverages resources from beyond the limitations of the medical system. It addresses the totality of health-related considerations within the population of a company, a university, a community, or an entire nation, using tools that can draw on all their considerable assets—operational, financial, and cultural.

THE GIFT OF LONELINESS

Which brings us to the public health impact of loneliness. For many years now, I have sought to address loneliness both as a public health issue and as a challenge to what it means to be a happy, healthy, contributing member of society, to thrive and flourish. Loneliness is not an illness, like diabetes or depression, although it's been implicated as a cause for these and other illnesses. There is no formal medical diagnosis for loneliness, no blood test or biomarker that indicates its presence, and no recommended course of treatment. So how do we make sense of it?

Loneliness is defined by social psychologists as the feeling that there is a gap between the connections we would like to have with other people and what we actually experience. Loneliness is experienced as "something missing." It is a completely subjective feeling. Only you can say that you are lonely. If you feel lonely, you're lonely.

Loneliness can't be measured by counting how many people you are regularly in contact with. The objective state of little or no interaction with others is a different circumstance, often described as social isolation. While isolation can lead to loneliness, it doesn't always. Conversely, we can't protect ourselves from loneliness simply by being around lots of other people. That can lead to feeling "lonely in a crowd," something almost all of us have experienced at one time or another. Similar feelings of loneliness can come from being in a failing marriage, a toxic workplace, or a new city, despite the many people we may cross paths with.

The definition of loneliness, however, still doesn't answer the important question of how we make sense of it, or how we relate to its gnawing discomfort. The most useful way to think about loneliness that I have found is this: Loneliness is a natural biological signal, like hunger or thirst. It is a flashing warning light on our mental dashboards that indicates a problem. Just as the gnawing in our stomachs tells us we should eat, the ache of loneliness tells us we should connect with other people. The late social neuroscientist John Cacioppo proposed in 2014 that feelings of loneliness perform a valuable function for our highly social species. "Just as physical pain is an aversive signal that evolved to motivate one to take action that minimizes damage to one's physical body," he wrote, "loneliness is an aversive state that motivates us to take action that minimizes damage to one's social body."

Gavin de Becker's bestselling *The Gift of Fear* extols the value of our gut instincts, the distress signals that help us avoid physical danger. In a similar way, loneliness is also a gift. Natural selection over millions of years has designed our bodies to send us danger signals when we are deprived of important resources—food, water, *and* reliable connections to others. Think of babies, who are unable to meet their own physiological needs. They cry in response to bodily signals of thirst, cold, hunger, and loneliness. As we grow, we learn to respond appropriately to most of these signals. We drink some water, put on a coat, have a bite to eat. But our danger signals for loneliness are often suppressed by social disapproval. Feelings of loneliness are something you're expected to grow out of, like fear of the dark or of monsters under the bed.

Imagine a society that stigmatizes thirst, cold, or hunger as something shameful that adults shouldn't be feeling. That's what modern society has taught us about our loneliness signals. Repressed feelings always find alternative outlets in human behavior. There are enormously profitable industries devoted to channeling our repressed response to loneliness signals toward food, alcohol, video games, TV, gambling, pornography, and any number of other sensation-seeking diversions. Modern life is a loneliness engine, a machine that converts our discomfort into behavioral, attitudinal, and physical changes. We are only now beginning to add up the engine's cost in human suffering, lost productivity, medical expense, and social instability.

Kendall Palladino, today the director of spiritual care at Yale New Haven Hospital, tells a story about when he met Mother Teresa in 1994. At the time, Kendall was a seminary student doing volunteer work at her Missionaries of Charity hospice in Calcutta. He was eager to tell Mother Teresa of his plans to attend medical school and then travel to developing countries to treat people with leprosy. Mother Teresa's surprising response, he says, changed the course of his life. "Why do you want to do that?" she asked him. "There is a poverty in your country that is just as severe as our poorest of the poor." She told him, "In the West there is a loneliness, which I call the leprosy of the West. In many ways, it is worse than our poor in Calcutta."

The conditions Mother Teresa so keenly observed in 1994 have only gotten worse since then. We need to take stock of the long-term implications if we fail to recognize loneliness as one of the world's most important public health problems. Growing feelings of disconnection from ourselves and others, especially for those already marginalized, will greatly accelerate the already rising rates of addiction, depression, and suicidality while also increasing the prevalence and lethality of heart disease, diabetes, and dementia. We will die earlier and more miserably, and this sicker society of the future will find its institutions sicker, too. Workplaces, schools, and communities will face a growing crisis of civility as they lose the capability to resolve differences and solve problems cooperatively. Economic growth will be stunted because the profitable exchange of goods and services has always depended on social capital and the ability of people to establish shared visions and take calculated risks for the prospect of mutual gain.

When you consider the power of today's media—social and otherwise—to enrich their shareholders by dividing and isolating members of our society, you can recognize the enormous forces we are up against. Seventy-five years ago, when radio was the most advanced form of mass media available, political philosopher Hannah Arendt saw the exploitation of mass media as the goal of every totalitarian leader, in order to create legions of isolated and lonely citizens who are easy to manipulate.

In free societies, we see orchestration of mass isolation being hailed perversely by social media manipulators as the inevitable result of freedom of choice in the marketplace of ideas. Studies have shown that inflammatory misinformation on Facebook, often amplified by troll farms backed by hostile foreign governments, got six times more engagement (and therefore earned much more advertising revenue) than posts shared by reputable news sources. An internal Facebook document obtained by *MIT Technology Review* showed that "in the run-up to the 2020 election, the most highly contested in US history, Facebook's most popular pages for Christian and Black American content were being run by Eastern European troll farms."

Filled with divisive misinformation, the foreign troll farm content reached 140 million US users per month because Facebook's content-recommendation system had pushed their messages into users' feeds. Similar misinformation later spread about the COVID-19 vaccines, prompting millions of people to put their health at risk by avoiding vaccinations.

Andrew Bosworth, chief technology officer of Facebook's parent company, Meta, claimed in a 2021 interview that if social media users want to share inflammatory and unreliable information on Facebook, "that's their choice. . . . They are allowed to do that. You have an issue with those people. You don't have an issue with Facebook. You can't put that on me."

That's the world that awaits us if we do nothing at this critical time. It's a world in which intentionally or not, social media companies and their advertisers make millions of people angrier, more fearful, more anxious, sicker, and lonelier. And it's not just big tech. Inside every democratic society, there are economic and political forces that enable new ways to exploit disconnection and isolation for profit and power and use mass loneliness exactly as Hannah Arendt had predicted so many years ago, in ways that weaken society from within.

So what do we do? Where do we begin? How do we reconnect with our loneliness signals amid all this noise? Do we have it in us to recognize loneliness as a gift handed down from our ancestors, as a useful reminder that we experience our full humanity in the company of other humans? How do we learn to read our loneliness signals as helpful messages received from our inner selves? How do we learn to tune in to these signals as we would a radio signal, seeking timely and valuable information? How can we respond through productive actions that build pathways for self-knowledge, inspiration, and growth?

And if we locate this gift for ourselves, how can we share it? How can we invite others to awaken a constructive awareness of their own loneliness? How can we advocate for a society that inspires and supports productive engagement with loneliness, instead of one that profits from the pain of suppressing it?

Public health campaigns succeed whenever a social consensus forms around this kind of shared idealistic goal. It is how seat belt laws were passed, how drunk-driving deaths have been reduced, and how the unhealthy habit of cigarette smoking (not so long ago a widely accepted social norm) has been all but eradicated from every public place in the US and other developed countries. My main reason for writing this book is to raise awareness of loneliness to this level. I mentioned studies have shown that loneliness can be as dangerous to your health as smoking fifteen cigarettes a day, and we know how to get people off cigarettes. Now let's help them be less lonely.

Throughout these pages, there are many, many hopeful signs that point to how we can avoid this grim future. As you read, consider how you respond to your own pangs of loneliness. If you can acknowledge that loneliness is as natural and common a human experience as thirst or feeling cold, you can take a fresh look at your habitual responses to your loneliness signals. You can explore new and imaginative ways to engage with the world, and discover where in your life it would be healthier and more fulfilling to respond with activities based on creativity and connection.

My hope is that by the time you reach the final pages, you will have transformed your understanding of what it means to be lonely, what it means to be creative, and what it means to be connected—to be UnLonely. As I'll show, all three are central to our questions of what it means to be human, how we can share our unique selves with others, and how we can celebrate our common humanity.

2

The Power of Creative Expression

My personal route to studying loneliness has been a circuitous one. It began in 2002, with a children's art show in New York.

The death and destruction wrought by the 9/11 terror attacks had a traumatizing effect on New York City's schoolchildren, especially those whose homes and schools were located near the World Trade Center. In the weeks and months following the disaster, many children in New York were afraid to ride on public transit or even go outside. Psychologists invited into the schools saw all the symptoms of an acute trauma response in the children: difficulty concentrating, trouble sleeping, and withdrawn silence punctuated by outbursts of anger or weeping. Many students resisted discussing their feelings and didn't want to talk about 9/11 at all.

The breakthrough came when children of all ages, up through high school, were encouraged to express what they'd seen and experienced that day through art. Using pencil, crayon, paint, and photo collages, they created thousands of stunning personal visions of sadness, anger, pain, and confusion—and also hope and resilience. The children who couldn't discuss their feelings were glad to discuss their art. And in doing so, they were able to work through their trauma and begin their recovery.

"Children and artists have ready access to the imagination, enabling them to express the fantastic, inconceivable, or unspoken," wrote Robin F. Goodman, an art therapist and child psychologist. "We want children to know that their voices are important, and that art is an extraordinary way to give voice to concern. We want adults to see what children may not put into words."

On the one-year anniversary of the attacks, a collection of the children's pictures was put on display at the Museum of the City of New York. I came across a news account of the exhibit and found myself deeply moved by the accompanying illustrations. Eight-year-old Kevin Wang drew the twin towers made of hearts, with the hearts at the tops of the towers scattering and floating up toward the heavens. Ten-year-old Abbey Bender drew a self-portrait wearing the iconic "I Heart NY" T-shirt. She drew her dog beside her with a thought bubble over the dog's head: "More than ever!" Sixteen-year-old Rejwan Ahmed drew a somber self-portrait looking off in the distance, with the smoking towers in the background. He called his work *A New World*.

These images aroused powerful feelings within me, as strong a response as I'd had to any visual art I'd ever seen. I felt a connection to these young artists through their work. Their pain, hope, and determination reflected my own complex feelings in the aftermath of 9/11. At the time, I had become once again deeply engaged with writing poetry, after years of neglecting it. I'd written a lot of poetry during my college and med school years, in fact, right through my medical residency training, and I'd even won some awards for it. In the following years, I'd put poetry mostly aside as if it were just another youthful indulgence. Twenty years afterward, I found that the shared trauma of the terror attacks, along with their personal impact, had stimulated creative urges within me, something that I assumed had been long lost in my past. I dug up poems written years earlier, edited them, grouped them together around specific aspects of loss, and shared them with close friends. Their generous responses were encouraging, so I kept at it, writing fresh poems in response to the new realities of loss and vulnerability that I and others were facing.

I also had a profound professional reaction to the 9/11 children's art project. There was one particularly intriguing public health implication about it that caught my attention. Art had helped these children process their trauma, regardless of their race and socioeconomic status. When a medical treatment shows benefits across the lines of race and class, it's reasonable to assume that there is an underlying biological mechanism accountable for that therapy's effectiveness. Something important was going on in these children's brains when they made art, something that relieved their stress disorders and restored their mental well-being. It occurred to me that if these biological mechanisms could be better understood, the resulting insights could be used to design new art-related public health programs for trauma recovery.

When I shared the children's art with friends and professional colleagues, many of them responded by choking up or crying. It was as if these powerful images had pried open something sealed up inside them. They struggled to find words for why the children's art had made them so emotional. When I apologized for upsetting them, most told me no apology was necessary, that the images made them feel better. Some kind of important and impactful information was being exchanged through their engagement with these simple pictures. I had a growing feeling that I was onto something, although I wasn't sure what.

The field of art therapy was founded in 1942, and years of study refined its varied approaches in all the related "expressive therapies" involving music, drama, movement, poetry, and expressive writing. As I read the literature, I found there was very strong empirical evidence that these therapies were highly effective for the purpose of psychological healing. But in biological terms, there seemed to be no explanation for *why* expressive therapies are effective. I could not find a definitive neurophysiologic mechanism that explained why expressive therapies have healing effects. (This was twenty years ago, when the field of functional MRI scanning to identify specific regions of brain activity was in its infancy.) I also found that these therapies are typically reserved for treating individual patients as a complement to their other psychological or physical therapies. I saw nothing in the public health literature showing how expressive therapies could be adapted to reduce the risk for illnesses both physical and mental, to make people more resilient, to allow them to thrive and flourish. In short, could these innovative and intriguing approaches be used to improve community health and well-being when offered at scale?

To explore this question further, however, I had a difficult choice to make. The arts and health research I was doing up to that point was something of a hobby. It wasn't consistent with any of the work I was doing at Harvard or at any of the organizations I was advising on digital health technologies. If I truly wanted to define and develop new public health roles for art and other expressive therapies, I'd have to take the work outside my familiar world of academe, medicine, and health systems. After consulting with some good friends in the field, I decided to create a new nonprofit, the Foundation for Art & Healing

(FAH). Through FAH, I could serve as an advocate for broader use of the arts as a powerful health-enhancing brain activity and help build a strong case for funding new research to identify the underlying mechanisms of art's healing power. From a public health perspective, I saw that if we could identify the physiological benefits of these brain-changing activities more clearly, it would help us make a case for effective and scalable public health interventions that put them to use. I also knew that better understanding of the basic science wouldn't be enough. We would need to do what is regarded as translational research to make the intersectional achievements of arts and health accessible to all who might benefit. We needed to develop new knowledge that would take our findings from "bench to bedside to Main Street."

In its initial years, FAH had no employees. It was just me, a small board made up of supportive friends, and a few terrific artists I knew for whom the work resonated deeply. One small project at a time, we drew in people from the arts and medicine who rarely got the chance to interact. We explored the important work being done to integrate creative arts expression into the treatment of post-traumatic stress disorder (PTSD) among active-duty service members and veterans returning from the wars in Iraq and Afghanistan. We also partnered with the Jewish Community Center of San Francisco to launch an Art and Healing series of evening events with notable artists who shared their creative work and discussed how it could improve health and well-being. Then in 2011, I met a remarkable artist named Robbie McCauley.

Robbie is an Obie Award–winning playwright and actor who had written a one-woman show called *Sugar*, a largely autobiographical account of her experiences as a Black woman with type 1 diabetes. She told me how she used a political consciousness-raising technique called "story circles" to help her write the script for the show. She had invited groups of other Black women with diabetes to gather in a circle and, one by one, share their stories about living with the disease. She later incorporated portions of their stories into her script.

Robbie had a question for me. Before engaging in the story circles, she had always struggled to manage her diabetes and experienced frequent spikes in her blood sugar levels. Afterward, however, her illness felt more manageable, and she had far fewer blood sugar spikes.

"I don't know what's going on," she said. "But I can just tell you, I've measured my blood sugar, and it's under much better control since doing the story circles and now, working on the play. Why do you think that happened?"

I admitted I didn't know. But I promised to find out and get back to her with an answer. I contacted one of the senior physicians I had met during my medical residency, Alan Moses, who had since become chief medical officer at Novo Nordisk, one of the pharmaceutical industry's leaders in the research and treatment of diabetes. Alan suspected that Robbie's experience might have been related to the hormone cortisol, which is released in the body in response to stress. High levels of cortisol interfere with fat and carbohydrate metabolism, causing blood sugar to spike.

In Alan's opinion, it was likely that the story circle process exerted such a strong calming effect on Robbie that her body's production of cortisol was reduced, helping stabilize her blood sugar. As Robbie established a meaningful sense of connection with people struggling with similar challenges, her body responded to the emotional signals that she was *safe*. Her body reduced its cortisol production because she was no longer in a lonely state of threat.

Now I had a question for Robbie. Could she help me test an idea that she had put into my head? I consulted with her and with Vivien Marcow Speiser, a noted expressive arts therapist from Lesley University, to develop a six-session support program, our very first Creativity Circle program. We added creative expression to the traditional story circle model, along with some custom-designed features to support women with diabetes. A chance encounter at Boston's Logan International Airport with Andrew Dreyfus, CEO of Blue Cross Blue Shield of Massachusetts (BCBSMA), a professional colleague whom until then I had only talked with about rising healthcare costs, led to an energetic conversation on arts and health and ultimately a collaboration to explore it through funding from BCBSMA's foundation. Then, with the help of Dr. James Rosenzweig, who ran the diabetes treatment services at Boston Medical Center (BMC), we launched a small study to see whether what had happened for Robbie McCauley would happen for others. The BMC diabetes center invited twelve middle-aged, lower-income Black women with poorly controlled diabetes to be part of the study. All of them agreed to visit the center once a week for six weeks and participate in two-hour creative circle storytelling sessions that also included some mindfulness meditation and creative art making.

Each of the dozen women showed up in BMC's ambulatory care center's conference room for the first session and came to every one of the following sessions. That was a remarkable result in and of itself, because studies like this almost never achieve perfect attendance! At the start of the first session, and again at the end of the last session, we had a team of interviewers administer a portfolio of physical and mental health surveys, diabetes coping scales, and patient engagement measures.

The results showed that after just six weeks, there was a statistically significant improvement in participants' mental health as well as a dramatically improved feeling of an ability to manage their illness. And when we interviewed the women on the final day of the study, many of them spontaneously rejoiced in how the experience had eased their loneliness.

"We shared stories of pain, sorrow, good times, funny moments," a participant named Diana told her interviewer. "It felt good knowing that I was not the only one who would sneak a piece of cake or forget to take my meds. That gave me strength to help myself and not see myself as a failure." She felt sad that the program was over but hopeful about maintaining the human connection formed through the creative circles. "I pray that we will all be together soon to check up on each other and to continue to share our good times and our many bad times that diabetes has offered us."

For Diana, the creative circles achieved something that she had struggled with on her own. Being a part of a creative group gave her a new perspective on her illness. It gave her confidence she could deal with her illness more effectively, and it reduced her self-judgment when she failed. Six sessions had made her both healthier and less lonely.

PROJECT UNLONELY

Robbie's and Diana's stories help illustrate the three ways that loneliness can kill. Physiologically, the stress of loneliness increases cortisol levels, impairs the immune system's capabilities, and increases inflammation, all of which directly raise the risk of premature death from cardiovascular illness, cancer, dementia, and diabetes.

Psychologically, loneliness can lower one's self-regard and consequently the motivation for self-care, which raises the risk of habitual self-neglect, including the abandonment of positive behaviors like a healthy diet, exercise, getting enough sleep, and sticking with a medication schedule.

Behaviorally, loneliness rather ironically stifles social interaction with others, which exacerbates the first two effects but adds one that is perhaps even more pernicious. People lacking reliable human connection in a community or social network lose the "safety net" function of having attentive people around who care about them, who will ask if they're well and offer comfort and assistance if they're not.

In 2015, a groundbreaking study called "Loneliness and Social Isolation as Risk Factors for Mortality: A Meta-analytic Review" was published by Brigham Young University's Julianne Holt-Lunstad (my future co-presenter at the canceled 2020 SXSW panel). The paper caught my attention because it so clearly established the *medical* impact of loneliness. Julianne's analysis of 148 studies of mortality risk, involving a total of more than three hundred thousand people, concluded that people without strong social relationships were roughly 30 percent more likely to die prematurely than socially connected people, controlling for age, sex, health status, illness, and cause of death. The lack of social relationships was comparable in importance with other well-established risk factors for an early demise, such as smoking, sedentary lifestyle, and obesity.

That's when the full picture of loneliness as a public health crisis came into sharp focus for me. It's the picture of a vicious cycle, one in which loneliness contributes to making us physically ill and induces us to neglect ourselves and our illnesses, which in turn isolates us from those who could help us get well, deepening our loneliness and putting us at ever greater risk of illness.

At the same time, at FAH we were finding how creative expression can ignite a virtuous cycle in the opposite direction. Sharing your story through creative expression has the power to restore your sense of self-regard, support your habits of self-care, and bring you closer to others who can lend you further support for your well-being.

In May 2016, the FAH board approved my proposal to launch Project UnLonely as our signature initiative. By then it felt obvious to me that FAH was in a unique position to promote the convergence of creative expression and healing to address the growing epidemic of loneliness that few people were even talking about.

We established three goals for Project UnLonely. The first was to increase visibility and awareness of loneliness and its toxicity. The second was to reduce its stigma. We knew we could use the arts as a vehicle for achieving both goals. As one example, in 2017, with the help of Michael Paseornek, then president of Lionsgate film productions, we introduced the annual UnLonely Film Festival (UFF), a curated online platform for short films on the theme of loneliness. Unlike a typical weeklong film festival like Tribeca or Sundance, ours is a public health awareness platform, designed to run all year and make powerful, award-winning short films on loneliness available 24-7 at no charge. Films stream along with short educational videos and discussion prompts to invite viewers to engage more deeply. With Mike's ongoing support as public cheerleader, adviser, and judge, we've reached hundreds of thousands of viewers, harnessing the expressive power of film to bring compelling messages of connection and the importance of belonging into conference rooms, classrooms, and living rooms around the world.

The third goal of Project UnLonely was to design and distribute effective programming. The promising results from the Creativity Circle sessions we had developed for diabetes persuaded us it was a model that we could adapt to other conditions and circumstances with elevated risks of loneliness. Our years of prior work with the arts in treating illness and trauma had demonstrated the healing powers of telling your story and sharing some important aspect of who you are through creative expression. If we could use creative expression to ease the stress of loneliness, we could help people feel better and then become healthier through changes in their brains, bodies, and behaviors and through their networks of relationships.

It's important to note that when we discuss creative expression, we're not primarily interested in improving people's artistic skills. The benefits of creative expression don't require you to try to be another Van Gogh, nor is this practice limited to the visual arts. Creative expression can come in the form of a story or a script or a poem, a garden or a garment, a cake or an architectural model, a wood carving or a quilt, photos or film, a tapestry, a mosaic, or a stone fence. The alleviation of loneliness occurs in the biology of creation, in the dynamic intersection of memory, imagination, and making that lends authenticity to self-expression, which results in the experience of being witnessed and seen. We are all born with the gift of creative expression, and we enjoy its benefits by exercising the creative instincts that nature has granted us.

THE LONELY SELF

For many lonely people, a primary source of their disconnection from others is their broken connection with their inner selves. When we feel lost to ourselves or inside ourselves, for whatever reason, making a connection with others feels fraudulent, elusive, or impossible. That's why for lonely people a party or a crowd can feel like a very lonely situation. Social isolation can contribute to loneliness, but it's not the same thing as loneliness, because you can be very lonely and not at all socially isolated. That's why "Get out more and see more people" is a facile remedy that doesn't help most people suffering from chronic loneliness. Conversely, you can be socially isolated and *not* feel lonely. For some people, their needs for human connection can be satisfied with relatively little time spent with others.

People who aren't lonely tend to have intimate relationships with friends and family that help them maintain a healthy sense of self. Strong religious beliefs, meaningful work, serving others in selfless ways, and the practice of meditation are all associated with maintaining a similar connection. We have found that artistic expression of any kind, especially when preceded by a brief session of mindful meditation or activity, is a powerful tool for reconnecting with oneself. Then, through personal sharing and conversation, it provides a path to connect with others.

The act of creative or artistic expression involves a set of specific activities, each involving mental processes that foster this connection. First, the making of any type of art requires you to be fully present in the moment and to fully activate your imagination. In the act of creation, your imagination operates as a gateway between your conscious and unconscious mind, allowing what's otherwise inaccessible within you to emerge, to be engaged with and expressed. To achieve that, you must attain a level of focus that, similar to mindfulness meditation, allows you to access your imagination, probe your full range of thoughts and feelings, and reconnect with your essential self.

Then there is the resulting artifact—the drawing, painting, sculpture, poem, dance move, or garden planting—the palpable manifestation that conveys something unique and authentic about you, the maker, to yourself and to any observer. Finally, if your work of creative expression is shared with others, considered, and appreciated, you feel seen, recognized, witnessed, and accompanied. Through this authentic disclosure of who you are, you make a specific kind of connection that is difficult to achieve, especially in the modern vortex of inattention, distraction, and anonymity.

The poet Pablo Neruda once wrote an essay in which he described the intimacy and meaning of interpersonal exchange. He recalled how, as a child, he once traded a fragrant pinecone for a toy sheep with a neighbor boy he didn't know. The exchange was made through a hole in the fence that separated their two backyards. "To feel the intimacy of brothers is a marvelous thing in life," Neruda wrote. "To feel the love of people whom we love is a fire that feeds our life. But to feel affection that comes from those whom we do not know, from those unknown to us, who are watching over our sleep and solitude, over our dangers and our weaknesses—that is something still greater and more beautiful because it widens out the boundaries of our being and unites all living things."

To me this describes the essence of creative connection, in which what has been made is not only shared but received. It is what allows others to see themselves in us and us in them. The celebrated poet Edward Hirsch, who is also the president of the Guggenheim Foundation, was the one who brought Neruda's powerful story to my attention. He told me in an interview that the moment of simultaneous sharing and receiving of creative expression between two individuals is like "an electric circuit being completed and both people are connected." It's an exchange that lets our electricity flow, allows the lights of empathy and compassion to burn brightly, and illuminates our fundamental human connection.

The link between art and social connection is so powerful that there is some evidence that merely appreciating art, even while sitting all by yourself, can make you feel more socially connected. Recent studies of brain scans by Dutch neuroscientist Janneke van Leeuwen (who is also a visual artist) show that in the brain-processing activities required to interpret works of visual art, blood flow in the brain utilizes the same brain regions that influence our social interactions. The implication of this research is that art has a specific biological function: to help us make sense of our social world, to help us assess signals of threats and opportunities, and to prompt our social responses. If this is true, then it could be that any involvement with art and creative expression prompts the brain to construct mental models that make it easier to connect with other people.

For chronically lonely people, then, creative expression can provide a safe and attractive pathway back to connection. It doesn't require them to examine why they've become lonely. It doesn't demand that they make changes in their social habits to quell their loneliness. Creative expression simply prompts them to connect with their inner selves and then make creative choices for no other reason than the satisfying pleasures of playful exploration. The mere act of engaging with art stimulates their social brain activity, making them feel more inclined to share themselves with others.

Children are at a distinct advantage when it comes to enjoying these benefits of creativity, because almost all children are reflexively creative and eager to share. Their artistry is often drawn from their innocence and free-spirited expression. By nature, they are less self-conscious than adults, and less bound by the limitations of doubt and negativity. And as a culture, we celebrate the creativity of children. Back in 2002, I learned of the 9/11 children's art exhibit at the Museum of the City of New York only because it had created such a stir in the media. The exhibit even went on to land a book deal: *The Day Our World Changed: Children's Art of 9/11.*

Can you imagine an exhibit of works by nonartist adults drawing that kind of attention? Of course not. Just as we're expected to get over our feelings of loneliness when we become adults, most of us are compelled while growing up to surrender our childlike impulse to create. During our adolescent years in particular, our creativity is either nurtured if we show talent or squelched if we do not. We become very sensitive to other people's judgments during those years. I still have a vivid memory of my older sister hearing me sing and telling me I sounded terrible. It took decades for me to enjoy singing again, and even now I feel a bit self-conscious about it.

As we grow up, unless we excel in the arts or receive special encouragement, we tend to leave them to artists as a practical division of labor, the way we leave law to lawyers and banking to bankers. I've come to believe that for most people this is a terrible loss. Human beings don't outgrow their need to create any more than they outgrow their need for food, water, and human connection.

I believe we must begin to include creative expression throughout the life span, if only for the pure joy of it, the same way millions continue to play sports after childhood, even though they are not professional athletes. They play because it's fun and because it's good for their physical and mental health. Millions more adults need to create and share their creations for the same reasons—as an intrinsically enjoyable activity that supports their physical and mental well-being.

How do we get there? An accurate diagnosis of any problem is the first step. Most of us have an insufficient understanding of what loneliness actually is. In fact, there are many different types of loneliness, rooted in a wide variety of human experiences. In order to grapple with loneliness and to break away from common misperceptions surrounding it, you need to understand it in more nuanced ways and to recognize exactly what kind of loneliness you are feeling.

3

Our Loneliness Heritage

In 2019, I gave an early morning talk on loneliness at a senior center in Manhattan. Every seat in the hall was filled, though I suspect that the offer of a free hot breakfast might have been a bigger draw than I was. During the Q&A session that followed my talk, an older woman named Mary raised her hand. "You know," she said, "I come to these lecture events because people tell me it's a way to get out and meet people. But you just gave this whole talk about loneliness, and it did no good. I'm still lonely."

Mary choked up on the word *lonely* and then started crying. The people seated nearby rushed to comfort her. Some wrote out their phone numbers and asked her to call them. It was a touching moment that illustrates the power of vulnerability. Mary had divulged something personal and painful about herself, and the total strangers around her responded with empathy and concern. A simple, sincere statement of need, uncomfortable as it may have been for Mary, allowed her to "show up" more clearly for the others in the room, who immediately connected with her.

My response to Mary that morning was to first acknowledge how rarely we even name the problem for what it is: loneliness; the absence of what we are thirsty for. It's as if in even speaking the word out loud, we confirm our own worst fears of our deep and shameful inadequacy. Instead, we sidle up to the topic, saying, "I wish I had more friends," or even "It would be nice to go out more." When we *do* muster up the courage to mutter to others, "I'm lonely," in response we often hear very simplistic prescriptions for curing loneliness: get a pet, join a book club, volunteer at a senior center. These are all conceivably good things to do, but they don't necessarily address the underlying causes of chronic loneliness. The activities themselves are not an answer. How we engage in them makes all the difference.

If our engagement with others amounts to fleeting moments with people who remain strangers, that won't address our core loneliness issues. If we seek out the company of others simply to avoid being alone, we can come away from such experiences feeling even lonelier than before. The shame of loneliness can lead you to feeling very lonely in a crowd.

At the same time, being alone is not the same as loneliness. We even have a high-class word for it: *solitude*. You can live alone, with very limited engagement with others, and not be lonely at all. You can be very satisfied by your few connections, however sparse. Religious hermits, for example, are comforted by the presence of God. And when Henry David Thoreau was asked if he was lonesome living at Walden Pond, his reply was, "I am no more lonely than the loon in the pond that laughs so loud, or than Walden Pond itself. What company has that lonely lake, I pray?" This sentiment reflected the Enlightenment belief that solitude in nature brings one closer to God, while associating with others in society is the source of all evil and corruption. "God is alone," Thoreau wrote in *Walden*, "but the devil, he is far from being alone; he sees a great deal of company; he is legion."

The common confusion between loneliness and spending time alone often hinders our ability to communicate our experiences of loneliness or do something about it. Loneliness is broadly defined as the uncomfortable feeling of a perceived gap between the connections we want with others and the connections we feel we have. The definition leaves a lot to be desired because the perception of such a gap can be manifested in different ways.

Classifying experiences of loneliness into different types is as important as distinguishing, for example, various types of love. In English we use the word *love* for a lot of different things. We have romantic love, love of family, love of friends, love of humankind. When we see the concept of love described in these four distinctive ways, it's easier for us to appreciate the unique properties of each form of love. And so it is with the language of loneliness.

The typology of loneliness that I've come to rely on divides the experience into three distinct categories: psychological loneliness, societal loneliness, and existential loneliness. Each one feels very different, although they are often confused with one another. Each one manifests differently, and although people frequently experience more than one type of loneliness at a time, each requires a distinct approach when we attempt to address and alleviate it.

Psychological loneliness is what most people describe when asked if they are lonely. It is the experience of wishing someone else was there, a specific someone, a warm and fuzzy flesh-and-blood person they can feel reliably and authentically connected to. It is marked by a longing for an authentic connection to another person, someone to trust and tell your troubles to, someone who has your back in anxious times, someone to care about. Not to be confused with "alone time," "me time," or solitude—all experiences that can be sources of calm, inspiration, focus, or rejuvenation—psychological loneliness is an uncomfortable state of being, tinged with negative emotions, perhaps sadness, fear, shame, regret, anger, guilt, or self-doubt.

Often, people suffering from psychological loneliness are fearful of developing these kinds of intimate relationships. Their attachments to others are somehow inadequate, insecure, or unstable. Many who suffer from psychological loneliness are around other people all day. Their problem is that there is no one among all those people whom they truly trust or can confide in. Someone who is very popular and has many friends may still feel desperately lonely if they have a psychological fear of opening up emotionally to any one of those friends.

---○ PROFILE: **Psychological Loneliness**

"I don't feel very much like Pooh today," said Pooh.

"There, there," said Piglet. "I'll bring you tea and honey until you do." —A. A. MILNE

Pete is a freshman. Captain of his high school soccer team, he decided last minute not to play in college so he could focus on being premed. All the guys on his hall are on the soccer team. They're nice, but they travel as a pack from practice to meals to the gym; then they disappear to away games and tournaments two nights a week and all weekend. Pete's alone again in his room on a Saturday night, scrolling through his high school friends' Insta photos. They're all crushing the transition. His parents are college sweethearts who still get together every year with their college friends. He doesn't want to be the one to break it to them that college is not the time of his life. Pete has noted more than once the tragic irony of his high school yearbook having named him "The Friend I'd Most Like to Have."

We can experience psychological loneliness in a room full of people, including "friends." None of them happens to be the "best friend," partner, or family member—a person with whom we feel accepted and loved for who we are deep down, the person with whom we are longing to connect. This longing is innate, with us from infancy. Some of us may remember satisfying early longings with an imaginary best friend or a transitional object—a blankie, binky, or teddy that we cuddled to comfort ourselves, easing the feelings of disorientation and anxiousness from missing the warm glow of parental attention.

Research in psychology on what's known as attachment theory also illuminates this aspect of loneliness. We are born dependent on others, particularly our mother, for survival, and learn and develop through attachment, which may have its early origins in infant development, with various long-lasting effects on our psyche, personality, and nervous system. The unhealed trauma of a dysfunctional upbringing, followed by subsequent traumas and negative experiences in adult life, can damage a person's ability to create and sustain healthy human connections. Eventually, the dull pain of chronic psychological loneliness can seem preferable to the acute pain of bad relationship experiences. Someone with psychological loneliness may even feel threatened by the idea that they need to connect with other people, backing off even further.

The second kind of loneliness, **societal loneliness**, is the overwhelming sense of not fitting in or belonging, of being systemically excluded. It's the experience of being uninvited or rejected by either a peer group, work colleagues, neighbors, or society at large.

Societal loneliness can be envisioned through the questions often on the minds of those who experience it. As I imagine entering a room full of people, am I welcome? Is my arrival anticipated? Do I fit in? Will I be safe? With psychological loneliness we might ask, "Where are my people?" With societal loneliness we ask, "Where is my seat at the table?"

PROFILE: **Societal Loneliness**

I'm not antisocial. The society is anti-me. —ANONYMOUS

Yolanda is the first in her family to go to college. They gave her a huge send-off. The care package her aunties packed was still warm when she overheard her suite-mate complaining about the savory smell and snuck it out to the dumpster. She actually likes all of her suite-mates a lot—she would've loved to go to the concert with them if she'd had the money. She's not about to complain about her lack of pocket money to her mama or her older sister, who worked five jobs between them so Yolanda herself wouldn't have to work and could instead focus on her homework in high school. She pushes up her glasses and rereads her class assignment for the fifth time, glad no one else is counting. She prays every night to get through the next four years before someone realizes it was a mistake she got in.

The experience may be the result of overt exclusion, including bullying, discrimination, and rejection. It may be the by-product of a change in circumstances, unique trauma, or the very real subjective experience based on an unverifiable internal assessment that "I am not welcome here." And just as frequently, it is the internal response to verified micro- or blatant aggressions, based on wide-ranging social norms of gender, race, sexuality, ability, body shape—the list, sadly, goes on and on.

This form of loneliness burdens the individual with a different and harder-to-relate-to stigma. Psychological loneliness, the longing for another, more readily engenders sympathy or empathy on the part of a confidant. Talking about societal loneliness can amount to tattling or, on a deeper level, a less congenial soul-baring. For individuals lacking a confidant, to say nothing of a social network, such conversations are less likely to occur, exacerbating the associated negative health consequences. The negative emotions and thoughts springing from societal loneliness can be as lethal as other forms of loneliness or a precursor or accelerant to depression or substance abuse, or even morph into suicidal ideation.

Sociologists point out that groups naturally bond in part by defining who is excluded from them. Although exclusion is sometimes done with purpose and cruelty, it's also a group dynamic that can be exercised unconsciously by group members, driven by the common suspicion of those who are strange or different from us. Some of us perpetuate that in guidance of our children, albeit in a well-intended effort to make them safe, asking them to recall the phrase "stranger danger" when encountering someone they don't know.

Intended or not, exclusion puts the excluded person at risk of feeling this kind of loneliness. Many people experience this kind of societal loneliness when they may most want and need to foster connection, such as in a new school, workplace, or community. On a societal level, all forms of discrimination and bias inflict feelings of loneliness on those who are different due to race, gender, religion, sexual orientation, nationality, or disability, or merely because they don't conform to social norms for attractiveness or personal behavior. Societal loneliness is prevalent in the psychologies of many of the socially awkward loners who perpetrate mass shootings. Taken to scale, this type of loneliness is the hallmark of institutionalized racism or any other systemic and prevailing prejudicial or exclusionary bias.

Existential loneliness, the third kind, might also be called spiritual loneliness. This loneliness is part of the human condition. It arises from the fundamental mystery of life and its meaning on a planet Carl

Sagan once called "a lonely speck in the great enveloping cosmic dark." You may feel connected intimately to others, but something is still missing. We aren't born with the answers to questions such as, Where did I come from? Why are we here? Do we connect to what was here before us, to what will be here after we depart? Do we have a mission and purpose that connects us to the universal? Do we matter? Do our lives have consequence? Where do I fit in? Psychological loneliness can overlap with and feed existential loneliness. If you lack connection with people, you are at elevated risk of losing connection with yourself and with meaning in your life.

PROFILE: **Existential Loneliness**

He who has a why to live for can bear almost any how.
—FRIEDRICH NIETZSCHE

Marilyn has lived alone for years, and she prefers it that way. She and her husband fledged the kids and enjoyed some golden years before he passed in his sleep, just inches away. It sounds creepy, but it's how they both had told each other they wanted to go. Her children are grown and are busy with work and children of their own. They have moved far away and she doesn't hear from them very often. Her husband is gone, and so are her two siblings. Her arthritis bothers her every day and she knows it will only get worse with time. Marilyn's fridge magnet reads, "So many books, so little time," but she would be the first to tell you, a book is not going to make you get out of bed. She has little to look forward to in her declining years, has no expectation of an afterlife, and worries about whether her money would run out if she fell ill. Some days she wonders if anyone would miss her if she died tomorrow.

Our busy lives, which some might argue were created to avoid confrontation with this particular form of loneliness, seldom allow us to contemplate existential loneliness. Instead, we move through our days on an undercurrent of uneasiness.

We are born alone, we die alone. Granted, some form of aloneness is the human condition, but there are no walls, no border checkpoints, nothing to tell us where aloneness leaves off and loneliness begins. These are the thoughts that can keep us up late at night or keep us from falling back to sleep in the wee hours of the morning, our internal GPS calculating and recalculating our current locations, wondering whether there is something *more* in the enveloping darkness. We long to connect with something we believe is greater than ourselves. It can be a larger purpose or mission that gives our lives meaning. A spirituality or a religious connection, which moors us in the universe. Neither is mutually exclusive, and it is more than a coincidence that we find a version of the Golden Rule—do unto others as you would have them do unto you—in many of the major religions.

We can experience existential loneliness in the presence of others, even among those to whom we feel closely connected. This type of loneliness is prevalent in our workplaces despite the fact that we are typically not alone. Studies suggest it is worth our while—when confronted by middle-of-the-night mental wrestling matches—to address our existential angst. Individuals who believe their lives are meaningful are reportedly happier. Happier individuals are more resilient, less vulnerable to or more tolerant of the other kinds of loneliness, and coincidentally, healthier. Their satisfaction with their lives and their security about their place in the universe may effectively reduce any discomfort caused by a relative lack of intimate connections with other humans. They experience less or no pain when they are alone or in unfamiliar social settings. In other words, they are less lonely.

One of the devastating drivers for this type of loneliness is the existential quandary that we are oriented to imagine a life of meaning, purpose, and connection to others, even while death looms as an ultimate disconnection. Anxiety about our mortality often builds walls that keep us from connecting. We're so afraid of dying and the inevitability of the disconnection it represents that we may keep ourselves distracted to the point where we remain apart from ourselves. This disconnection from self can be the first determinative tear in the fabric of connection. Traditional religion has calmed this fear for most people for most of human history, but modern societies are more secular and less religious than any societies in the past. For many, living in an individualistic and reflexively striving culture in the absence of religion or a spiritual orientation opens up the void of existential loneliness.

What all these types of loneliness share is the gap in our perceptions between the way we want things to be and the way we experience them to be. On a practical level, it's useful to have more of a sense of what type or types of loneliness we are dealing with so that we can explore and manage those distressing feelings most effectively. It's important to differentiate between the lonely feelings that arise when we tell ourselves, "I don't know who I am anymore, or what matters to me," versus "I don't have a friend in the world," versus "I feel excluded at work." Only when we can identify the type of loneliness we are feeling can we begin to explore what is behind that feeling, and how best to respond.

In the treatment of physical pain, medicine has developed many proven methods for patients to assign numerical scores to their levels of pain on an hourly or daily basis. We need something like that for these three types of loneliness. Today, on a scale of 1 to 10, I might grade my level of existential loneliness at a 2, and my societal loneliness level at a 1, but my psychological loneliness is at a 7 because I'm still reeling from a recent relationship breakup. As with physical pain scores, when you can identify with specificity the nature and level of your discomfort, your path to healing appears clearer and more reliable. Assigning a number to your discomfort also provides a potentially more useful way to communicate it to others.

When I picture how these three types of loneliness interact within our minds, I think of a braid or a "triple helix" structure. While one type of loneliness may dominate your conscious reflection or unconscious sensitivities at any given moment, all three types may persist and influence us in varying amounts.

Once you take a moment to reflect on the varied implications of these three types of loneliness, it's easier to appreciate why Mary, the woman in my lecture audience, was unlikely to feel less lonely simply by attending public events. The mere fact that she lives alone and spends a lot of time by herself does not necessarily make her lonely.

To understand why Mary feels lonely, you would need to get to know her. Perhaps she lost her husband five years ago and has still not grieved the loss. Perhaps she's anxious about growing old and dying. Perhaps she's been hurt by past friends and loves, and is fearful to trust again. Perhaps she was very attractive in her younger years and now feels lost without the easy social acceptance our culture grants to good-looking young people.

This is why the common prescription—"Get out and be with people"—is often worse than inadequate. It's potentially very destructive. People can turn their frustration at their continued loneliness into rigid confirmation of their perceived lack of self-worth. Mary gave voice to a feeling many lonely people get when they try to salve their loneliness by joining a crowd. "I'm here with people, so why do I still feel lonely?" Without any understanding of the various types of loneliness and what gives rise to these feelings, lonely people are apt to feel inadequate and ashamed. They may conclude there is something wrong with them and give up on trying to connect with others, leading to ever-deeper levels of despair.

It's important to note that our sense of connection and engagement with ourselves and others is often fluid and dynamic. The pain of loneliness or the discomfort of anticipating loneliness prompts some people to become lonelier. Someone who is suffering from any combination of types of loneliness may prefer isolating themselves and shunning human contact except when absolutely necessary. People who struggle with psychological loneliness, who bear grudges or feel regrets about people in their past, may have decided they prefer their own company to that of others, who they've learned can't be trusted. People with societal loneliness, who are somehow viewed as different, may just as soon pass up group gatherings of all kinds, just to avoid the dread that if they show up, they may be spurned and excluded. And those with deep feelings of existential loneliness may feel loneliest when they're around people who seem happy and content with life, which triggers self-reproachful feelings of having failed to find joy, meaning, and purpose in their own lives.

We may isolate ourselves to cope with our feelings of discomfort around others, but the pain of loneliness is the price we pay. Recall my comparison of the ache of loneliness to that of thirst, as a bodily signal that a physiological need must be attended to. Human connection, like hydration, is a need that is dangerous to ignore. When we lack connection with other human beings, it takes a toll on our ability to function—to think, to feel, and to maintain our health.

Three things matter most in relieving loneliness, regardless of the particulars. First is to accept that the relationship you have with yourself is fundamental to addressing any type of loneliness you may be feeling. Second, you must reexamine the personal biases you use to interpret your experience of loneliness. When you begin to question the reasoning behind why you say "This is the way it is" about your loneliness, you will open doors to new possibilities for yourself. You can change your reality by changing your interpretation of reality. Third, and perhaps most difficult, is to tolerate the discomfort of moving forward. You must resist the natural urge to avoid the risks involved with both discovering and revealing who you are. This struggle is a universal experience, and the more you learn about it, the easier it is to accept that your loneliness is there to help you make meaning in your life. The French author La Fontaine observed that people often meet their destiny on the road they took to avoid it. He could have added that the road is often a lonely one, but it doesn't have to be.

THE EVOLUTIONARY THEORY OF LONELINESS

In the early 1990s, John T. Cacioppo was among the founders of a then-new field called social neuroscience, which studies the relationship between social experience and biology, particularly brain biology. He founded the University of Chicago's Center for Cognitive and Social Neuroscience and coauthored the first research papers to assert an evolutionary theory of loneliness. John and fellow researchers reasoned that feelings of loneliness might have evolved to encourage early humans to cooperate and avoid going off on their own.

For many thousands of years, long before farming and cities, humans subsisted as small and scattered groups of hunter-gatherers. In a world filled with dangerous predators, including other humans from rival groups, the only source of physical security for the human animal was to stay with the group. The group served as each individual's sole source of safety, shelter, and sustenance. Humans are the only social primates who cooperate in cooking and sharing food, a dietary advantage associated with the evolution of our larger brains and our dependency on group behavior for adequate nutrition.

The benefits of remaining in a group were so powerful that our bodies sent us pain signals to warn us when we were away from it. Feeling pain when apart or disconnected from the group is likely the glue that kept these small groups together. Over time, groups endowed with weaker loneliness signals would have likely died out. We are de facto descendants of people who stuck with the group and felt the pain of loneliness most severely whenever they strayed.

John Cacioppo was a brilliant scientist with a warm, engaging personality, who sadly died in 2018 at the age of sixty-six following a three-year battle with cancer. Back in 2016, I had a memorable meeting over coffee with him and his wife, Stephanie Cacioppo, a neurologist at the University of Chicago who coauthored many of John's research papers. Among the things we discussed was how it is the quality of our social connections, not the quantity, that determines how lonely we feel. If we don't feel safe or securely connected with the people around us, loneliness will persist. That's the evolutionary basis for feeling lonely in a crowd of strangers.

With the development of civilization and complex societies, emotions rooted in Paleolithic survival helped us adapt successfully to this entirely different way of living. For example, we no longer fear predation from big cats. Instead, that fear response has been adapted to make us careful around modern bodily threats—busy streets and dark alleys. Our primary source of fear has extended from speedy predators to speeding automobiles.

But there's a catch. Our brains evolved the fight-or-flight stress response to give our bodies bursts of energy and hypervigilant focus to protect ourselves. The stress response floods our bodies with hormones and other bioactive molecules to get us revved up. Whether we're dodging an oncoming car or a rampaging bear, those molecules may save our lives. But when the brain's stress response keeps producing those same compounds day after day in response to the anguish of sustained loneliness, our systems stay revved up for fight or flight—until they wear down.

John's book *Loneliness: Human Nature and the Need for Social Connection* detailed what he called the insidious catch-22 of chronic loneliness. Although loneliness signals a need, like hunger and thirst, it is different because some types, especially psychological loneliness, can't be relieved without the cooperation of at least one other individual. The catch-22, John wrote, is that "the more chronic our loneliness becomes, the less equipped we may be to entice such cooperation."

Studies reveal that lonely people in a prolonged brain state of fight or flight show less empathy and reduced ability to accurately "read" other people's intentions. The part of the brain that maintains self-control—executive function—is impaired, so they may react inappropriately when they misread other people's social signals.

John reasoned that this is why jilted lovers so often engage in destructive obsessive behaviors they later regret—driving past an ex's home each night, phoning or texting at odd hours or even stalking them. But it's also why middle-aged adults who are chronically lonely "have more divorces, more run-ins with neighbors, more estrangement from family." Their reactive, defensive form of thinking creates a self-fulfilling prophecy in which people really do learn to avoid contact with them. Unhealthy, life-shortening eating and drinking habits are typical sources of respite. "Is it any wonder that we turn to ice cream or other fatty foods when we're sitting at home feeling all alone in the world?" John asked. "We want to soothe the pain we feel by mainlining sugar and fat content to the pleasure centers of the brain, and, absent self-control, we go right at it."

And here's what is perhaps the worst effect of all. Your loneliness isn't just your problem. Feelings of loneliness tend to spread among people like a network of contagion. In 2009, John researched the phenomenon with Nicholas Christakis, a social scientist and physician who heads the Human Nature Lab at Yale. They found evidence that simply being around lonely people is associated with having a higher level of loneliness oneself, similar to the risk of contagion from being around someone with an infectious disease. If you have a friend of a friend who is lonely—two degrees of separation—your risk of loneliness is still elevated by 25 percent. Even at three degrees of separation, you are 15 percent more likely to be lonely if a friend of a friend of a friend is lonely.

As much as some of us might be resigned to loneliness, we all come up against the immutable fact that we are innately social animals. Connection is essential to our humanity and to our well-being. When we are too lonely for too long, the way we make sense of the world changes, leaving us increasingly at risk for even greater levels of loneliness. We fail to thrive and flourish, we get sick, we spread the affliction to others, and we die before our time.

TOCQUEVILLE'S CURSE

When Alexis de Tocqueville wrote his lengthy report *Democracy in America* for a European audience, he noted both the benefits and hazards of living in a society without an aristocracy. One of those hazards was loneliness.

In traditional European societies, everyone had a fixed place in the hierarchical social order. Therefore, everyone considered themselves as belonging in terms of loyalty and obligations to others, including God. These loyalties and obligations were enforced by strong social institutions—the Church, the state, and the family.

Tocqueville noted that Americans, by contrast, "are in the habit of always considering themselves in isolation, and they willingly fancy that their whole destiny is in their hands." The effect on each individual, he wrote, "constantly leads him back toward himself alone and threatens finally to confine him wholly in the solitude of his own heart."

The potential for disastrous loneliness in modern societies was first explored by the father of sociology, Émile Durkheim, who published a classic study of suicide in 1897. Using data gathered in German-speaking Europe, he noted that suicide rates were much higher among Protestants than among Catholics. He speculated that the Catholic Church exerted stronger social control and cohesion among Catholics in those countries, which might make individuals more resilient and better supported in difficult circumstances like bankruptcy or imprisonment.

Durkheim formed a theory based on the different ways societies regulate the lives of their people by integrating them into the society's fabric. In modern free societies, where individuals are at risk of not being integrated enough, they may suffer from what Durkheim termed an "egoistic crisis." Some in crisis will kill themselves because they believe their lives are meaningless and of no consequence to the lives of others. Durkheim's conclusion was that freedom is not an absolute good. In fact, people don't do particularly well when they are provided infinite amounts of freedom. If society doesn't set up stable expectations for people's behavior and life course, he wrote, they risk experiencing anomie, an aimlessness rooted in the weakening of referential shared assumptions, which can drive them to despair and self-destruction.

Princeton professors Anne Case and Angus Deaton cited Durkheim's work in coining the term "deaths of despair." They point to the decline of traditional institutions that have maintained human connection in the past—religion, marriage, and stable workplaces—as the root cause of increased deaths from suicide, alcohol, and drug overdoses among middle-aged noncollege white people in the United States.

"Our account echoes the account of suicide by Émile Durkheim," they wrote, "of how suicide happens when society fails to provide some of its members with the framework within which they can live dignified and meaningful lives."

For example, marriage has lost its earlier social status as the assumed prerequisite for a happy and valuable life. This has certainly been liberating for many people, but it has also raised the risk of increasing loneliness in two ways. Fundamentally, more people choosing to stay single means more people are socially isolated, which increases the risk of loneliness for each one of them. Secondarily, the loss of marriage as a social norm has been devastating to many people who have not found a meaningful alternative. In Durkheim's analysis, it's too much freedom for those people, which puts them at increased risk of anomie and despair. Modern society has set free each human being to make their own meaning, but it has yet to wake up to the growing crises of loneliness and despair emerging among millions who are disoriented and struggling with that much freedom.

Over the course of many millennia, humans have been very resourceful in satisfying their innate Paleolithic needs through civilizational substitutes. For example, white-collar work and automation have freed most of us from strenuous physical labor, but our bodies still require the regular activity they were designed for. So we take walks, we hike, we bike, we go to the gym. We find socially appropriate ways to meet our innate need to exercise our joints and muscles.

Now we face a new challenge. The traditional social bonds that have forever fed our innate need for closeness and connection are weakening. But we have yet to devise reliable adaptive tools that meet these needs as effectively as gym equipment meets our need for exercise. We evolved as a social species, and we get sick when we abandon the behaviors that ensured our ancestors' social survival. It's time to confront a long-overdue question: Is there a kind of mental and emotional workout that can strengthen our social selves as reliably as gym workouts strengthen our physical selves? Could regular engagement in creative expression be a part of such a human connection workout?

THE CREATIVE IMPERATIVE

An apocryphal story about Ernest Hemingway tells of how he bet some bar buddies he could write a short story that could make them cry in just six words. He won the bet with this story: "For sale: Baby shoes, never worn." Whatever depth and detail this story lacks is more than made up for in imagery, impact, and memorability.

I have my own six-word short story whenever I'm asked for a brief prescription for what we can do about loneliness: "Be curious. Make something. Have conversations." Like Hemingway's story, that's hardly a complete picture. But it is useful because it is so easy to remember and also because, like Hemingway's six words, it triggers a sense that these simple suggestions are connected to larger, more complex and compelling ideas. Each of these three steps serves to stimulate your brain, the way you make sense of things, and your behaviors toward connectedness—beginning first with the essential connection you need to make with your feelings and your true self, and then moving outward in connection with others.

Be Curious

By "Be curious," I mean that when you are experiencing the pangs of loneliness or perhaps engaging in unhealthy behaviors in solitude and secrecy, you should try questioning those feelings and your choices in response. What are the sources of your loneliness? Is it new or familiar? What type of loneliness is it—psychological, societal, or existential? Are you feeling all three, or is one more acute today than the others?

To be curious about loneliness is to recognize, perhaps for the first time, the specific feelings and behaviors that are symptomatic of your loneliness. To stretch the thirst analogy just a little further, while it's true we know to drink something when we feel thirsty, it's also true that many people walk around each day chronically dehydrated. They don't recognize the common symptoms of mild dehydration—fatigue, headaches, and constipation. And so they continue to feel a little off, oblivious to their need to drink more water.

By being curious about our loneliness, we can begin to give curiosity the attention it deserves. Curiosity is another one of those things that are central to our humanity. Why do we wonder why the sky is blue or what happens during an eclipse? Why are we interested in other cultures and eager to travel to explore them? Why will we watch a bad movie to its conclusion, just to see how it ends?

My earliest memory of my own curiosity involved a toy electricity kit my parents gave me when I turned seven. It used a battery, a switch, and a variety of wiring configurations and little flashlight bulbs to demonstrate the effects of various ways the wiring could be done to determine how brightly the bulbs would glow. I was so deeply immersed in experimenting with that toy and in puzzling over the fact that when the two bulbs were wired to each other in a straight line they were only half as bright as when they were wired with each on its own loop of wire and parallel to each other, that when the battery began to run down, I took the whole kit and kaboodle with me into my bedroom closet. I closed the door so that alone in the darkness I could repeat the experiments and enjoy the sense of wonder at my discovery, despite the weakening battery.

I was fortunate growing up to have the celebration of curiosity all around me. Both my parents were scientists, research chemists interested in biological questions like how bones grow and how certain nutrients like calcium are absorbed in our digestive system and then work in the body. Even at a young age, I recall conversations around the dinner table about some of the fundamental issues they were interested in as well as descriptions of the experiments. Although I couldn't follow all of it, my parents were always happy to answer any questions and to try to explain as simply as possible what they were working to sort out.

Perhaps surprisingly, many of the questions made sense even to a child and captured my attention. For instance, to cure the bone disease rickets, which is caused by a deficiency of vitamin D, does it matter whether you replace what was missing all at once or in smaller doses over a longer time? And if it's smaller doses over time, does it matter whether you give the dose once a day, once a week, or once a month? I came to see not only that science was driven by curiosity, but that knowing the answers to some of the questions could make a real difference in some very practical ways. Like having stronger bones, or in the case of my electricity experiments, knowing that even with the same-strength battery, a light bulb could burn twice as brightly if it was wired in a specific way.

My childhood curiosity led me to a useful understanding of electricity that I've never forgotten. If you were to pay attention to your feelings of loneliness in the same spirit of discovery and curiosity, you would likely come to certain new understandings about loneliness, your relationship to it, and the various ways things in your life could be wired to affect it. And that could be very, very useful.

One psychological view of curiosity involves what is known as the information-gap theory. When we are given an interesting but incomplete piece of information, it arouses in us an adverse sense of deprivation—again, like thirst—that motivates us to find the answer. That's the itch of curiosity that demands to be scratched, and scratching that itch is a very effective way to learn.

When I teach my public health courses, I give my students just enough of the lesson to stimulate their thinking and arouse their curiosity. In that way, I'm not merely transferring what I know. They are experiencing the new knowledge as their own personal discovery, which makes it impactful and memorable. In the course I teach at Harvard on loneliness, I go even one step further. I invite the students not just to think about what could address loneliness at a personal or societal level, but to anticipate the barriers that might arise in putting those solutions into practice. Then I prompt them to get curious about how to overcome those obstacles in reliable ways. "Don't worry," I tell them. "We'll address best practices later." Their learning depends on getting curious about obstacles first.

"Thirst for knowledge" is a real thing. It's the source of attraction to any riddle or crossword puzzle—incomplete information in need of a solution. And now I've given you a puzzle of a different kind. I've presented you with several new ways to consider your loneliness. My intention here and in the pages that follow is to continually arouse your curiosity with information that is always just a little incomplete— until you consider how it may pertain to you, to other people you know, to the groups you belong to, and to society as you understand it.

Make Something

Trying to figure out what's going on within our rational minds or in our emotions is a necessary first step, but it still will not fully clarify who we are in the world, what the world means to us, or how best to navigate it. In fact, in our culture, when we get curious about something, it's common practice to imagine we can look up the answer, ask someone, or think really hard about it and see if we can puzzle it out. There is nothing wrong with that approach, except that it works better for some things we are curious about than it does for others. If we were curious about the melting point of lead, we could look it up or do a simple experiment to find it out. Ultimately, reconnection with ourselves or others seems to require something other than discovering and adhering to a set of scientifically derived principles. That's because there are other ways we as humans make sense of things than rationally analyzing them. Our emotional ways of making sense of things, which we may not even be conscious of, can have a profound and meaningful impact. The placebo effect is just one example of that. In this often-observed phenomenon, if we expect a pill to help alleviate our pain, it's more likely to do so than if we don't, even if the pill is made of sugar. Daniel Kahneman, the Nobel Prize–winning psychologist, pointed out that most of our immediate decisions are made on an emotional basis, whether we are aware of those emotional and nonrational influences or not, and then we construct a rational analysis to justify them. So how do we reach into that part of our "sense-making" apparatus, which often we aren't even in touch with? And why is it so important to do so?

To be connected to others, we have to recognize that the sense of connection is more than an abstraction. We have to answer for ourselves who we are to others, who they are to us, where we fit, what gives us purpose, and how we want to live.

For most of us, though, to create the kinds of connections we want involves sharing deeper, more fundamental aspects of our "story," of who we are, than our love of ice cream. But when we are lonely because we have changed in some way, or left something or someone behind, or moved somewhere new, or experienced something traumatic, or started to question our purpose or value, we may not know who we are anymore. We may be fundamentally disconnected from ourselves. How, then, could we possibly connect with someone else?

I have found that an incredibly powerful way to first explore and then share one's story is through artistic expression—creating something tangible that expresses who you are, or an aspect of who you are, and sharing that thing with others, or having it attended and acknowledged by others.

The experience of creating has often been described as a kind of ecstasy, perhaps because it opens a cognitive and emotional flow between the conscious and unconscious mind. Making choices according to what pleases you aesthetically brings both sides of the brain together in a delightful tango of imagination. Making something happen in the present moment, as the clock ticks each minute to the next, simultaneously arouses your awareness of both the past and the future. In terms of the future, you have a vivid, imagined vision of what you want your work to be like when it's completed and how it may be perceived, while at the same time you are drawing on past experiences and emotions to inform each creative choice along the way. The feelings may be intense, but they are happening on the relatively safe terrain of creative construction, where you, as the maker, are in charge.

For accessing the past, recollection may offer the warm glow of nostalgia or the ache of regret. For the future, expressive making can capture the breathless enthusiasm of optimism and hope or the piercing stab of anxiety and dread as you anticipate life's challenges and obstacles. The past and future connect in the present moment, in the making of an artifact that allows something tangible and meaningful to be shaped and shared.

You don't need to be a skilled artist to have this creative experience open to you. You simply need to find a creative medium for transmitting important information about yourself, for encoding it expressively, in whatever art form you prefer, so that the result can then be decoded by someone else. When you do that, you complete that figurative electric circuit Edward Hirsch describes and you're both connected. The point—what works about the arts in alleviating loneliness—happens in the act of creation, in the fact of self-expression, and in the experience of being witnessed or seen. The word *poetry* (one of my own preferred art forms) is derived from the Greek word *poesis*, which means "to make." A poem is a "made thing," no different from a painting, a quilt, or a garden.

How and why does this work? Artistic expression involves specific activities, each unfolding in time and involving mechanisms that facilitate connection. In the process of making, the maker has the ability to be in the moment—to be in touch with musings, impressions, and emotions, often otherwise difficult to access; to craft a symbolic artifact that is a repository of very personal and high-value information that then becomes a means of, or a catalyst for, telling one's story.

In a world of seemingly inexorable distractions and with our mind's response of continuous partial attention, creative activity secures for you a tiny sanctuary of calm and focus. Making art can become a form of mindfulness meditation, with many of the same benefits. As Eastern religions have long known and as research has confirmed, being present in the moment quiets the mind and relieves stress. It puts you in touch with thoughts and feelings—both the challenging ones and the inspiring ones—and facilitates reconnection with one's essential self.

Then there is the art itself, the made object or narrative vehicle or otherwise constructed opportunity for telling one's story that inevitably, without our having to shape or edit or do anything about it, conveys something authentic and unique about the maker. The artifact can be a literal rendering of a scene or circumstance, but it doesn't have to be. Whatever it is, however abstract, expresses the maker's way of seeing or feeling, their imagination; their delight in color or craftsmanship; their point of view; their heritage; their uniqueness; their originality.

Creative expression also gives us the positive experience of making choices and making our own meaning—which seems particularly apropos in an age of weakening social norms and constraints. I'll go out on a limb and say it: Remaining engaged in creative expression may very well be an essential survival skill of this century. By creating and sharing, we train our brains to feel excited and inspired at the sight of a blank sheet of paper, rather than feeling victimized by the burden of having too many choices. And it also offers an opportunity to reveal to others how we make sense of the world, inviting them to interact with us regarding it.

Have Conversations

Once the foundational work of making is established, there is still more to be done. We need to talk about it, to have conversations. The research on mindfulness shows us the positive impact on body and mind of "here and now" experiencing, but the arts also involve the sharing of our art with others. Our art creates a bridge to another and is thus a tool or enabler for a form of connection.

Here's how it works. If you share your story, your feeling, your way of seeing, your artistry, your expertise, your appreciation or passion for something, and that story is attended and acknowledged by others, you feel recognized. You have made some kind of connection by being who you are. When the receiver connects with the art that the creator has had the generosity to share, both people feel less lonely.

A connecting conversation is one in which you share your story. You put something at risk. You are willing to tolerate the emotional discomfort of disclosing something private, knowing that you may be judged or critiqued, and perhaps you may suffer the pain of rejection or abandonment, or of simply being ignored as inconsequential, boring, or worse.

Exchanges of this kind progressively build trust between two people. It's in this process that we begin to see ourselves in others and to have them see themselves in us. We may find common ground, even when we may have fundamental disagreements, because we each have risked and shared something vulnerable through what we have created. In the exchange, we make sense of ourselves in relation to others and the world at large.

Connection is not a mystery. It only seems mysterious because many people aren't aware of how it works and how to achieve it, and that can feel like walking into a dark room, fearful of tripping over the furniture. Psychologist Arthur Aron claims that two people can fall in love by discussing thirty-six playful but revealing questions such as:

Given the choice of anyone in the world, whom would you want as a dinner guest?

Would you like to be famous? In what way?

Before making a telephone call, do you ever rehearse what you are going to say? Why?

What would constitute a "perfect" day for you?

These are not questions that delve too deeply into the personal details of your life. But answering each still involves some risk. The questions you ask in meaningful conversation should reveal your values and where you find meaning in life. That is how you know someone. That is how you are known. This is the same type of revealing that happens when you share a work of creative imagination with someone else. That work is infused with very specific information about you, encoded in the medium you choose and decoded by someone else. It's a powerful tool for connection and available to anyone.

THE FIVE TERRITORIES, EACH A LONELINESS LANDSCAPE

One early morning in March when I was fifteen years old, I came downstairs to find my father sitting on the living room sofa, white as a sheet and in obvious pain. He asked me to wake up my mother, to try not to upset her, but to tell her to call the doctor. I stayed with him until the police arrived. This was before emergency medical technicians responded to 911 calls. The cops knew what they were doing, and worked quickly and professionally to assess the situation, to get an oxygen mask on him, and to radio ahead to the emergency department of the local medical center. As they loaded him onto a stretcher, I retreated to the dining room, peering out from around the corner. I was frozen with a feeling of embarrassment, a sense of deep shame that I couldn't do anything to help my dad.

My mother went to the hospital with him, but I went to school and spent the day in a daze. That afternoon, as I approached the house, I saw my sister outside, cleaning out the car and crying. Then I knew. My mom told me that my dad had died of a heart attack not long after he'd gotten to the hospital. I never got to say goodbye to him. He was forty-seven years old.

I look back now on that time and recognize how this traumatic experience had left me deeply lonely, and from all three types of loneliness. Psychologically I was bereft. I had lost a friend, a confidant, a caregiver. My dad was someone who had known me, accepted me without judgment, and cared deeply about me. Now I was alone without him. It was a deep and personal blow, and the knife-edge of loss was all the sharper because I didn't have that same sort of closeness with my mother or two sisters. A hole had opened up. Years later I wrote a poem that likened his loss to the crater in the Arizona desert where a meteor left a circular dent a mile wide and five hundred feet deep. Psychologically, I was dented. There had been a sudden removal, creating a crater in the center of my psyche.

My societal loneliness in the aftermath of my father's death stemmed from my social redefinition. Overnight, people we knew acted different toward me. In their minds, I'd gone from "typical adolescent" to "fatherless child." The Pittsburgh Jewish community that my family was part of was very supportive, and I found their response very reassuring, the comfort of being connected to a group. But it was disorienting to be so suddenly re-sorted into a variety of preestablished assumptions that altered how people behaved toward me and how my behaviors were interpreted. Losing my father changed how I was seen and treated by strangers, which gave me a lonely and isolating sense of uncertainty about how I would be judged and responded to.

On the existential level, my dad's death confronted me for the first time with the profound indifference of the universe. My father was such a decent person, who had worked so hard all his life, and this was his reward, to have his life cut short at forty-seven? How did that possibly make sense in a world that had any fairness or justice? What did that mean for me? Would I die at that age, too? Would I leave a family bereft and abandoned? What would the point of any of that be? To invest so much, to care so much, and then to have it all come crashing down? Where did my own pathetic efforts to have a life fit into that narrative of uncertainty and fragility?

I had so many questions, and no one to discuss them with. None of the people around me right after my father died, mostly older relatives, really wanted to have that conversation. To be fair, I'm not sure I wanted to have that conversation, either. Existential loneliness can be especially difficult to share with others, and the resulting sense of isolation can intensify its pain.

That spring when I was fifteen was a trauma that in many ways made me who I am today. The loneliness that descended on me in the weeks and months after my father's death helped shape my subsequent choices and determined the course of my life. I'd been left adrift, disconnected and unsure of how my life connected to the bigger story of what the universe had in store for me.

What I wish I'd had at the time was some guidance about how to cope with the loneliness I was feeling. In many ways, this is the book that I wish I could have read after my father died. It wouldn't have made losing him any easier, but it would have helped me navigate my way during the many times when I felt despondent, rudderless, and lonely.

Trauma of this kind is what I regard as one of the five territories of loneliness. The other four territories are illness, aging, difference, and modernity. I call them territories because they are realms of common human experience where it's easiest to get lost in loneliness without a map and guide.

In the next five chapters, I will examine each territory and its distinct emotional challenges, medical symptoms, and behavioral tendencies, as well as scientific insights and opportunities to explore creative expression and reconnection as the response. Along the way, you will meet some remarkable people. There is the army veteran who overcame his PTSD through the decorating of papier-mâché masks, a group of children who wrote and produced a show called *Hemophilia: The Musical*, a hospital administrator who managed to create laughter from her mastectomy, and many others who are using the joy of creativity to make human connections.

4

Trauma

Captain Jason Berner was a Marine combat engineer in his twenties when he was deployed to Iraq annually from 2004 to 2007. Over those years, he lost several men in his unit to improvised explosive devises (IEDs). One such device had been buried in the road where the unit was walking, and Jason himself had stepped right on it. The IED failed to detonate for some reason, and instead went off several seconds later, sparing Jason while killing one of his men.

I first met Jason several years later when he was being treated for post-traumatic stress disorder at Walter Reed National Military Medical Center. I arrived there with a film crew for a documentary we were making called *Can Art Be Medicine?* The facility where Jason was being treated, the National Intrepid Center of Excellence (or NICoE, as it's called), had a major push to look at both mindfulness and art therapy as adjuncts to more traditional modes of care in its treatment of PTSD. We did interviews with two of the psychiatrists there, along with other practitioners and patients.

In his interview with me, Jason told me about his course of treatment for his anxiety disorder and memory flashbacks, which are symptomatic of PTSD. He'd begun art therapy, he said, but only after some initial reluctance. He'd discovered that working with paint and clay had helped him express himself in ways where words had been failing him for years. "Each time I did something with art therapy, I felt better," he said. "Because there was something in me that was dying to get out. And through art, I was able to express it."

As a severe psychiatric disorder, PTSD is relatively rare. But posttraumatic stress is not. Each of life's traumas deals a blow to our connections with others—the sudden death of a loved one, catastrophic illness, a near-fatal car crash, an abusive relationship, bullying at home or work, a house fire or natural disaster. About one-third of people who experience these traumas will remain irritable for some time afterward, unable to sleep and disturbed by thoughts, images, and emotional memories of their experiences.

Most people with strong relationships in their lives will "metabolize" traumas over time. They integrate traumas in their memories as unthreatening events that are now behind them, although they still recall the accompanying sadness and loss. Talking over the events and having new life-affirming experiences with friends and family assist in this process of memory integration. But if your social supports were weak before the traumatic event, your acute stress reaction to trauma can be prolonged. If you are lonely to begin with, you risk having no one close to you to help you metabolize your memory of the trauma. You're also less likely to have the positive social experiences that balance out the terrible thing that happened to you. Instead, you may suffer doubly from the harsh unhealed emotional memories of the trauma itself, and then from the lonely anguish of ruminating over those uninvited and intrusive thoughts in isolation.

It's a lonely feeling for anyone when we have strong unexpressed thoughts bottled up inside us. For people suffering from post-traumatic stress, those feelings can spiral into what I call the vicious cycle of loneliness. The aversion to reexperiencing traumatic events can lead people to disconnect from others. Think of someone so badly hurt by a past love affair gone wrong that they shut off their feelings to avoid the risk of reexperiencing that pain. In the more extreme cases, stirred-up memories of past traumas can trigger flashbacks of emotional pain and uncontrollable physical fright reactions. To avoid that risk, someone suffering from post-traumatic stress can get progressively lonelier as their world gets progressively smaller. In that smaller world, it's even harder to find ways to express those difficult thoughts, prompting more loneliness, further social withdrawal, and ever-deeper loneliness.

WHAT WE CAN LEARN FROM WOUNDED WARRIORS

Psychiatrist and researcher Charlie Marmar began working with Vietnam veterans suffering from PTSD in the 1970s and 1980s. He observed how men who had been fairly well connected socially before the war gradually grew more withdrawn upon their return. "First, they withdrew from family and friends," he told me in an interview. "Then they often used alcohol and drugs to numb themselves further. And then finally in the more advanced stage of the illness, they might withdraw geographically and physically." Some of the men he treated wound up moving to remote areas of Hawaii, living off the land in extreme isolation, just to avoid the risk of having painful memories triggered while in contact with other people.

Marmar now heads the Steven A. Cohen Military Family Clinic, a PTSD treatment and research program at New York University Langone Health, where he also chairs the psychiatry department. Over the past twenty-five years he has led a wide range of clinical studies researching the causes of PTSD and treatments for it, including both psychotherapy and new medications. He also serves on the advisory board of NYU Langone's Center for Psychedelic Medicine, which is investigating the use of MDMA (recreationally used under the names ecstasy and Molly) to assist in the treatment of PTSD and other stress-related psychiatric problems.

Research has documented how the anxiety associated with all post-traumatic stress can make people hypervigilant. They are often unable to relax or even sleep because they feel they are in constant danger. If that sounds strange, consider any common phobia you may have—of heights or of snakes. Now consider how well you would sleep if you were perched on a cliff or believed your bedroom was crawling with snakes.

Phil Klay, a former US Marine, won a 2014 National Book Award for his short story collection *Redeployment*. One story in the book is told from the point of view of a sergeant who has returned home from Fallujah, where three members of his platoon had been killed in brutal house-to-house fighting. Walking the streets of Wilmington, North Carolina, the sergeant in the story feels exposed and alone without his platoon. He's seized by hypervigilance: "In Wilmington, you don't have a squad, you don't have a battle buddy, you don't even have a weapon. You startle ten times checking for it and it's not there. You're safe, so your alertness should be at white, but it's not."

For people whose nervous systems are running continuously on high alert in this way, the damage goes beyond lost sleep and compromised health. Loud noises can provoke a cascade of fight-or-flight reactions that would be vitally important in a military context, but in a civilian context are perceived as irrational and often transgressive. Veterans have crashed their cars and put others in danger because they were "combat driving"—zigzagging and accelerating around perceived threats in calm suburban traffic because they'd been triggered.

Social cognition becomes distorted over time for people with PTSD. They tense up when they see a stranger walking toward them even in broad daylight. They may be prone to misinterpreting other people's words and behaviors, responding to innocent comments and gestures with suspicion or outright hostility. Assuming that strangers are out to get you is rational in a war zone, but it looks like paranoia in a civilian setting. Those with PTSD tend to have atrophied social skills, because as they learn to avoid people who may trigger a flashback, the few folks remaining in their orbit gradually learn to avoid them.

Often on edge, wary of others' intentions, and growing ever more isolated, sufferers of PTSD are at high risk of taking their own lives. The suicide rate for veterans of the US military is twice that of the general population. When one study of two thousand veterans over a four-year period sought to identify the key risk factors for suicidal thinking, it concluded that the primary indicator is loneliness.

The vast majority of people who suffer from post-traumatic stress recover from it without ever developing the disabling PTSD. Out of a US adult population of more than 220 million, about 10 percent of all women and 4 percent of all men will suffer from PTSD at some point in their lives. However, one of the major risk factors for developing the disorder is suffering from post-traumatic stress without strong social supports in your life. Loneliness can set you up as a candidate for PTSD.

Albert Szent-Györgyi, the Hungarian biochemist and Nobel laureate, once said, "The brain is not an organ of thinking but an organ of survival, like claws and fangs. It is made in such a way as to make us accept as truth that which is only advantage." By this he meant that our brains are continually working to detect threats and respond to them. The brain interprets sensory input and assesses threat levels by relating the input to what those cues signaled in the past, because that's all the brain has to go on. After suffering a traumatic experience, your brain as an organ of survival will stay on high alert until it can accept that the danger has passed—that a loud noise is no longer an exploding IED but a truck backfiring.

But when you have been severely traumatized, the emotional memories of that painful experience are hard for your brain to separate from its immediate reaction in the present moment. The brain can't readily identify and store the memory of a traumatic experience as something safely in the past because of the powerful feelings of helplessness and terror that accompany being injured, assaulted, abandoned, or bearing witness to violence. Until the memory of the trauma stops arousing painful emotional reactions, your brain will accept as truth only that tremendous danger is still present and react accordingly.

The course of treatment for PTSD points to how important narrative storytelling is to everyone's mental well-being. To heal from post-traumatic stress of any kind, you must learn to tell the story of what happened repeatedly until the story loses its emotional grip. The brain uses a process called memory consolidation to preserve our recall of emotionally meaningful past events. Memory consolidation is why most of us can remember what we were doing on 9/11 but few remember anything about 9/10. The brain struggles to consolidate traumatic memories as past experiences because traumatic memories so often awaken the ghosts of the emotions felt at the time of the trauma.

The objective of talk therapy is to provide a safe environment for retelling the trauma narrative enough times that the memories of the event no longer provoke that overwhelming emotional response. "You can't change what happened," Marmar says. "If you were sexually assaulted, you were sexually assaulted. As Shakespeare said, what's done is done and cannot be undone. The events that occurred are not plastic, but your subjective reaction to them is." The function of repeated retelling is to fill in missing gaps in memory in order to create a cohesive story of your experience that you can readily recollect. In this way, you *reconsolidate* your memory of the event, this time in a way that is less agonizing.

Healing from any post-traumatic stress calls upon you to turn a fragmented set of troubling memories into a consciously formed life narrative. You first recall the details of what life was like for you before the traumatic event. You may ask, "Who was I before I was deployed to Iraq? Who was I before I was assaulted? Before I lost someone I loved in the pandemic?" Next, you tell the story of the traumatic event itself. Finally, you tell how the experience changed you. "What has my life journey been since the trauma?" The brain can finally relax because it now has a reconsolidated memory of what happened that is coherent and unaccompanied by overwhelming emotions.

Building this new trauma narrative requires finding the words to reframe the story, and that can pose a major obstacle to talk therapy. Traumatic memories often leave their victims unable to articulate their complex and contradictory feelings. The fear of reexperiencing these agonies can put memories beyond words. Bessel van der Kolk, a psychiatrist and researcher who cofounded and chairs the Trauma Research Foundation in Boston, tells how traumatized crime victims are often unable to give useful testimony in court against their assailants. Sometimes their memories are too fragmented and confused to be credible. Other times, the victims attempt to give testimony in unemotional ways that avoid triggering a PTSD episode, in which case they come across as evasive. For these same reasons, military veterans with PTSD will sometimes have their medical claims rejected.

In experiments at Harvard Medical School in the 1990s, van der Kolk and his team performed brain scans of volunteer subjects while triggering PTSD flashbacks. The scans showed heightened activity in the visual cortex and in the limbic system, particularly the amygdala, where certain emotions reside. At the same time, there was markedly decreased activation in the brain's language center. A portion of the brain's left frontal cortex called Broca's area went offline as the flashback was triggered. This is the same brain region that deprives stroke victims of their ability to speak when its blood supply is interrupted or reduced. Someone with Broca's aphasia will have particular trouble attaching words to the kinds of tangible recollections required for memory reconsolidation.

"Confusion and mutism are routine in therapy offices," van der Kolk wrote in his bestseller, *The Body Keeps the Score*. "We fully expect that our patients will become overwhelmed if we keep pressing them for the details of their story." On average, approximately one-fifth of PTSD sufferers drop out of talk therapy, which is one reason there is growing advocacy for the use of psychedelic drugs for extreme PTSD cases. Since 2017, the FDA has acknowledged use of the illegal recreational drug MDMA as a "breakthrough therapy," but its use remains tightly restricted. When taken prior to a therapy session, MDMA causes the release of "feel-good" hormones such as dopamine, serotonin, and oxytocin, which tends to make patients more self-reflective and open to working through traumatic memories that previously had been too painful to discuss.

Expressive arts have also proven to be extremely valuable in helping traumatized individuals make progress in therapy, but without directly retelling their trauma narrative in words. Engagement through visual arts, music, drama, poetry, or dance allows people to communicate with their unconscious, nonverbal minds, and by making a creative representation of a troubling memory, the maker can offer the mind a new narrative about the traumatic memory, beginning to reconsolidate the memory without words. Sharing the made artifact or performance becomes a channel for communicating the memory and making a safe, authentic emotional reconnection with other people.

Recall how the children in lower Manhattan were suffering from post-traumatic stress after 9/11. Many had no words for the disturbing memories of what they'd seen and heard that day. In the weeks that followed, some struggled emotionally because their minds couldn't consolidate their memories into cohesive narratives. That was the source of their post-traumatic stress. It was why some came to school each day feeling disconnected and withdrawn, given to sudden outbursts of anger or sadness. Until the children were prompted to express their stories in crayon and paint, and then to have conversations about what they had made, they could not access their trauma narrative.

Melissa Walker is an art therapist who has worked for many years with service members suffering from both PTSD and traumatic brain injuries, which can further limit the efficacy of talk therapy. Of the many forms of therapeutic arts Melissa has worked with, she has found that one of the most effective for military service members is the making and decorating of life-size papier-mâché masks. "Finally, these invisible wounds don't just have a name, they have a face," she said. "It allows them to come to grips, literally, with their trauma." She estimates she has worked with more than a thousand service members in painting masks to express what words cannot.

In a TED talk she gave in 2015, Melissa told of a soldier who jumped into a bunker during heavy fighting in Afghanistan and was confronted by the vision of a bloody human face. The solider knew the terrifying image wasn't real, but the bloody face kept reappearing before his eyes, multiple times each day and even in his sleep. Fearful of being considered weak or sick, he told no one about the vision. For seven years it was his lonely secret and his constant companion. He even gave it a nickname: BFIB—Bloody Face in Bunker.

Through his art therapy work with Melissa Walker, the soldier was prompted to paint a mask to represent BFIB. Creating art from such a painful vision was difficult, but it proved to be transformative for the soldier's mental health. When he began referring to the mask itself as BFIB, his visions of BFIB lost their grip on his psyche. By remaking BFIB into a tangible artifact he could hold in his hands and discuss with others, the soldier found it was no longer a ghostly and shameful secret. He put it in a box at the hospital, and when his treatment ended, he left it there. A year later, with his PTSD symptoms subsided, the solider reported that since he'd made the mask, the vision of the Bloody Face in the Bunker had reappeared to him only twice. Both times, he added, the face had been smiling.

How is such a transformation possible? Let's take a closer look at the brain scan research done by Janneke van Leeuwen, referenced in chapter 2. She and her research team reviewed the "social brain atlas," which was created by Daniel Alcalá-López and his colleagues from twenty-six published functional MRI studies of the brain networks associated with social engagement. Van Leeuwen then correlated those areas of brain function with the cognitive processes required to support neuro-aesthetic tasks, like assessing the meaning of a work of art, and then integrated those findings into a single aggregate brain map. The team discovered that these areas of neuro-aesthetic processing, collectively known as the artistic brain connectome (ABC), closely overlap and interact with the known networks of the social brain connectome (SBC), which regulate our physiological responses to social encounters. Theoretically (and this is still far from proven fact), when soldiers make art in an environment filled with creative works of all kinds, the activation of the ABC in the brains of these soldiers enhances the functionality of their brains' SBC, suppressing their fight-or-flight responses to traumatic triggers and improving their brains' access to feelings of empathy and compassion.

Humans are innately both social and creative, but never before has brain science detected such a clear connection between these two primal traits. Could it be that creative expression is far more important to our humanity and our connections with others than we realize? When we engage in creative expression, even while sitting alone reading poetry or looking at a book of art prints, the mental effort adjusts our brain reactivity patterns toward more positive social perceptions and behavior.

When Captain Jason Berner was first invited to make his own mask for art therapy, he told us in an on-camera interview how he had dismissed the idea. "Here I am, a strong, physically demanding warrior," he recalled later. "Why do I have to do art? I plan battles. I plan wars. I take life, if necessary, if absolutely necessary. I'm not doing art." In time he relented, and the mask he made reflected his prideful self-concept as a warrior and the vulnerability it concealed. He painted his mask bright red on the outside, with an angry furrowed brow and slashes of yellow on the cheeks that resembled Native American war paint.

"The thing I like about the mask is that it represented the many different levels of who I viewed myself as," he told me, holding the mask in his hands. "When I was weak, emotionally and psychologically, I was able to project a strong front."

Jason's training told him, as commander of his unit, that his men were his responsibility. He was their protector. But now he had to live with the memory that several of them had died, while he had been spared. The experience of making the mask, choosing its color design, and discussing its meaning had given him a safe place to engage with emotions that had long been beyond words.

"I never would have talked about what this meant," he said. "I was shielded in some ways. I was protected. I was able to express it in a way that was safe for me . . . to create something that makes it okay to feel the way I feel and help take that burden away."

COMPLEX PTSD

Treatment also revealed that Jason's life traumas had begun long before he'd taken up arms to protect his country. When he was just nine years old, Jason's parents brought him to a house party where he saw a motorcycle gang member stab a man over drug money. As a teenager, he explained, his role in his family included "protecting my mother and little brother from my father and his alcoholism and dependencies." Jason's father frequently battered all the members of his family when he was drunk, and Jason assumed at a young age that his job as eldest son was to protect his mother and brother. He also feared that if his father ever killed his mother, he would be next.

In art therapy, Jason used clay and paint to fashion a heraldic coat of arms that reflected his role as protector. He chose chivalric symbols for valor, courage, and justice: a pair of crossed swords behind a shield, a lion, and a set of weighing scales. Holding the coat of arms in his hands, he explained, "It represents all those people I've been protecting my entire life."

These particular details of Jason's PTSD recovery lead us to an entirely different terrain within the territory of trauma: *complex* PTSD. These are the stress disorders caused by long-term exposure to traumatic injury: chronic childhood abuse (emotional, physical, and sexual), chaotic dysfunctional upbringings, abusive adult relationships, and hostile neighborhoods and workplaces.

In children, a category called adverse childhood experiences (ACEs) recognizes that early traumas in childhood can have deep and sustained impacts on future health issues, including loneliness. There are more than fifteen experiences that rank as ACEs, including incarceration of a parent, domestic violence in the home, and having a parent with a substance abuse disorder. A landmark 1998 survey known as the CDC-Kaiser ACE Study showed that adults who as children had one or more of these experiences were at a significantly higher risk for both mental and physical health problems as adults.

However, health screening for ACEs is problematic because they are so common. The study showed that only 36.1 percent of respondents reported having no adverse childhood events. As many as 30 percent of adults reported physical abuse in their upbringing, and more than one in four women were victims of sexual abuse. Substance abuse was present in about one-quarter of all families, mental illness was present in one out of five families, and 12.7 percent of survey respondents said they witnessed their mothers being treated violently.

In 1988, when Harvard Medical School researcher and psychiatrist Judith Herman first introduced the concept of "complex PTSD" as distinct from event-based PTSD, she noted the "utter aloneness" of her patients' self-perception. She has since gone on to become a leading expert in trauma and domestic abuse. Her seminal book, *Trauma and Recovery*, describes complex trauma as "an affliction of the powerless.

At the moment of trauma, the victim is rendered helpless by overwhelming force."

Childhood neglect and abuse are so deeply traumatizing because every child victimized by adults wants to believe at the same time that adults are the child's protectors. The brain, doing its job as an organ of survival, registers this extreme state of cognitive dissonance as a primal threat to survival. That is why people who have been traumatized in their youth, like Jason Berner, are more susceptible to PTSD as a reaction to traumatic events in adulthood. Because the original traumatic experience is not comprehensible, similar situations must be assumed to be a source of danger until proven otherwise. For someone with complex PTSD, events that serve as reminders of the original trauma will be perceived through this filter as threats to survival.

When I consider the power of early trauma to affect social cognition and decision-making in later life, I think of my own experience at age fifteen, in the aftermath of my father's sudden death from a heart attack. I recognize that I suffered a kind of trauma that day that few young people ever experience. I vividly recall hiding behind the dining room doorway, *speechless* with fear and confusion as my father was taken down our front steps on a stretcher and loaded into the back door of an emergency vehicle. I had no words for the horrible implications of what I was witnessing. An hour earlier it had been just another school morning. Now my father, a warm and loving man, a dedicated research scientist whom I loved and admired, was leaving our house feet-first as a pale and helpless heart attack victim. It was the last time I'd ever see him alive.

My overwhelming feeling at the time was one of embarrassment and inadequacy. I blamed myself for what had happened. I felt guilty that I'd been unable to keep him alive. He died on my watch, and I had been powerless to stop it. I knew this feeling wasn't completely rational, but I felt it strongly nonetheless, and I was too embarrassed by it to discuss it with anyone. I worked hard to put it out of my mind, and to a certain extent was successful, which allowed me to keep moving forward in my young and disrupted life. This was a generation in which people didn't talk about these things, anyway.

In the following years, I was haunted by the loneliness of unresolved grief. It turned out that my father had been the glue holding our family together. Without him, we each grieved separately. Each of us withdrew to our own lonely island of sorrow. My mother had always struggled with depression, and when she lost her husband, her depression took over. From what I remember of the years until I went away to college at Princeton, my mother spent most days chain-smoking in bed. I not only lost my father, who had always been the more nurturing and attentive parent, but also lost my mother.

We are an adaptive species, of course, so I went outside my immediate family for human connection. My close friendships with two high school pals, Mark and David, were very important to me. I was particularly close to Mark and much preferred spending time at his house with his family than with my own. But neither Mark nor David lived to see their twenty-first birthdays. David died at age twenty from a sudden and fatal medical crisis that his family avoided talking about, and Mark died less than a month afterward; he'd had a rock-climbing fall in Oregon. He was still alive when helicoptered to the local hospital but didn't survive his injuries. In both these cases I felt sadness and loss, but also the nagging feeling that I had let them down, failed to do something to make a difference—that they had died on my watch.

I tell this story not as a "woe is me" tale, but to underline how intimately acquainted I am with traumatic memories for which there are no words. I had coped with the loss of my father by finding supportive friendships with Mark and David, with Mark's parents' home as a kind of sanctuary. Then Mark and David were gone. Late in my junior year of college, I made some conscious choices that were shaped by my grief. As much as I loved poetry and the arts, I made a practical career decision to apply to medical school. The safety and security of that career path, and a general sense that I would be doing something that could be useful, made more sense to me after I'd lost my two friends. At that point I hadn't connected the dots to realize I unconsciously thought that by mastering medicine I might have the skills to keep people close to me from dying. Or that by saving others, I might be able to make amends for having been unable to save those I loved.

Later in adult life, in my twenties and thirties, although I dated actively and at one point lived with someone, I wasn't fully there. I was still in a different place, one of loss, shame, sadness, and uncertainty. Some survival-oriented part of my brain had come to the conclusion that it wasn't such a great idea to actually allow yourself to be invested emotionally in other people, because it was just too devastating when they died. I had a series of love relationships that I bailed on, one after the other, when they became too close. My social cognition had been distorted by trauma. Where others could let themselves fall in love, I felt triggered by the emotional memory of having lost my father and my friends. As intimacy grew in these relationships, I threw up emotional walls just as reflexively and irrationally as the traumatized vet who reaches for his weapon when he hears a loud noise at the shopping mall. I think of the pain and puzzlement in the faces of the young women I loved, as they saw me inexplicably withdraw from our relationships. They had no idea, and I had no understanding, of the unresolved grief I carried into every intimate relationship.

My traumatic memories of loss remained unconsolidated, and they rang fearful alarm bells about the dangers of close attachments. In my state of hypervigilance to avoid future pain, I had no way to accommodate the incontrovertible fact that everyone in a close relationship risks losing that relationship to death. Mortality is the human condition. I was smart enough to graduate magna cum laude from Princeton and then get top honors and acknowledgments in medical school, but traumatic memories so distorted my cognition in the area of intimate connection that I was powerless to reason my way out of it. In therapy, the process of memory reconsolidation gives this power back to traumatized individuals so they can tell the story of their trauma without pain. Healing allows them to own their stories, rather than having their stories own them. My story owned me, and I owned loneliness.

The role of loneliness in the diagnosis and treatment of complex PTSD is only beginning to be understood. A study in 2011 showed that among young women who had been exposed to physical or sexual abuse before the age of fourteen, there was a high correlation between the severity of their PTSD symptoms and their personal appraisals of loneliness, as they agreed with statements such as "I am disconnected from people" and "Even though I have friends, I still feel lonely."

Another study, published in 2019, provides case studies suggesting loneliness plays a major role in sustaining the symptoms of complex PTSD and in impeding progress in its treatment. The authors noted, "Loneliness and complex PTSD appear to interact iteratively, each capable of reinforcing the other, via deleterious mutually enhancing feedback cycles." This is very similar to my observation about the vicious cycle of loneliness. Post-traumatic stress can make you lonely, and loneliness makes the treatment of PTSD more difficult. The combination of social avoidance behaviors and loneliness puts people being treated for complex PTSD at risk for alienation and suicidal ideation, much like the military vets Dr. Marmar had treated.

The study authors cited the case of a young woman suffering from complex PTSD due to childhood sexual abuse. Her loneliness and lack of social support had put her at greater risk of being vulnerable to sexual predators, which exacerbated her condition.

Persistent loneliness, the authors write, is also a common roadblock to progress in PTSD therapy in such cases. "When intimate and relational loneliness are prominent and the individual lacks external emotional and social supports, attempting such processes in psychotherapy is extremely difficult and odds of ineffective therapy increase." The study's authors suggest that because loneliness is frequently easier to address than other complex PTSD symptoms, interventions for loneliness should be more commonly considered for the treatment of PTSD, when offered in parallel to more conventional approaches. This makes intuitive sense because a patient with better relationships and social supports will have greater prospects for success in PTSD management overall. It's what I would call a recommended reversal of the vicious cycle into a virtuous cycle.

THE PYRAMID OF VULNERABILITY

PTSD is commonly thought of as a military mental health condition because the US Department of Defense and the Department of Veterans Affairs have done so much groundbreaking work in its recognition and treatment. However, for the civilian population that suffers traumas every day, increased awareness of how to recognize and respond to feelings of post-traumatic stress would make an enormous contribution to the mental health of the nation.

The Pyramid of Vulnerability is a traditional public health model I often use in my teaching about loneliness. It is based on the concept of triage, which sorts the population into three tiers according to their risk level for any medical condition or health concern. In the case of loneliness, the top tier of the pyramid is occupied by people whose loneliness is so profound that it is causing them significant life-damaging consequences. In the bottom tier, at the base of the pyramid, are the vast majority of people who feel lonely from time to time but are not really affected by it. The middle tier constitutes the most interesting group, because they are at risk of falling victim to life-damaging loneliness for any number of the reasons I've discussed. The goal of screening for "new onset" loneliness is to identify those in the middle tier and provide them with support and interventions to help them reduce their loneliness, so that they can reenter the general population in the pyramid's base.

Pyramid of Vulnerability for Loneliness

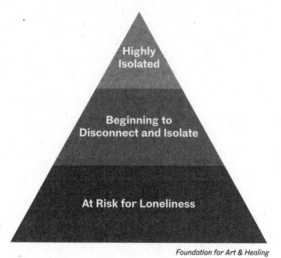

Foundation for Art & Healing

If we apply this pyramid model to the specific loneliness of post-traumatic stress, we can see that the middle tier is populated by people who have experienced serious trauma and are at risk of developing disabling PTSD and the severe loneliness that frequently accompanies it. Many of those people would benefit from engaging in connection-oriented activities that would help resolve their post-traumatic stress. They could be spared the incalculable personal suffering of PTSD, and society could be spared the tremendous healthcare costs of PTSD treatment.

For the general public, located in the bottom tier of this pyramid, the appropriate intervention is improved education that raises awareness of the risks and symptoms of stress and loneliness following a traumatic event. The US government, for instance, distributes "psychological first-aid" handouts at natural disaster sites that describe proven best practices for how to give and receive support during the trauma of being dislocated. The advice in these handouts would be helpful to anyone who's been injured in an accident, victimized by a violent crime, or suffered any other kind of trauma.

We all experience traumas in our lives, which is yet another compelling reason to maintain a strong personal network of social connections. We never know when a sudden setback might send us reeling and put us at risk of isolating and becoming severely lonely. The value of your social connections becomes clear when you need them the most. That's why, generally speaking, a society with less loneliness and more connection will have a healthier and more resilient population.

To help avoid the loneliness of post-traumatic stress in your life, you can try the framework I've proposed for creative expression: be curious, make things, and have conversations.

- First try to be curious about your feelings following the event. Recognize the potential for loneliness and the type of loneliness you might be feeling. Psychologically, are you avoiding your feelings and engaging in unhealthy behaviors? What about societal loneliness? Are you feeling that it's harder to "fit in" or to belong comfortably in the same social circles since the event? Has the event left you feeling spiritually or morally bereft and isolated?

• Next, try to make something. If you can find the words, write out what you're thinking and feeling. Perhaps keep a daily journal or a dream journal. Or make something in any medium that gives you comfort and a feeling of accomplishment. As long as it's linked somehow to wherever your curiosity takes you, cooking a recipe you've never tried before, adding a new section of flowers to your garden, or building something new in your house can be just as creatively expressive as painting a picture.

• Have conversations about what you've made and the thoughts and feelings that are embedded and intertwined with it. Then reach out in the areas where you have detected the ache of loneliness. If it's relevant to your situation, try talking about your loneliness-related unhealthy behaviors with someone, or take the risk of connecting with someone you feel might be avoiding you. Have a spiritual conversation with a trusted source if that's what's ailing you.

As tough as it may be, recognize the importance of discussing the trauma with close friends and confidants. You are reconsolidating your memory. In each of these cases, your objective is to consign the event to memory, to develop a trauma narrative that can be retold without pain and no longer puts you at risk of spiraling into the vicious cycle of negative feelings, withdrawing from others, and loneliness. Seeking help from a medical professional or through psychological counseling is always a good idea in the aftermath of a traumatic event, but it's also true that there will never be enough appointments available to deal with all the pain of life's adversity. That's what FEMA recognizes by offering general mental health advice and information in its disaster relief efforts. The risks are great, and the available professional resources are rarely adequate. The problems of trauma and loneliness require scalable and broadly available public health responses because there is not nearly enough individual care to go around.

PANDEMIC AS A GLOBAL TRAUMA

The global pandemic that began in 2020 has been a trauma for millions of people due to loss of work, loss of relationships, and loss of loved ones who died from COVID-19. The US rates of loneliness hit historic highs in 2019, and then the forced isolation of the pandemic's onset raised those rates even higher. Millions of people endured agonizing months without seeing friends and loved ones, without the casual everyday social interactions of going to work and school, and were deprived of the pleasure of parties, concerts, clubs, and restaurants. Those who were traumatized by the sudden isolating loss of rituals and routines that gave their pre-pandemic lives texture and meaning will experience a much longer recovery period. As with other post-traumatic stress and disordered grieving syndromes, they are prone to suffering ongoing anxiety, hypervigilance, a sense of vulnerability, and increased risk for depression, addiction, and suicidality.

At the same time, the pandemic offered an object lesson in how it's much easier to talk about loneliness when one realizes how many other people are experiencing it. It also brought with it an important opportunity to destigmatize loneliness. Once we can admit to being lonely because the entire world is struggling with the trauma of it, we improve our chances to navigate it while reducing both its prevalence and toxicity. Unembarrassed acknowledgment of our loneliness is a powerful force that connects us, ameliorating physical and mental harm while also giving us the endurance to make it through a tough time.

For the chronically lonely, the agony of loneliness frequently includes their dark suspicion that they deserve it. They suspect they're not worthy of making authentic and reliable connections with others because they are damaged goods. Losers, in short. On the other hand, with loneliness becoming a widespread and acknowledged problem during the pandemic, those who were already lonely could feel somehow affirmed. With so many people sharing the same circumstances, there is a natural reduction in stress levels and an enhancement of positive moods and emotions like optimism, patience, empathy, and forbearance.

The experience of loneliness is highly personal and subjective. So the pandemic's effect that I noted earlier—"same storm, different boats"—left some people taking on water and drowning, while others found calm and safe harbors. For many, the solitude granted them by the pandemic lockdowns spared them from the loneliness of their working lives. Businesspeople who used to spend weeks at a time on the road were glad to spend time at home with their children. There were fortunate couples for whom working from home afforded them the opportunity to grow closer. A survey of two thousand people in the UK showed that during the 2020 lockdown months, 43 percent of survey participants engaged in activities that made them feel accomplished. They had more time for hobbies, including creative arts. They exercised more, read more, and took online classes. Many survey participants recalled the period of forced solitude as one of increased self-care, self-growth, and self-connection.

And for those who did not fare so well, there is a phenomenon called post-traumatic growth—PTG—in which people who endure the psychological struggle of adversity often see positive growth following their recovery. Researchers who have studied PTG have found several areas of personal growth most commonly experienced, almost all of which are strongly related to alleviated loneliness. Recovery from trauma, for example, often results in closer connections with others, especially with people who have also suffered. Another common PTG effect is an increased sense of personal strength and self-esteem. Still others who have experienced PTG emerge with a greater appreciation for life in general and a deepening of their spiritual beliefs.

In each of the four other loneliness territories that follow, there are some elements of trauma to be found, in varying degrees, which is why the matter of post-traumatic growth is worth mentioning now. Loneliness can also be, like trauma, both a scourge and an opportunity. This is not to discount the pain of loneliness, nor does it suggest that the life circumstances that might be making you chronically lonely are in any way "good" things.

The objective of trauma recovery is not to forget the past but to set oneself free from the emotional grip of the memory. If you can tell your trauma story without pain, then you own your story, your story doesn't own you. In a similar way, loneliness is not something to be denied or ignored. By accepting loneliness as a useful bodily distress signal, you can see the pangs of loneliness as invitations to explore and grow. Transforming your relationship with loneliness in this way can truly transform your outlook on life and the human connections it offers. Your feelings of loneliness are there to serve you, not torture you, no matter the territory in which they are encountered.

5

Illness

In 1992, Lillie Shockney was an oncology nurse at Johns Hopkins Hospital when she was diagnosed with metastatic breast cancer. Then in her thirties, married with a young daughter at home, Lillie knew enough about the illness to count her blessings. She had a strong support system of family and friends to see her through this personal crisis. That's why what happened next came as such an unpleasant surprise.

When Lillie called her friends with news of her diagnosis, she heard awkward silence on the other end of the line. At work, even among her nurse friends, she saw deer-in-the-headlights reactions when she told them she had cancer. In the weeks that followed, friends didn't call as frequently as before, and some went completely silent. When Lillie phoned some of them, her calls went straight to voice mail and her messages went unreturned.

Lillie had been working with breast cancer patients since the age of seventeen, but nothing had prepared her for the loneliness that came with her diagnosis. She felt hurt and abandoned, but she also understood. News of serious illness can make well people feel very uncomfortable. "They're thinking, if it can happen to you, it can happen to me," Lillie told me in an interview. For some people, illness stirs up frightening reminders of their own mortality. Connecting with a friend with cancer may feel to them like a connection with death.

Around that time, there was an award-winning series of public-service TV commercials promoting automotive safety. The spots featured a pair of crash test dummies named Vince and Larry who cheerfully had their heads smashed, torsos impaled, and limbs torn off in crash tests without wearing safety belts. Vince and Larry emerged from the wreckage joking as they reattached their limbs, but the ad closed with a serious admonition: "You could learn a lot from a dummy. Buckle your safety belts."

Lillie saw one of the ads and was struck by inspiration. "I said to my husband, 'I have to find the funny in this,'" she recalled. "I need to share the funny, so I can get my friends back on track with me, so I can get the support that I need from them."

Lillie called around to her friends, and rather than try to explain her loneliness and need for friendship, she asked for their help. Following her upcoming radical mastectomy, she would soon be fitted for a right breast prosthesis. Like the crash test dummies Vince and Larry, Lillie's prosthesis would need a name, and she was open to suggestions. She asked everyone to contribute and vote on their favorite name for her prosthesis. Ideas soon came rolling in, and Lillie's conversations about the silly contest had the chance to turn to more meaningful subjects. Within weeks, she had a name for her prosthesis (Betty Boob), and she also had her friends back.

Loneliness can take a tremendous toll on people with illness. When Linda Topf's multiple sclerosis gradually robbed her of everyday mobility, she witnessed her connections with other people suffer and decline as a result. The illness left her feeling cut off from the rest of humanity. "I felt that people didn't want to listen and couldn't ever understand my life experience," she wrote in her book *You Are Not Your Illness*. "This sense of isolation, of being separate from people who are well, can be as painful as any of the worst treatments or symptoms that we might have to endure. It is loneliness in its most profound form."

For every kind of illness, there is a risk of a specific kind of loneliness. For Lillie Shockney, it was abandonment by her friends. For Linda Topf, it was the separateness of disability. All illness has that power, to set us apart in some way, to make us feel we no longer belong among those who are well. "Illness is the night-side of life, a more onerous citizenship," Susan Sontag wrote in *Illness as Metaphor*. "Everyone who is born holds dual citizenship, in the kingdom of the well and in the kingdom of the sick."

Loneliness arises when we find ourselves ill and are unable to move comfortably between Sontag's two kingdoms. There is much to be gained in each one. In the kingdom of the well, we explore and expand the possibilities that are part of the familiar narrative of living. We take steps, deliberate or not, toward ways of seeing, being, and believing that shape the attitudes and behaviors that enable our accomplishments, both personal and public. In the kingdom of the sick, there is no less an opportunity for enabling accomplishment, even when done outside the spotlight of our social bias toward focusing our attention on what's positive.

"Ruins, for me, are the beginning," said Anselm Kiefer, the German painter whose work is deeply influenced by growing up after World War II in a town destroyed by Allied bombing. "With the debris, you can construct new ideas. They are symbols of a beginning." In major illness, with its forced reframing of our physical and emotional land-scapes, there are important ways we can notice and get curious about things that were invisible beforehand. How we use this new informa-tion can determine whether illness and other traumas can be shaped into post-traumatic growth. Can we find within it some points of clar-ity, which like a piton used in climbing can prevent us from falling while also enabling the upward ascent?

DANGERS OF A LONELY HEART

In the early 2000s, I served as a medical adviser to Health Buddy, a company that was involved in some of the first efforts to use digital interactive technologies for the purpose of telehealth. We put digi-tal scales in the homes of people in imminent danger of the extreme shortness of breath from severe heart failure that requires urgent med-ical attention. Each scale was linked online to a centralized call center staffed by nurses. Our objective was to remotely monitor each subject's weight on a daily basis to detect any sudden gain that would indicate the start of dangerous fluid buildup in the lungs. Through early inter-vention with increased doses of medications, Health Buddy could re-duce the overall rate of costly hospitalization among this particular population.

The project soon showed very encouraging results. Hospitaliza-tions of all kinds among the subject population dropped by 50 percent. We were delighted that this initial phase had worked so well, and the program expanded nicely as news spread of its effectiveness. It took a few years before it occurred to me that the early interventions with adjusted medications occurred only rarely. It seemed unlikely that the relatively small number of interventions would account for such a dramatic drop in hospitalizations.

I came to suspect the difference was related to loneliness. Many people with severe heart failure live a fairly isolated existence. The simple act of monitoring the scales in the people's homes had given many of them a sense of being connected, allowing them to feel that Health Buddy and the caring nurses employed there "had their backs." The daily weigh-in and brief but personal contact with the call center made them feel less lonely, and likely more motivated to do the two things most vital to heart failure management: avoid high-salt foods and adhere to their medication schedules.

Back in the pre-internet 1990s, I'd seen similar results while working with a company called Access Health, which ran a round-the-clock call center staffed by registered nurses. The people who called to discuss their health problems frequently raised all sorts of emotional and stress-related issues, and many were clearly lonely, although they rarely dared to utter the word. At the time it was a pretty big eye-opener for me. Like many medical practitioners in the early days of digital health, I thought the primary value we were providing was in dispensing timely clinical information, educating callers on the different types of headaches, for instance, and informing them that not all head pain indicated something serious. And yes, we did dole out that information, but only incidentally to offering callers what many were truly looking for: comfort and connection. The conversations with the nurses, the reassurances they offered, and their willingness to stay on the line had a tremendously calming effect on callers. It made me wonder how many emergency room visits are billed solely because people often have no one to talk to when they feel a strange ache or pain.

As with the work I'd done years earlier with autoworker data in Michigan, I saw how public health, properly carried out, reduces human suffering as it reduces medical expenditures and makes much better use of scarce resources like emergency room personnel. These and other experiences led to my growing conviction that clinicians as healers needed to pay careful attention not just to physical signals but also to certain emotional and social factors in order to fully support their patients' health.

In 2018, I collaborated with a Fortune 200 company to use their annual employee health survey to create a loneliness score for each worker in the same way they asked about smoking and alcohol use. When we correlated loneliness scores with medical claims, we were surprised to see that the lonely employees had the same rate of hospital admissions overall, but twice the frequency of readmissions and preventable admissions. And while the lonely employees had the same number of opioid prescriptions as their better-connected coworkers, they had three times the rate of diagnosed opioid use disorders, a clear signal of increased addiction risk. All this contributed to the provocative finding that in aggregate the lonely employees had 22 percent greater per capita medical and prescription drug costs than those who were not lonely.

It's likely that many of those addictions and hospitalizations were due to daily stressors, chronic illness, and mental health issues poorly attended to by lonely people. Illness invites loneliness, and loneliness in turn presents a litany of obstacles to remaining well. The direct and persistent harmful physiological effects of loneliness are a serious health threat to anyone already suffering from an illness, all in addition to the way loneliness erodes the maintenance of the positive health behaviors that are critical to managing the illness. And to make it even worse, lonely people lack the safety net of attentive friends and family members to guide them supportively through the health challenges they encounter, leaving them more vulnerable to their ill effects.

The impact of loneliness on people with chronic illness (most of which is lifestyle related) constitutes what might be the world's fastest-growing health problem. In most advanced economies, healthcare expenditures are dominated by the cost of treating potentially preventable chronic illnesses such as heart disease, diabetes, respiratory conditions, dementia, and others. As much as 90 percent of annual US medical expenditures are for people with chronic and mental health conditions. Healthcare spending in 2021 totaled $4.3 trillion, representing 18.3 percent of US gross domestic product.

The cardiovascular ailments of heart disease and stroke are by far the leading causes of death in the world's most highly developed nations, the same nations where loneliness is also widespread and growing. The World Health Organization estimates that cardiovascular diseases take almost eighteen million lives each year, making it the leading cause of death globally. Four out of five of these deaths are from strokes and heart attacks, and fully one-third occur prematurely in people age seventy and under. Imagine if we could make meaningful progress in reversing the rising levels of loneliness and its attendant medical costs, how in addition to the reduction in human misery those funds could be allocated toward improving education, transportation, and crumbling infrastructure, and mitigating climate change.

Many of the well-known physiological effects of loneliness—elevated blood pressure, increased inflammation, reduced immune response—are highly detrimental to cardiovascular health. (A major UK study published in 2018 that tracked the records of almost half a million people pointed to loneliness increasing the risk for heart disease by as much as 50 percent.) And that's not surprising. The fight-or-flight state of arousal brought on by loneliness stimulates production of cortisol, which raises blood pressure as it prepares the body to either fight or flee from danger. That's useful for a body with an urgent need for self-defense, but the sustained fight-or-flight stress signaling of loneliness can have damaging long-term physiological consequences.

A 2015 study of gene expression in leukocytes (white blood cells that make up part of the immune system's response to infection) showed that among both lonely humans and isolated macaque monkeys there was a decreased expression of genes involved in antiviral response and an increased expression of genes involved in inflammation. Long-term fight-or-flight stress signaling from loneliness can raise your inflammation levels while having a negative effect on immune system function. That's a worrisome finding, particularly in light of growing research that implicates inflammation as a causal factor in a wide variety of physical and mental illnesses, which in aggregate are responsible for the majority of health impairment and death worldwide.

In 2018, the American Heart Association (AHA) sponsored a pilot study that was one of the first to draw a direct correlation between loneliness and increased hospitalization and mortality from heart disease. More than two thousand Minnesota residents with heart failure were surveyed, and although only about 6 percent reported feeling a high degree of social isolation, members of this relatively small population were 3.5 times more likely than their non-lonely counterparts to die during the study's eight-month follow-up period. They were also 70 percent more likely to be hospitalized, and 60 percent more likely require emergency room visits. (Among survey respondents who perceived themselves as only moderately isolated, there was almost no difference from the non-isolated respondents in terms of mortality and hospitalization rates.) It was one of several studies that led the AHA to release a scientific statement in 2022 declaring social isolation and loneliness to be associated with a 30 percent increased risk of heart attack or stroke, or death from either. A statement by the chair of the writing group, Dr. Crystal Wiley Cené, added, "Given the prevalence of social disconnectedness across the U.S., the public health impact is quite significant."

One thing I found particularly interesting about the 2018 study was that it employed an easy-to-use survey device called the PROMIS social isolation short form (Patient-Reported Outcomes Measurement Information System, a set of data-friendly survey standards developed by the National Institutes of Health [NIH]). One of the limiting factors in all survey research is that longer survey questionnaires usually give more accurate data, but they also tend to reduce response rates. The PROMIS social isolation short form, on the other hand, has been shown to be effective in identifying very lonely individuals by scoring their agree-disagree responses to just four simple statements:

I feel left out.

I feel that people barely know me.

I feel isolated from others.

I feel that people are around me but not with me.

These four statements could serve as a very effective screening device for many populations. The study's senior author, Lila Rutten of the Mayo Clinic, expressed hope that by screening for "perceived social isolation" (defined as the subjective feelings of loneliness and social disconnection) she could "lay the groundwork for understanding how such patients might be better cared for and supported." For example, quick scoring on responses to these four statements could determine whether a patient is in need of enhanced care, social support, or perhaps a mental health evaluation. There are other relatively short surveys that have been used to measure loneliness, including three questions extracted from the full twenty questions of the UCLA Loneliness Scale, that could provide a similar type of tool, used in the same way.

For people with any type of serious preexisting condition, routine screenings of this kind may be essential to saving lives and reducing costs of care. We've seen where simple interventions through human connection can make a big difference in the severity of chronic illness for many patients. If loneliness is screened for in this way and then addressed with the same degree of concern as smoking cessation has been over the years, how many millions of lives and billions of dollars in healthcare costs could be saved? We'll come back to this simple "screen and refer" strategy to get people started down the path of being more connected and less lonely in a variety of settings, not just medical ones, as we move through the different loneliness territories.

The famously cynical George Bernard Shaw once remarked, "The universal regard for money is the one hopeful fact in our civilization." Reductions in both monetary costs and human suffering need to be reliably proven for any public health measure to be considered sustainable. Interventions for alleviating loneliness done at scale have little chance of being funded and replicated unless savings can be documented in terms of reduced distress, improved ability to function, and medical dollars saved.

This economic argument is a provocative and important one. An AARP study shows that treatment costs for lonely Medicare beneficiaries are about sixteen hundred dollars per year above average costs. Effective programs to address loneliness should be paid for as a portion of the medical cost savings they achieve. CareMore Health, a division of Anthem, the country's second-largest private health insurer, was a pioneer in having clinicians screen patients for social issues like loneliness. Because CareMore assumes the financial risk for its patients' care, reducing loneliness is beneficial both to its patients' well-being and in reducing CareMore's costs. When CareMore enrolled more than one thousand seniors at risk of loneliness in a program of regular contact through phone calls, home visits, and social events, emergency room utilization for participants fell by 3.3 percent, and hospital admissions were 20.8 percent lower. Public sector insurance programs like Medicare Advantage and Medicaid continue to develop incentive reimbursement systems to encourage more of this kind of programming.

TWELVE STEPS AND BEYOND

The same vicious cycle of loneliness described among people with PTSD in the previous chapter can be found among people with most kinds of serious illness. Loneliness makes people sicker, and as their illness advances, they grow more isolated, which can lead to distortions of social cognition and despair that no one cares about them. Self-esteem erodes to the point where isolation presents a true danger to self-care and survival. Psychotherapist Alisa Robinson describes this downward spiral as she has seen it in her clients:

> *Imagine this—you feel lonely and sad. You don't like the feeling. It feels horrible. So you try not to think about it. You read books, keep busy at work, drink a couple of glasses of wine, eat a few doughnuts, whatever you can to avoid the feeling. But you haven't actually done anything different to make a change. The next time you notice yourself feeling lonely, you realize that*

you have been feeling this way for quite a while and nothing is different. Now you feel even worse. You might not only feel lonely, but now your self-esteem starts to suffer. You feel more hopeless, more lost and confused.

And it's not just physical illness. Mental Health America, a national advocacy group, has invested a lot in providing online surveys with titles such as "Do I Have Depression?" and "Do I Have Bipolar Disorder?" More than five million people have filled out these surveys, and at the end of each survey, there is an additional set of questions that asks each respondent to name the kinds of help they would like. Among survey respondents who scored a high probability of having mental illness—whether it's depression, bipolar disorder, PTSD, or another illness—the most commonly checked box is: "I want to connect with someone just like me."

For anyone dealing with the loneliness of illness, connecting with "someone just like me" makes a lot of sense. From my early years of medical practice, I had come to see how Weight Watchers has often been very effective for people struggling with weight issues. I just hadn't fully connected what they do with addressing loneliness.

Obese people are frequently marginalized in our appearance-obsessed culture. They feel shamed and excluded, and many isolate themselves, turning to overeating as a form of self-medication, while poor body image turns them away from healthy behaviors like exercise. The soothing effects of processed foods high in fat and simple sugars tend to stimulate the same pleasure centers in the brain that are affected by addictive drugs like cocaine. From the earliest days of Weight Watchers, weekly group meetings with weigh-ins cultivated a sense of belonging among members that gave them the motivation and support they needed to change their eating habits. In a similar way, 12-step programs call on members with addictions to be part of a group that listens to each other's stories, offering support and recognition.

Twelve-step groups also encourage each person to find a "sponsor" who serves as mentor and coach, available around the clock for support. So in both of these clinical scenarios, there is a sense of connection fostered among the members of a group, which then helps them chart a collective path toward better health behaviors. It also raised the "chicken and egg" question in my mind as to whether loneliness, or a feeling of disconnection, was an initial driver for overeating or out-of-control drinking in the first place.

Back in 2014, when we did our six-session Creativity Circle pilot program for twelve women with diabetes at Boston Medical Center, the participants' comments attested to the value of not feeling alone with a chronic illness. One participant, in acknowledging the difficulties of needing a daily finger-prick to test her blood sugar levels, told us, "This program has helped me look at my life and decide I need to make better choices. No one likes to have to stick themselves every day—no one. But this is the only way I will live a long life, if I test myself, eat right, focus on other things that I want to do. And I learned no one is exempt. Doesn't matter if you're smart or educated or have money. People get diabetes. Then it is up to you to decide what to do about it. I don't want to gamble with it."

The measurable positive health effects of support groups have been known for a long time. More than thirty years ago, Dr. Matthew Budd, a pioneer in Mind Body Medicine at Harvard Medical School and an important teacher and mentor of mine in the early stages of my career, developed and led a series of programs at Harvard Pilgrim Health Care called "Ways to Wellness," for people with psychosomatic and stress-related illnesses such as tension headaches, musculoskeletal pain, and gastrointestinal distress. He noted that people in these support groups soon started having fewer symptoms, improved their management of their disorders, and scheduled fewer office visits seeking treatment.

Why would that be? Matthew believes it reflects the importance of narrative to the functioning of the brain. We train the brain to perceive the world through the stories we tell and the types of language and linguistic structures we use in those stories. Loneliness is characterized by a lot of negative self-talk reflecting low self-regard: "No one would want to help me" or "What's the point of trying?" If that's what you tell your brain all day, your brain will begin to function as if it were true. Involvement in support groups at Harvard Pilgrim, on the other hand, provided participants with a healthier and collectively constructed alternative narrative about their psychosomatic illnesses. Each participant, by making connections and having conversations with "people like me," was able to develop a more positive story about their affliction. That made them feel less lonely, reduced their body's stress levels, and helped them heal. It also led to fewer office visits, less use of other healthcare resources, and lower costs.

My friend Tom Insel, a psychiatrist and once the head of the NIMH, told me a story about a college-age drug trial participant with a severe case of obsessive-compulsive disorder (OCD) that defied medical treatment for more than a year. Then something remarkable happened.

When Tom began his medical career at the NIMH, he ran trials on a clinical unit. The young man, Kyle, was part of a study on whether a new serotonin receptor blocker called clomipramine might help people suffering from OCD. Kyle was a bright young man in danger of flunking out of the George Washington University because his obsessions and rituals prevented him from completing his schoolwork.

The trial was what is known as a double-blind crossover trial. For half of the study, each participant would receive either the real drug or a placebo, and for the next half they would receive the opposite. Neither the subjects nor the experimenters knew whether they were in the placebo group at any given time, so as to reduce any bias in measuring outcomes. Crossover trials of this kind make it easier to recruit participants because everyone is assured of receiving the experimental drug for at least half of the trial.

During the first four weeks, Kyle's condition improved markedly. His obsessions were less intrusive, his rituals abated, and he was able to do his schoolwork. During the later weeks of that first period, Kyle met a young woman named Sarah, and the two of them started hanging out together on campus. Around the midpoint of the study, when the treatment protocols were swapped, Kyle and Sarah's relationship grew closer, and they fell in love. It was during this second four-week period that Kyle's OCD ratings fell all the way to zero. His OCD symptoms disappeared, even though he had stopped taking clomipramine.

"His scores for obsessions, compulsions, and mood were all in the normal range," Tom writes in his book *Healing: Our Path from Mental Illness to Mental Health*. "Kyle was elated. I was devastated. Sarah nearly ruined the study. Whatever their relationship gave Kyle was clearly better than clomipramine." All the other people in Kyle's trial group relapsed to varying degrees when they started taking the placebo.

For Tom, this experience marked his introduction to the idea that social connection could be a profoundly important intervention for mental illness. He took this understanding into his broader work on mental health and started to see studies that confirmed it in surprising ways. For example, although people living with schizophrenia are often described as socially avoidant, newer evidence suggests their avoidance arises from becoming overwhelmed by face-to-face experiences, in which they cannot control the amount of stimulation coming from close quarters and eye contact (a little like the experience of people on the autism spectrum). In fact, people with schizophrenia are often intensely lonely. They crave connection, but only in the proper contexts, ones in which the intensity of the connection can be controlled.

As mental health problems (which include depression, anxiety, suicidality, and dementia) grow at alarming rates in most developed nations, Tom has come to accept that connection is essential for recovery, and mental illness itself is "a medical problem that requires a social solution." And yet, he notes, "Of all the things that we psychiatrists and psychologists do not understand about people with [serious mental illness], loneliness may be at the top."

Earlier I cited the study of complex PTSD that proposed initiating psychiatric treatment by addressing loneliness first, because a patient in a spiral of chronic loneliness is poorly suited to deal with the more challenging aspects of PTSD treatment. This same concept of "loneliness first" might be applied to other scenarios of medical treatment as well, especially in cases of people who are objectively socially isolated—living alone, with little or no family or close friends. When treatment of medical issues addresses the patient's loneliness, it can help develop some regular contacts in the patient's life to offer support and encouragement during that treatment.

These conditions are frequently accompanied by other health problems—including substance abuse and obesity. And like obesity and substance abuse, loneliness has certain bidirectional effects that can lead to downward behavioral spirals, particularly in people with mental health issues. Addiction and obesity can make you feel lonely, and that loneliness can also be a cause of substance misuse and overeating.

When it comes to proving the cost-effectiveness of specific loneliness interventions (ranging from adopting service animals to volunteering programs), we should prioritize those most likely to be scalable for sustained long-term benefit. That's why I find programs that integrate creative expression, mindfulness, and conversation to be so promising. These approaches quite literally alter our brains in ways that change how we make sense of the world, allowing their benefit to grow with time and practice as we explore our new realities.

However, what all these promising interventions are lacking is sufficient published research providing conclusive evidence of their efficacy. Medical research on complex and multifaceted conditions like loneliness relies on outcome measures like QALY—the quality-adjusted life year. This is a simple index to quantify the value of health outcomes, combining the value of a year of life and the quality of life within that year. The trouble is we don't have documented QALY numbers for many of the best loneliness interventions that are already widely accepted as beneficial. Without such studies attesting to their value, many institutional purchasers of health services are reluctant to pay for them.

Other outcome measures like "Healthy Days Measures," developed by the CDC, could conceivably be used to measure the impact of loneliness interventions. They rely on a person's recall, by asking questions like "During the past 30 days, approximately how many days did poor physical or mental health keep you from doing your usual activities, such as self-care, work, or recreation?" That "look back" approach has merit but also limitations, as it's well known that people's ability to recall things accurately is often influenced by the same factors, like loneliness, that we are trying to assess.

At the same time, there has been a steady move away from strict adherence to the conventional medical model for treatment of many so-called lifestyle-related illnesses such as heart disease, diabetes, some neurologic and chronic pain disorders, and mild cognitive impairment, recognizing the interaction of many factors. In fact, if loneliness could be approached in the same way as weight gain or smoking (as risk factors that could lead to or exacerbate medical complications) and provided with the appropriate interventions, we might see substantial improvement on overall health in the population. Loneliness should always be considered a comorbid condition that could be addressed in tandem with treatment for any illness. Even those who aren't lonely would benefit from education and awareness building. That way, if loneliness starts to become a factor in their lives, whether because of the illness or in some other way, they are better prepared to respond.

This is where primary care can play such an important role. We could approach loneliness in primary care visits with screening tools, much the way we already approach depression with the PHQ-9 questionnaire, which has become a healthcare standard. Patients could be screened for loneliness with one of the questionnaires mentioned earlier, perhaps the PROMIS social isolation short form or the three-question short form of the full UCLA Loneliness Scale.

Using such questionnaires for screening means that patients who score high for loneliness will require further evaluation with a longer survey and with subsequent conversations about the depth and quality of their social connections. These loneliness scales are of limited usefulness because they are one-dimensional, and loneliness is multidimensional. Two individuals might have the same high score for loneliness but require completely different interventions because the specific nature of each one's loneliness puts them at risk for different health problems. For example, research shows that patients feeling higher levels of loneliness among their peers are more likely to suffer from social anxiety disorder, while patients with the same high level of loneliness, but experienced around family members, are more commonly associated with eating disorders and self-harm.

Primary care team members need to tease out the nature of each patient's loneliness and gain a greater understanding of their health risks. Such conversations are prone to be difficult ones, given the stigma that surrounds loneliness. The conversations should be conducted by someone on the team with good communication skills who has received some training in how to talk about loneliness with caring and empathy, in a non-triggering way.

What would be most useful at that point are more sensitive questions that would help clinicians identify more precisely what kind of loneliness the patient is experiencing. Since 2020, I've been working with a team of social science researchers at Penn State University on a Multidimensional Loneliness and Social Connection Scale (MLASC). The research project, led by a friend and longtime collaborator, health psychologist Joshua Smyth, has validated questions that probe the experience of loneliness and quality of connection across five distinct social contexts: as an individual, with a significant other, with peers, with family, and with the subject's community, including the workplace. For each of these five contexts, there are brief subsets of questions on either loneliness or social connection, which can be used in any combination for a variety of clinical and research purposes. Further research into loneliness can use one or more of these survey question sets to focus on specific areas of study. The MLASC survey could also be used to fine-tune interventions for loneliness, ensuring individuals receive personalized guidance to address the types of loneliness that burden them most. It's rare that one size fits all in offering people the guidance they need to be healthy and well, and that's certainly the case for loneliness.

When primary care teams can gain a clear picture of patients' specific sources of loneliness, they can direct those patients toward effective resources to assist them. This approach is already used extensively in the United Kingdom, where it is referred to as "social prescribing." After the patient's social circumstances have been evaluated through further conversation, they receive a recommended set of activities to choose from to help them increase social connectedness. Besides the 12-step and other support groups, socially prescribed activities include programs such as nature walks, crafts, creative arts, sports, school tutoring, and other community volunteer activities. Nearly all these programs are already available in most communities, but the UK experience is that patients with chronic loneliness are more likely to try them when they are prescribed by their primary care team. For some lonely patients, the doctor's recommendation in itself will make them feel cared for in a new way and represent a small step toward closer human connection.

"THE LONESOMEST DISEASE"

In its November 21, 1953 edition, *The Saturday Evening Post* ran the headline "I've Got the Lonesomest Disease!" The article was written by a woman named Helen Furnas, who had a rare version of a very rare disease: hemophilia. Helen's type of hemophilia, known today as type C, was a milder form that affects both males and females. Her problem was that in 1953, nearly all doctors assumed hemophiliacs were male. She wrote, "I have to carry in my already overstuffed handbag a specialist's elaborate analysis of my condition with instructions about what to do if accident strikes or surgery is needed. Without that paper any strange doctor whom I warn that I'm a bleeder just tickets me as neurotic. Chances are he never saw a bleeder in his whole professional career. All he knows about hemophilia is that the book says only males have it."

Her article went on to detail the sorrows of isolated farm families whose children had the disease. She wrote hopefully that the newly founded Hemophilia Foundation had begun to develop member networks of local chapters: "The prime contribution of such organizations is personal, getting the word to hemophiliacs and their families: 'You aren't alone. Thousands of us like you have got together to buck one another up. Get in touch with Bill so-and-so in your town. He knows the answers.' Otherwise this hemophilia, both statistically and personally, is the lonesomest disease in the world."

Such "lonesome" diseases are categorized by the FDA as rare diseases, defined as any condition that affects fewer than two hundred thousand people nationwide. The FDA list of seven thousand rare diseases includes familiar names like hemophilia, cystic fibrosis, and Tourette's syndrome, along with many more obscure conditions, including malignant hyperthermia and visual snow syndrome. It is estimated that about one out of every ten US residents suffers from one or more of these conditions. Because of their rarity, these diseases are often misdiagnosed by doctors, misunderstood by the public, and neglected by major pharma companies. Just seeking appropriate treatment for a rare disease can be a source of intense loneliness and social isolation. Learning to manage a rare disease is especially lonely for children and teenagers, who are already at a vulnerable stage in their lives.

Patrick James Lynch was a twenty-one-year-old theater student when his eighteen-year-old brother, Adam, who, like Patrick, had hemophilia, died of a brain bleed. People with hemophilia are at risk for this type of spontaneous bleeding, and as happened to Adam, they can be fatal. To control that risk, they need to adhere to strict medical protocols, often requiring regular infusions of blood-clotting factors that can replace the ones that are missing. They also need to be vigilant in their avoidance of activities that could lead to bleeding—those that, like certain contact sports, have far less risk for others with normal bleeding physiology. Imagine how hard it would be for anyone to stick to those kinds of self-care routines, let alone someone at a stage in life in which fitting in with peers and social activities is so important to healthy development. Devastated by the loss of his brother, Patrick also recognized that Adam's death might have been avoided if he'd taken better care of himself. Patrick went on to cofound Believe Limited, a creative agency and production company devoted to multimedia entertainment and engagement programs for people impacted by rare diseases, including bleeding disorders. The idea was that if families could see stories like their own told in artful and empathic ways, their experiences with rare diseases would be less lonely and easier to deal with.

I became aware of Patrick's story in 2018 when BioMarin, a drug company that specializes in treatments for rare genetic disorders, reached out to us for assistance with one of his projects. BioMarin had funded Patrick's idea of holding a musical theater boot camp in New York for teenagers with hemophilia. Two dozen winners of an essay contest would be flown in on a Friday for a seventy-two-hour music theater intensive with rehearsals, and then they would perform their production on a real Broadway stage on Monday, which is the day off for the regular shows. Our role was to lead sessions on the health-enhancing value of creative expression, and to evaluate the effect that the boot camp had on the participants.

Drawing on their personal experiences, the teenagers collaborated with musical theater professionals on a six-song show called *Hemophilia: The Musical*. It's an amazingly fun and funny show (the video of the performance is easy to find online) full of insights about the lonely struggles of young people whose medical condition prevents them from doing so many of the things that most teenagers take for granted. The show also struck home a universal theme kids with hemophilia know better than most of us: fitting in can be hard for everyone at times. To be unlonely in this world, we each need to find "our" people, the ones who accept us as we are and welcome hearing our story.

At one level, having a rare disease feels psychologically lonely, like any other illness, because you are isolated by your pain, your course of treatment, and the limitations the illness inflicts on you. Beyond that, with a rare disease you can also feel a deep societal loneliness of being different from everyone, including people with more common ailments. When stigma is attached to a rare disease, as with leprosy, or HIV in the 1980s, the results can be devastating levels of loneliness in all three kinds—psychological, societal, and existential.

I worry now about the loneliness experienced by the millions of people suffering from what is called long COVID. These are the estimated 10 to 20 percent of people who have recovered from COVID, often having had mild or moderate symptoms, but months later are still experiencing strange incidences of brain fog, fatigue, and other mysterious lingering aftereffects. Researchers studying long COVID don't know for sure why so many people continue to suffer COVID's disabling aftereffects. With no biomarkers to offer a definitive diagnosis, there is no consistent way to track the severity or document responses to treatment.

As a result, people with long COVID, who are more likely to be middle-aged than over sixty-five, and twice as likely to be female as male, are apt to feel marginalized and ignored by the healthcare system. (Until October 2021, there wasn't even a numerical diagnostic code for long COVID that would enable treatments to be covered by health insurance.) Especially worrisome is that some of the reported symptoms of long COVID include insomnia, anxiety, and depression, all of which put those people in the middle of the Pyramid of Vulnerability for loneliness. Unaddressed, this puts them at risk of falling into the vicious cycle in which isolation and loneliness beget more loneliness, leading to significant health impairment from the loneliness alone.

AT THE END OF LIFE

Two years after Lillie Shockney had welcomed Betty Boob into her life, she was diagnosed with cancer in her left breast. This time, she and her husband knew how to handle the email announcement. "We said that we found out today Betty Boob is getting a roommate and we need you to help us select a name." Another name contest resulted, and with it came Lillie's realization of what her creative approach to her illness had accomplished. Through humor, she said, "I was able to neutralize this scary discussion of cancer."

For more than two decades, Lillie led two weekend-long retreats each year for women who had terminal metastatic breast cancer. One weekend retreat was for women with their significant others. The second retreat was for women not in relationships, who would bring a female caregiver—their mother, their sister, sometimes a best friend.

For three days and two nights, the women discussed how their lives would end.

The most common source of worry for these women, Lillie found, was the pain and suffering at the end of life. She has strong ideas on how best to manage palliative care long before it's time for hospice, in order to preserve quality of life for as long as possible. She always felt that she was doing a valuable service to her patients in these discussions.

The second-largest worry, however, was about the children the women would leave behind. Many at these retreats were in their twenties or thirties and would be leaving behind toddlers and young children with precious few memories of their mothers. For this worry, Lillie recognized her words of comfort in response weren't nearly as helpful.

"I got tired of saying, 'I'm so sorry that you won't be here for your children,'" she recalled. Determined to stop repeating what wasn't working, she wondered what was possible. How could she help these dying women fulfill their desire to be a part of their children's lives as they grow up?

She hit upon the idea of providing sets of greeting cards for every milestone in their children's lives—birthdays, bar or bat mitzvah, confirmation, getting their driver's license, high school graduation, marriage, having children of their own. She brought hundreds of cards to each retreat, so that the women could select their own, then take them home and handwrite the message they wanted their children to read on those special days in the far-off future when they would no longer be around.

One day in 2016, after Lillie had been leading women through this card-writing process for nearly twenty years, she received a call at work from a young woman who'd called the Johns Hopkins general number knowing only Lillie's first name.

"I'm so thankful you're still there," the woman said. "There's a story I want to tell you." Fourteen years earlier, when the woman was only ten years old, her mother had died while under Lillie's care. "My mom was in and out of the hospital a lot, and each time she came home, my aunt Sarah would come over to help take care of her. And I would hear my mother say to Aunt Sarah, 'Lillie said to do this,' and 'Lillie said to do that.' But I didn't know who Lillie was, until after my mom passed away and Aunt Sarah became keeper of my cards."

For every important day in this young woman's life, her aunt Sarah gave her a card from her mother. On the day she got her driver's license, she read in her mother's handwriting, "Please drive like Aunt Sarah. Do not drive like your father."

Three weeks earlier, the woman told Lillie, she'd gotten married, and her aunt Sarah handed her a fourteen-year-old envelope, yellowed at the edges. It was a beautiful wedding card from her mother. All down the left-hand side of the card's interior was loving marital advice. At the bottom, her mother had written, "When your dad lifts your veil and kisses your left cheek, you will feel me kiss your right cheek."

The woman on the phone said to Lillie, "That's why I had to find you. I had to tell you, I swear I felt my mother's kiss. I have always felt my mother's presence and guidance through these cards."

She asked Lillie if she could expect any more cards, and Lillie assured her that there were more if she was planning to have children. There would be a card when she was expecting, in which her mother described how she felt when she was carrying her daughter. And when the baby arrives, Lillie told her, "There's a letter from your mother describing how she felt the first time she held you with all of her hopes and dreams for you in your life." There was even something waiting for the deceased woman's grandchild.

"When your baby is a toddler," Lillie told the woman, "there is a tape of your mother reading nursery rhymes and children's stories, so your children will know their grandmother's voice."

When we die, we take our loneliness with us, but the broken connection of our passing leaves our survivors lonely for our company. The letters from the women in Lillie's program, as artifacts of creative expression, have forged an irrevocable connection with their survivors, and in some cases, with the grandchildren they've never met.

Many years ago, I knew a British-born financier whom I'll call James. He retired in late middle age, and he and his wife moved to New York, where they were very involved in the Buddhist practice of insight meditation. James had taken up painting later in life, more or less as a hobby, but after he was diagnosed with cancer, painting became his full-time occupation. He worked in his studio all day, applying broad swaths and wild swirls of brilliant colors across his large canvases. His condition became terminal, and after he ended treatment, he continued to paint.

I had planned to visit James for a video interview in his studio, but his condition went downhill before we could arrange it. A week before he died, he left me a voice mail, explaining that although he was too weak to lift a brush, he could still concentrate on his art. "I'm still painting," he said. "I'm painting in my mind."

I kept James's message on my phone for years afterward. I would listen to it from time to time, just to feel the connection with him, and to feel his intense connection with his creative self during his final weeks of life. Whenever I heard the message, I felt less lonely.

6

Aging

Marinella Beretta's neighbors near Lake Como in Northern Italy said they hadn't seen her in at least two years. Piles of uncollected mail had stacked up outside the locked gates of Marinella's modest suburban villa when, in February 2022, the local fire department was called to investigate some fallen trees on the unkempt property. Inside the house, firefighters discovered Marinella's decomposed corpse seated upright at her kitchen table. An autopsy determined she had died of natural causes more than two years earlier, at the age of seventy.

No one missed Marinella Beretta when she died. If she had any living relatives, none ever came forward. Neighbors said they assumed she had moved elsewhere, as many local people had when the pandemic descended on Italy in early 2020. Marinella had sold her villa years earlier to a Swiss investor under the Italian *usufrutto* law, which allowed her to remain at the property rent-free for the rest of her life. It was the investor who called local police and asked them to check on neighbor complaints about fallen trees. That was the only reason Marinella's body was discovered.

Marinella Beretta caused a greater stir in death than she ever had in her life. There was a media frenzy in Italy about how society had failed her and was failing the elderly. In 2018, government statistics had revealed that 40 percent of Italians over the age of seventy-five were living alone, and their numbers were growing. Officials expressed sympathy but offered few solutions. "What happened to Marinella Beretta in Como, the forgotten loneliness, hurts our consciences," the government's minister for family and equal opportunities said in a statement. "Taking care of each other is the experience of families, institutions, of our being citizens. No one should be alone."

There had been a similar hue and cry about the problem of old age and loneliness years earlier in France. A three-week heat wave struck the country in August 2003, and more than fifteen thousand people died, "mostly old people and often lonely old people," according to one press account. In Paris in particular, old people living alone in tiny, poorly ventilated attic apartments died of heatstroke without anyone noticing they were missing. The body of a seventy-seven-year-old man who had lived in one such apartment for twenty years went undiscovered for two weeks until people in the building finally notified authorities of the stench coming from the top floor.

While the French government scrambled to improve its disaster preparations in the aftermath of the heat wave, some studies of the disaster pointed to the much larger social problem it had revealed, the problem of increasing elderly isolation and loneliness. In Paris and its suburbs, eighty-six of the heat wave victims couldn't be identified because they had no family and none of their neighbors even knew their names. It took a team of genealogists to locate distant family members for most of these victims, but twenty of them remained unidentified when they were laid to rest.

Stories of unattended deaths of old and isolated people frequently emerge during natural disasters such as heat waves, floods, and hurricanes. It happened during Hurricane Katrina and the flooding of New Orleans in 2005. It happened during COVID surges all through 2020 and 2021. Calamities of all kinds remind us that lonely aging people are among the most vulnerable people in our society, but unlike other vulnerable people, such as children and the disabled, society largely ignores the old and lonely. Carla Perissinotto, a geriatrician who was among the first to study the health threats to seniors associated with loneliness from a medical practitioner's perspective, believes social attitudes toward aging magnify the effects of the stigma of loneliness. "We want to ignore older people," she said in 2017. "We don't want to talk about what it looks like to not age successfully. We only want to hear about healthy aging."

Aging puts us all at very specific kinds of risk for each of the three types of loneliness. In terms of psychological loneliness, aging can be a drumbeat of losses, one after another. Lost identity looms for many after retirement. Hearing loss, reduced mobility, and cognitive decline can all contribute to an increased sense of isolation. Then there's lost vitality, lost looks, lost friends, and lost family members. If you are lucky enough to live a long life, you will suffer the continual losses of friends and loved ones who die before you. In particular, the death of a spouse or close friend can create unresolved grief that easily descends into an unrelieved state of loneliness. As author Philip Roth wrote in his 2006 novel, *Everyman*, "Old age isn't a battle: old age is a massacre."

Societal loneliness, the second kind of loneliness, comes to older adults in the form of being marginalized in a culture that worships youth, health, and competition. Societal loneliness is especially acute among those who are poor, infirm, or struggling with their mental health. If you have a reason for being societally excluded, as an immigrant, as a person of color, or because of your gender identity, aging only adds to that sense of loneliness. One study of the 2003 Paris heat wave victims noted that many of the unidentified bodies turned out to be those of destitute foreign-born men. Within French society, it's common for elderly men from ethnic minorities to suffer social exclusion. For some of those men, the exclusion contributed to their lonely deaths.

And then there is existential loneliness. With aging can come existential questions. Was my life meaningful? Do I have a legacy? Who will miss me when I'm gone? There is a rising awareness that the end is near, that a dark curtain out there is about to fall. We don't know what's on the other side of that curtain, and that awareness of vulnerability can be a source of great anxiety and loneliness if you have no one you trust to talk to about it.

At the same time, it's a common myth that loneliness is spreading among old people largely because so many of them live alone. In truth, old people in economically advanced societies frequently live alone because they want autonomy and privacy, while still enjoying social interactions with friends, family, and neighbors. Research has shown that as we get older, we don't need to maintain connections with more than a few close friends and loved ones. We no longer feel the need to mix with lots of people the way we might have when we were younger. That's why the pain of loneliness during the pandemic was reported far more commonly among younger adults, for whom social distancing and closed restaurants were far more damaging to the accustomed forms of human connection.

Aging for many people can be a period of great discovery and freedom to explore things they were unable to do earlier in life. Jungian analysts regard the early years of aging as a middle passage between the first adulthood, when our choices are primarily shaped and influenced by the perspectives, needs, and consideration of others, and a second adulthood of autonomy, self-realization, and giving back to the tribe as a volunteer. For many, this second adulthood becomes a time when existential loneliness can be engaged with and resolved, a task some have called "climbing the second mountain."

I meet a lot of older adults transitioning into something like that, and I count myself among them. You see older people as active first-time participants in charitable work because aging has given them a new perspective, one more willing to support others. Wisdom really does seem to come with age, and for a lot of older people, that wisdom includes accepting their place in the passage of time and of generations. There's a certain level of self-knowledge and self-acceptance to be found in old age, which can prepare many of us, as we age, to deal with feelings of psychological, societal, and existential loneliness without having our lives spiral downward. I can imagine the creation of "Second Mountain" support groups for seniors in which these issues are openly discussed and various activities such as mentoring and volunteering are actively encouraged.

And yet, the specific problem with loneliness in old age is that it can have devastating health effects on vulnerable older people. Loneliness exacerbates poor health behaviors in seniors, even around something as simple as getting adequate sleep. Many recent studies have linked inadequate sleep to loneliness, and in John Cacioppo's evolutionary view of loneliness, poor sleep is also related to the hypervigilance and anxiety survival response of being isolated and vulnerable. If you're lonely, the theory goes, our programming tells you to sleep with "one eye open." When loneliness fragments sleeping patterns in this way, neural activity is reduced in brain regions responsible for social engagement behaviors. Sleep deprivation and exhaustion, in turn, can intensify feelings of loneliness in a downward spiral. And yet, in medical circles there has only recently been an increased awareness of sleep deprivation as a health indicator among older people. It is still not common practice for health practitioners to track sleep in older patients and make recommendations for improvement.

Previous chapters have shown how loneliness can exacerbate the ill effects of most chronic conditions, ranging from heart disease to depression. In old age, these conditions can quickly become serious acute illnesses because of the natural decline of your physical resilience and your cognitive capabilities. If you've aged out of your regular social networks, if friends and family have moved away or passed away, the vicious cycle of loneliness can set in slowly: feelings of vulnerability lead to anxiety, which leads to isolation, which leads to distorted social cognition, which leads to increased feelings of vulnerability and isolation—all of which puts seniors at elevated risk for mild cognitive impairment, depression, substance abuse, and suicide. A 2012 study led by Carla Perissinotto revealed that over a six-year period, aged adults who were lonely suffered a 60 percent increased risk of functional decline in everyday activities and a 45 percent greater risk of death.

Navigating the territory of aging is tricky because so many of the risk factors of loneliness are difficult to measure. Poverty poses an increased risk of loneliness for aging people, for example, but it's a bigger problem in some poor communities than others. Older men are more at risk than women of severe loneliness, in part because they are less likely than older women to admit that they are lonely. And although cognitive decline and dementia are risk factors for causing loneliness, there is also strong evidence that loneliness itself can be a contributing *cause* of mental problems. A health and retirement survey tracked more than twelve thousand older respondents over ten years and revealed that, after controlling for all other factors, loneliness was associated with a 40 percent increased risk of dementia.

Rich or poor, male or female, living alone or with your spouse, your risk of developing dementia is significantly higher if you are lonely. Part of the aging journey, if you're lucky enough to reach your golden years, should include a healthy awareness of all the traps and challenges embedded in the three types of loneliness. Suffering loss and grief may be inevitable in this territory, but the suffering of loneliness is not.

AGE AND SOCIAL ISOLATION

After a heat wave killed 739 older people in Chicago during the summer of 1995, the Centers for Disease Control and Prevention reported the conditions of vulnerability most common among the victims. Almost all of them were poor and lived alone without working air conditioners. Most already had illnesses that prevented them from leaving their homes each day. And most were socially isolated, without close social contacts living near them.

Poverty was a common factor among the older Chicagoans who perished, but some poor communities were hit harder than others. Chicago's Latino residents, which represented about one quarter of the city population at the time, accounted for only 2 percent of heat-related deaths, even though as a group, they were disproportionately poorer and sicker than the city's overall population.

When sociologist Eric Klinenberg studied the individual cases of Chicago's heat wave victims, he found that the death rate among older people in the majority-Latino neighborhood of Little Village was much lower than in the adjacent majority-Black neighborhood of North Lawndale—despite both neighborhoods having similarly high rates of poverty. What had protected Little Village's older people from the heat wave?

"Chicago's Latinos," Klinenberg explained, "tend to live in neighborhoods with high population density, busy commercial life in the streets, and vibrant public spaces. Most of the African American neighborhoods with high heat wave death rates had been abandoned—by employers, stores, and residents—in recent decades." In his book *Heat Wave*, Klinenberg showed how it was much lonelier to be old and poor in North Lawndale than in Little Village. During the 1995 heat wave, the difference cost many old people in North Lawndale their lives.

When a neighborhood is abandoned by everyone able to leave, the few people remaining behind include many vulnerable older people with few friends and family, who have reason to fear opening their doors to strangers. The heat wave itself was a natural disaster, but as Klinenberg pointed out, "Hundreds of Chicago residents died alone, behind locked doors and sealed windows, out of contact with friends, family, and neighbors, unassisted by public agencies or community groups. There's nothing natural about that." The heat wave, he said, "made visible the hazardous social conditions that are always present but difficult to perceive."

In 1999, another heat wave struck Chicago, and this time the city government was better prepared. For people without air conditioners, free bus transportation was available to designated neighborhood "cooling centers." City workers contacted elderly residents by phone and police did door-to-door checkups on those living alone. As a result, a much smaller number of Chicago residents died in the 1999 heat wave. The death toll of 110 suggested both the effectiveness and the limitations of such an emergency response.

When the COVID-19 pandemic struck in 2020, however, the city failed to take similar steps to protect vulnerable older people. Street maps showing patterns of COVID-related deaths in Chicago closely resembled twenty-five-year-old maps of Chicago heat wave fatalities. In both instances, deaths were highly concentrated where the loneliest and most vulnerable older people live, in Chicago's low-income South Side and West Side neighborhoods.

The Chicago experience suggests that with thoughtful planning, adequate resources, and effective operational logistics it's not that difficult to save lives in aging and isolated populations. You need to identify the population, make contact, assure them of support, and provide ways for the most vulnerable among them to escape what may be hazardous living conditions. Telephone outreach and home visits are simple and appropriate interventions that can make a big difference for aging people whose conditions are in that precarious middle tier of the Pyramid of Vulnerability, where any added difficulty in their lives (a heat wave or a viral contagion) could land them in the pyramid's top tier, requiring emergency medical care.

In the United Kingdom, the Campaign to End Loneliness, led by the What Works Centre for Wellbeing, has sponsored local coordinated efforts to reconnect older isolated people with their neighbors. In the borough of Wirral, in northern England near Liverpool, local government championed a project called the Great Wirral Door Knock, in which teams of social workers, emergency responders, and volunteers went to houses identified as likely to be homes of lonely people. Guided conversations opened by asking people what they liked about living in Wirral, and from there went on to offer information about help and support that was available. Each team carried medical consent forms in case referrals needed to be made. In one neighborhood, after a number of people told the volunteers that recent bereavement had caused them to feel isolated, a bereavement support group was formed. One Wirral resident said, "If the volunteer hadn't knocked on my door, I would have carried on living in misery."

In 2017, CareMore, the California-based Medicare and Medicaid provider discussed in the previous chapter, began a Togetherness Program to screen older plan members for loneliness during their physical exams. Seniors were asked about loneliness during their medical checkups, and those who said they were lonely were offered either home visits or regular phone calls from CareMore personnel. A third option was to join one of the Nifty After Fifty gyms attached to Care-More medical centers. The group exercise classes were an immediate hit, and a number of second and third marriages were the result of connections made there.

The greatest impact, however, was from regular phone contact between CareMore and those members who were most at risk of loneliness. One case involved an elderly CareMore member with mental illness who ended up severely isolated and lonely because he was so difficult to be around. His condition worsened as he skipped his medical appointments and stopped taking his psychiatric medications. It took regular contact on the phone with CareMore to finally get the man to come in for a medical exam, and eventually he agreed to resume his medications. This is a great example of how compassionate "social care" can be added to traditional medical care in a synergistic and powerful way, spotlighting an important path forward for quality and cost of care, not to mention the patient's experience.

Preventive care of this kind has been spreading, thanks to the growth of the US government's Medicare Advantage program, which provides insurers with monetary incentives to keep aging populations well. Providers with strong scores for cost reduction (who are also rated highly for member satisfaction) can earn higher rates of per capita payments, which is why there has been dramatically increased interest in loneliness among both for-profit insurers like Humana, Aetna, and UnitedHealth Group, and traditional nonprofits like Kaiser Permanente and a variety of nonprofit regional Blue Cross Blue Shield health plans. It's an exciting prospect for elevating the national conversation about loneliness, because some projections predict as many as half of all Medicare recipients will be Medicare Advantage members by 2030.

SCAN Health Plan, a California-based nonprofit with the specific mission of "keeping seniors healthy and independent," has its own Togetherness programs, which during the pandemic evolved to include virtual online classes for seniors with common interests and tech support to help members connect online via Zoom. The aim of SCAN's Togetherness programs is to treat loneliness and isolation as health problems for which each member has an individual prescription. "We want to normalize the fact that there are so many people . . . that are hiding that they are lonely," said Chief Togetherness Officer Lisbeth Briones-Roberts.

SCAN, or Senior Care Action Network, was among the first health providers to recognize the health risks of loneliness. In 2017, SCAN sponsored a survey on aging and loneliness that revealed the stigma of loneliness among older people. Almost 60 percent said they personally would be reluctant to admit feeling lonely, even though more than 80 percent said they knew at least one person who was lonely. About 6 in 10 agreed with the statement that they wished they had more friends, and 24 percent said they believed they weren't important to anyone.

The CEO of SCAN is my friend Sachin H. Jain, who previously served as CEO of CareMore and led the development of its Togetherness Program in 2017. One important change made to SCAN's Togetherness program, Sachin says, has been to increase the number of regular phone calls with seniors that are made by senior volunteers.

"We actually decided to focus our efforts on engaging seniors to help other seniors," he said. "You know, it's one thing for me as a healthy-ish forty-one-year-old to call a seventy-five-year-old and listen to their stories. It's another thing for someone who's seventy-five to talk to another seventy-five-year-old." The peer-to-peer idea originated at CareMore, where one important marker of success was a 25 percent increase in members seeking treatment for urinary incontinence, an embarrassing condition that can lead to isolation, avoidance of social events, and loneliness.

The need for callers exploded with the pandemic, and SCAN was unable to recruit enough senior volunteers to meet demand. "So then we open-sourced it to the entire population of employees," Sachin said. "We told them, 'Every one of you can become a Togetherness worker.' And it actually connected many more employees to the mission of the company. It's a form of corporate citizenship that I think is really remarkable."

It speaks to Sachin's ultimate goal: to create a social movement around loneliness as a serious health issue. He told me, "I'd like to see more healthcare providers start addressing senior loneliness as their responsibility." I couldn't agree more. Even with the incredible amount of information available online, patients often look to their doctors to get a sense of what really matters most as they navigate how best to stay healthy, what to prioritize, and which behaviors and habits to address. If physicians began to view their patients' social health as equal in importance to their physical and mental health and acted accordingly in delivering advice and care, many people would live longer and more satisfying lives.

CREATIVE PROGRAMMING
FOR SUCCESSFUL AGING

Older people often find themselves in close proximity to one another by happenstance, often because older residents have stayed in a community after younger people have moved out, or because certain types of residences (high-rises with elevators, for example) attract older people. This can be a very good thing. They're in close enough proximity to form meaningful friendships, if they have activities to bring them together. Urban planners and others often refer to these clusters of older people as NORCs—naturally occurring retirement communities. It was in one such NORC, an apartment building in the Bronx, New York, where the Foundation for Art & Healing piloted one of the first of our Successful Aging Creativity Circle programs.

The success of the Creativity Circle groups for people with diabetes inspired us to develop a similar workshop format centered on the shared experience of aging. Once again, we introduced an element of creative "making and sharing" into each of the six weekly sessions, hence the name Creativity Circles. One week might call for a twenty-minute interval with drawing, the next week with making something with clay, and the next week with expressive movement. Each week offers a different theme that would serve as a prompt for creative expression and group discussion.

For example, the theme of session four is brain health. The group facilitator leads a discussion about how to take care of our brains and what takes a toll on brain health, and then takes a brief poll of how participants assess their own brain health habits related to getting enough sleep, remembering things, or dealing with boredom. Participants discuss the need for connection and friendship, and make lists of things they might do to bring more social interaction into their lives. Everyone is asked to consider committing to taking one step in the coming week. It might be something as simple as a phone call with a friend they haven't seen in a while.

A ten-minute session of guided breathing meditation follows, and then a twenty-minute session of creative making, using collage on construction paper to create two separate pieces of art. The first collage represents their current state of mind—the stressed mind, the responsible mind, the daydreaming mind. The second collage represents how they would like their mind to be, what kind of balance they would like to have. The participants share their work with each other and discuss how the creative choices they've made represent their stresses, their worries, and what they'd prefer to occupy their minds with. Through their artworks, created in the space of a few minutes, total strangers are able to connect with one another and share some of their most intimate inner thoughts.

From a scientific perspective, we'd say this workshop deploys three distinct "interventional modalities," all three of which have a strong base of evidence in fostering human connection. The first is mindfulness meditation, through a guided imagery exercise. The second is creative expression, the effects of which we've already discussed. And the third modality is social-emotional learning, which takes place as participants share their story through conversations, with their creative expression work serving as an empowering catalyst and focal point.

That's the theory. Its impact in practice, based on the survey responses from our first few pilot groups, was especially gratifying. As with the story circles for women with diabetes, many participants in these early Creativity Circle groups felt a reawakened urge to connect with others, and did so over the six weeks of the program. They grew in confidence around managing their emotions and dealing with the challenges and burdens of their lives. Their behaviors also measurably changed. Engagement with other community organization activities increased, as did their efforts to connect and stay connected with existing friends. Some incorporated mindfulness meditation and creative expression into their lives more frequently and in ways they never had before.

There was one memorable survey response from a woman I'll call Eileen. She said in her follow-up: "Now I'm all involved in arts and crafts here. I've started a group. I'm joining another group. It's lifesaving. I have to admit to you, sometimes I feel it's not worth living, because there's too many problems and it's so overwhelming. But when you have some drawing and pleasure and fun, and you're doing your passion, you can live."

We had designed Creativity Circles so they wouldn't require an art therapist or any other licensed mental health practitioner to lead the eight sessions. Our aim was to create a curriculum available to anyone with basic skills in leading group events, and if the curriculum was faithfully followed, the participants would benefit. To test that idea, in 2019 we partnered with the SHARE Network, a community outreach center developed and managed by University of Chicago Medicine on Chicago's South Side. Jason Molony, a program manager at SHARE, gathered a Creativity Circle group at the St. Brendan Apartments, a senior citizen residence located in Englewood, one of the high-crime, low-income neighborhoods that suffered high rates of fatalities among isolated elderly people during Chicago's 1995 heat wave. We were excited about this event, because it would be the first Creativity Circle to run without our direct involvement. The St. Brendan group would tell us whether what we had designed was truly scalable.

The initial session had a slightly rocky start. The participants, all over age sixty, weren't sure what they had signed up for, and Jason, trained in social work, had never led a group of this kind. When he began distributing materials for the class, including colored pencils, there were nervous comments about the prospect of doing art. One participant, an elderly man, stood up and left, muttering about "kindergarten stuff."

Jason said he felt a change in the group once he led them through the first meditation. "There's some real magic in the combination of mindfulness, guided discussion, and the arts," he said. "I got to see it play out in real time, the kind of power it brought to that room." He asked the participants to approach the sessions "with an open mind and an open heart."

Everyone at the St. Brendan workshop had known each other for years, if only to say hello to each other at the mailbox. But even those who were friendly with each other didn't really know each other's stories. During the session on the theme of "legacy," several of the participants opened up about the particular grief they felt from having had one or more of their children pass away before they did. "It just morphed into a conversation about that level of loss and grief. And that's powerful stuff. They've lost kids, they've lost spouses, they've lost friends," Jason said. "There's so much grief. It was a conversation they might not normally have."

That is an essential function of the Creativity Circle, to create a context for conversations that might not normally occur. All support groups create that kind of context, of course, but not everyone wants to attend a support group for grieving or loneliness. Creativity Circles were designed to address loneliness and other difficult issues in ways that are attractive, unintimidating, and even fun. Through guided meditation and creative expression, the sessions nurture the practice of sharing and connection without necessarily calling attention to loneliness. In that sense, Creativity Circles might be to loneliness what restaurants are to hunger. They offer an enjoyable experience that satisfies a human need, and in an appealing context for human connection.

Restaurant reviews rarely discuss hunger, and similarly, the initial survey data from Creativity Circles rarely addressed loneliness directly. Instead, participants reported new levels of self-confidence in managing their emotions and dealing with issues related to aging. These results were very similar to those from the pilot program in New York. We were excited because Creativity Circles don't provide explicit instruction in any of these competencies. We surmise that the experience of being mindful, making creative work in response to carefully crafted prompts, and then having meaningful conversations fulfills human needs in ways that reduce anxiety, improve social cognition, and nurture self-confidence.

Based on these positive results, we reached out to the AARP Foundation, who granted us the funding and expert advice we needed to run Creativity Circles with community partners at nine locations in Illinois, New York, and Maine in March and April 2020. When the pandemic forced their postponement, we adapted the Creativity Circles curriculum for online delivery via Zoom. We expanded the number of weekly sessions from six to eight, but reduced the time allocated for each session to one hour, assuming it would be difficult for participants to stare at a screen for much longer. We also developed a strong tech support capability, and all nine eight-week workshops were delivered in the fall of 2020 without a glitch. As confirmed by the responses from 102 participants (ranging in age from 50 to 101), each was a roaring success.

Respondents reported experiencing the same increases in self-confidence at managing their emotions and coping with the difficulties of aging as did the participants in the original in-person pilot workshops. They also reported increases in making efforts to connect with friends, take up new creative pursuits, and engage in mindfulness meditation on their own. There was little dissatisfaction with the online format. "This pandemic has made me miss touching and hugging my friends and family," said one participant. "At least I can connect to people using technology."

In the course of the eight weeks, the majority of the respondents increased their engagement with other outside activities. It's as though these relatively brief online sessions had helped them reset their sense of possibility for connection in their lives, and even more important, they acted upon it. "What I found to be most beautiful is this organic connection that just happens, usually around the third or fourth session," said Jenil Bennett, a community health aide with SHARE who facilitated two of the online workshops. "People start to open up and really share about their lives, their experiences, and how to cope with aging. There is a bond when complete strangers become part of this close-knit group."

The participant responses also suggested we'd made a mistake by shortening the length of each program session for online delivery. Participants told us they wished each session had run longer. They also said the program should have more sessions, and that they wanted more programming of this kind. I don't think any of us could have predicted that response. Those and other insights about online programming were gifts of the pandemic. We came away from the calamity having developed an alternative method of delivering Creativity Circles that is highly scalable, while providing most of the same benefits as our original in-person design.

The success of the online program also opened our eyes to the possibility that Creativity Circles serve as a true lifeline for aging people at risk of being socially isolated by poor health, disabilities, or remote locations. As one participant commented, the weekly online encounter with meditation, creative expression, and conversation might give older people a deep sense of human connection that is otherwise unavailable to them. One participant commented, "The group gives me something positive to think about. It is a bright spot in my life and has given me more contact with people."

Along those lines, we also developed Reflect and Connect Calls, a program that substitutes the art-making of Creativity Circles with art appreciation and discussion in small teleconferencing groups or one-on-one phone calls. We also developed a program for sharing a work of art (like streaming one of the short films from our UnLonely Film Festival) and then reflecting on it through mindfulness meditation and conversation.

At the same time, I hope that Creativity Circles will continue to flourish in face-to-face settings because they are especially helpful in building meaningful friendships through shared experiences. At St. Brendan, activities coordinator Milton Wright told of how, before each week's session, he would post all the artwork from previous weeks on the activity room walls. "After three or four weeks, we had a nice little gallery going on," he said. "I think it created an atmosphere where people felt comfortable making art because there it was up on the wall. It was something to be proud of." In 2022, when St. Brendan resumed bingo nights and other communal activities, several of the women asked about bringing back Creativity Circles, even though almost two years had passed. "They were talking about what a good time they had, doing those art projects and sharing feelings," Milton said. "It was a good environment for them to kind of open up."

The mission of all these efforts is the same: to help keep older people connected, so that loneliness doesn't put them at elevated risk of mental and physical impairments. Every year is a good year for aging people if they remain at the bottom tier of the Pyramid of Vulnerability for loneliness. It's a win for public health, and for each at-risk individual, if they spend yet another year with only the ordinary occasional loneliness innate to the human condition. It's a reminder that good health is much more than the absence of illness. Connecting with others is part of the full picture of good heath, one of thriving and flourishing in the later years of life.

HARD-TO-REACH MEN

One disappointing outcome of our Creativity Circles rollout is that only 9 percent of program participants have been men. That's unfortunate because our survey results show that male participants have benefited from the program just as much as female participants. The problem might be one of perception. I think back to the combat veteran Jason Berner, who initially resisted art therapy because it was at odds with his self-identity as a warrior. How many men are turned off by Creativity Circles for similar reasons, because they think there's something unmanly about making collages and talking about what they mean? At the St. Brendan Creativity Circle, it was a man—one of the few who signed up—who promptly quit when he saw the colored pencils and associated them with child's play.

Participating in the Creativity Circles involves some acknowledgment of vulnerability, and that can be a problem for men. Without indulging in gender stereotypes, I have to point out that psychologists recognize aspects of traditional masculine values that can set older men up for loneliness. For example, male friendships tend to be "side by side" in shared activities and work relationships, in contrast to the "face-to-face" friendships of shared feelings and emotional disclosure among women. With old age and retirement, men commonly lose these friendships as shared activities fall away and work relationships end. As their support networks wither, men often withdraw in old age, and many risk entering the vicious cycle of isolation leading to loneliness and loneliness leading to still-deeper isolation.

The evidence continues to mount that loneliness and social isolation in older men is a serious problem, one that is exacerbated by the shame and stigma men feel about being lonely. A common traditional male response to stress and suffering is "grin and bear it." The CDC study of 1995 Chicago heat wave fatalities revealed that men were more than twice as likely as women to die, even though the vast majority of older Chicagoans are women. In general, women are much more likely than men to retain their social relationships as they age, and so under the stress of the heat wave, they were more likely to have helpful friends checking in on them. In addition, if the need arose, women were more likely to actively seek assistance. Men, by contrast, were less likely to have anyone checking on them, and less likely to ask for help even if it was available.

Calvin Mosley, a social worker who works with homeless veterans in Chicago, frequently encounters this cycle. Some of these men in their prime had families and good jobs, and were involved in their communities, but with age they tended to alienate the people close to them. "Maybe they were too hard on their family," Calvin said. "I think about this one World War II veteran, because I was really close to him. He told me how he pushed his family away." The man was so strict and demanding that his children wanted nothing to do with him when they grew up. When his wife died prematurely, he was alone in the world.

Studies have shown that postretirement men who no longer feel a purpose in their lives are prone to depression and loneliness. Calvin says that when he talks to homeless men, he listens for signals of either despair or integration in their conversations. If the events in their day are integrated into some form of meaningful purpose in their lives, they are not at risk for loneliness. But those who express a sense of despair and meaninglessness are.

Jason Berner overcame his aversion to making art only when he could see the practical function it would serve in helping him get well. This makes me wonder if there's a way to increase the appeal of Creativity Circles to men by adding some elements of practicality and purpose. Can the curriculum be designed in a way that makes male participants feel their creations are serving some clear instrumental purpose? I think of the AIDS quilt, and how the meaning of creating each piece was magnified by the way it contributed to a massive international effort.

Perhaps there is a larger creative project that could engage older men in the same way, so that the benefits of the Creativity Circle process would be available to them as they serve a useful purpose. I still don't have an answer.

"I COULD DRUM HER OUT OF DEMENTIA"

Sometime in the early 2000s, I went to a friend's party way back in the woods of Sonoma County, California, where so many of San Francisco's hippies had retreated when they got older. Pot smoke hung heavy in the night air, and the host's pet potbellied pigs wandered around at his guests' feet. I struck up a conversation with a man in his late fifties with short dark hair graying at the temples, whose eyes lit up when I told him of my work in the arts and health.

"Well, I'm pretty interested in that, too," he said. In fact, he added, he'd given testimony in Congress on the subject. Given the setting, I wasn't too sure how likely that all was, but then he went on. "I'm a drummer," he explained. "My grandmother had Alzheimer's and couldn't speak or recognize me. But when I played certain rhythms on my drums, she'd say my name. It's like I could drum her out of her dementia."

We spoke for a while longer, and although his story intrigued me, I still found it a little hard to believe he'd testified before Congress. Then another guest told me who I'd been talking to. He was Mickey Hart, longtime drummer for the Grateful Dead.

Mickey had appeared in 1991 before the congressional Special Committee on Aging, at a hearing titled "Forever Young: Music and Aging," where he advocated for drum circle workshops to be held in nursing homes and retirement communities. Among the benefits, he said, "would be immediate reduction in feelings of loneliness and alienation."

Oliver Sacks also testified at that hearing, which was held not long after his memoir, *Awakenings*, had been made into a major motion picture starring Robin Williams and Robert De Niro. In his experience, he said, music therapy worked best for people with dementia when it evoked pleasant memories. "It must be the 'right' music," he said. "The music which holds significance, has meaning for the individual." In that way, he added, "the demented patient can be restored to himself; can recall, re-access, not only his powers of speech, his perceptual and thinking skills, but his entire emotional and intellectual configuration." I met Dr. Sacks a few years later, and although we never became close friends, he was a thoughtful adviser to the Foundation for Art & Healing in its early days, and we visited several times in his writing workshop in Manhattan. He said something marvelous about music, that it could act as a prosthesis for the brain, and like a prosthesis restore something vitally important to allow beneficial functioning.

In the decades since then, there's been a slowly growing appreciation for what music and dance therapy can do to restore memory and function for people living with dementia. The science of dementia suggests that the things learned earliest in life are most easily revived—and that includes the childhood delights of music, dance, visual arts, and crafts.

There is growing evidence that we can reverse early-stage dementia through intensive social connection programs that include creative arts engagement. Again, the brain research findings of an overlap between the "art brain connectome" and the "social brain connectome" provide a scientific basis for how the arts can change memory and the recollection of faces and events, changing how we can relate and connect to others. I'm excited about a number of innovative programs and initiatives in this area. One early noteworthy example is "Alzheimer's Thursdays," an art appreciation group for people with Alzheimer's at the Museum of Modern Art in New York that began in 2007, with the support of the MetLife Foundation. That pioneering initiative opened the door to a wide variety of museum-based programs to address cognitive impairment in creative ways, efforts now championed by the American Alliance of Museums. Then there is TimeSlips, a group started by MacArthur award winner Anne Basting, which is building an international network of artists and caregivers with the mission of "bringing meaning & purpose into the lives of elders through creative engagement." Studies of TimeSlips programs in nursing homes have shown evidence of increased alertness and more frequent positive interactions with staff among those with mild to moderate dementia. A TimeSlips program offered in an art museum in Switzerland showed improved mood among both participants with dementia *and* their care partners.

CAREGIVING

So much of the focus on aging and loneliness examines the risks of older people living alone. However, there is a special loneliness for older people in the role of taking care of a spouse who is in mental and physical decline. This is true also of older people who are caregivers for siblings, for roommates, and for their adult children with mental and physical disabilities.

In 2019, we worked with a Jewish community center on Long Island, New York, to design and offer a six-session Creativity Circle program for family caregivers. The difficulties we encountered illustrate the challenges faced by caregivers every day. First, the community center had a tough time recruiting a group of twelve caregivers. Most people they approached were either daunted by the moderate time commitment of one to two hours per week for six weeks or said it was too much trouble to travel to the center. Many caregivers couldn't find the time to do something fun that was for their own self-care. It's possible that some of the people who would have benefited the most from the Creativity Circle were those who simply felt too overwhelmed to attend.

Other caregivers asked about the availability of what's known as adult day care for adults with dementia. The caregiver could participate if they could bring their care recipient with them and have them get support while the caregiver engaged in our program. When the program finally ran, only a few of the caregivers were able to attend all the sessions, and although it was an overall positive experience for them, it was not something we could do again until we could address some of these roadblocks.

Aging spouses who are caregivers must juggle three roles at the same time—medical point of contact and "on the scene" practitioner, logistics aide, and loving spouse. The first two roles often crowd out the third. With so much medical information available online, the complexity of deciding what's best can be overwhelming, especially when combined with the tangled US system of health insurance. (I've experienced firsthand some small sense of that feeling when friends have asked for my informal medical advice or to assist them in getting care.) Then there are the at-home medical care tasks, sometimes involving activities that can be intimidating for those without clinical training. The logistical demands of caregiving are an additional source of strain. How do I get their medications? How do I find the special food they need and store it in the refrigerator? How do I learn to change dressings? Spousal caregivers face the constant worry that they are not doing enough.

All these practical issues tend to overshadow the third: What's my emotional relationship to what's going on? In cases where spousal caregivers may feel overwhelmed, they may experience negative emotions, like anxiety over whether they can keep up, fear that they aren't getting it all quite right, or even resentment over the situation they now find themselves in. That resentment can also trigger a sense of guilt—"What's wrong with me that I resent doing this caregiving for someone who has cared so much for me?" Those feelings, along with the isolation that often comes with providing hours of support a day, often add loneliness to the caregiver's burden.

Research shows that caregivers, like everyone, are less lonely if they have strong networks of social support. Studies have also shown that the quality of the marriage is a factor in caregiver loneliness. If a marriage was not solid when one spouse was diagnosed with dementia, the caregiving spouse will tend to feel especially lonely, because they now are taking care of someone about whom they have resentments that will never be resolved. Even in loving marriages, the task of caregiving can lead to depression and loneliness.

"When I've spoken to older adult male partners who are caring for their female spouses, they often share how they struggle with a sense of responsibility," said Kate Krajci, a Chicago social worker who specializes in work with people with dementia. "They feel guilty about leaving their spouse with anyone else. Some say things like, 'I made a vow six years ago that I had to do this, this, and this.'" These men feel guilty about enjoying themselves outside the home, even for activities as simple as meeting friends for coffee. "They sacrifice any kind of respite they might get, even if it's just going out shopping, because of this responsibility they've taken on."

While it's true that female caregiving partners often feel this way, too, they are also more likely to have stronger support networks. As we've seen with other examples of women struggling with loneliness, they are much more likely than male caregivers to ask for help when it's needed and talk about their feelings with intimate friends and family. Men who become isolated caregivers either lack that network or don't accept available support from family, friends, and social service providers. They end up communicating daily only with the spouse who has dementia and may not even recognize them. That can lead to exceptionally painful forms of psychological loneliness.

Krajci added, "Especially with forms of dementia that affect language ability, I hear consistently how 'we can't connect the way we used to,'" she says. "I hear that consistently from both the person living with the dementia, as well as the caregiver." For caregivers, the loss of conversation magnifies their sense of isolation and loss about who their spouse once was, which can lead to deep depression and a profoundly lost sense of self.

The stress of caregiving can be very intense for anyone, not just aging people and their spouses. For younger adults who are called on to balance work with both child-rearing and caregiving for an unwell and aging parent, loneliness can be a significant problem. When you have so many serious obligations competing for your time and attention, your own needs for self-care, like connecting with friends, are at risk of going ignored.

My colleague at Harvard, Arthur Kleinman, is a leading medical anthropologist who says that care is a fundamental and universal feeling, no different from other feelings such as pain, suffering, and joy. He wrote a book in 2020, *The Soul of Care*, after serving as caregiver to his wife during her ten-year decline and death from Alzheimer's. Care, he told an interviewer, is "an elaboration of the love that we have for others. That's why I believe this is not just an emotion, but a moral emotion. It's an emotion that centers our life. That's why I use the term, the soul of care. I wanted to use the idea of soul as an inner feeling of value and emotion tied together, that sort of orientates us, centers us. And I think that's what care is about. It is a crucial part of who we are in relation to others, and as such, it's about as universal as anything you'll find."

AGING AND GRIEF

Children's book author Maurice Sendak gave his final interview on National Public Radio in 2011, less than six months prior to his death at age eighty-four. He told Terry Gross, the longtime host of the *Fresh Air* show, that he wasn't afraid of death. "I cry a lot because I miss people," he said. "I cry a lot because they die and I can't stop them. They leave me and I love them more."

He was still grieving his companion of more than fifty years, who had died in 2007. Then, earlier in 2011, two of his closest friends, a married couple, died, one shortly after the other. "They were not that old," he said. "And so it's what I dread more than anything is the isolation." Addressing Terry Gross, he added, "Almost certainly, I'll go before you, so I won't have to miss you."

In 2021, the American Psychiatric Association added "prolonged grief disorder" to the DSM, the *Diagnostic and Statistical Manual of Mental Disorders*, which formally classifies mental disorders. Prolonged grief disorder can be diagnosed when someone is grieving a death that occurred over a year in the past and continues to experience such intense longing for the deceased (or becomes preoccupied with thoughts of the deceased nearly every day for more than a month) that their grief damages their social relationships and work performance.

"If you've recently lost someone close to you, it's very important to check in with yourself," APA president Vivian B. Pender said at the time. "Grief in these circumstances is normal, but not at certain levels and not most of the day, nearly every day for months. Help is available."

The loneliness of what's been called disordered grieving, complicated grieving, or disenfranchised grieving has been studied for a number of years. In my opinion, there is no objective time period after which normal grieving develops into prolonged grief disorder, because we are social creatures, and what is ordinary in some social contexts might be regarded as disordered in others. Among the most common symptoms are intense emotional pain, emotional numbness, feeling that life is meaningless, and intense loneliness. These are feelings that might be common within the first year of losing a loved one, but the DSM states that the disorder may exist after that, when the duration of intense grieving "exceeds expected social, cultural or religious norms and the symptoms are not better explained by another mental disorder." It is estimated that as much as 15 percent of bereaved people will develop prolonged grief disorder, which suggests that on any given day, between 2 and 3 percent of everyone in the world is experiencing it.

By some estimates, an average of nine people feel grief at each person's passing. We are only now beginning to get a handle on the enormous trail of grief left by seven million deaths from COVID-19 around the world. For much of 2020 and all of 2021, social distancing prevented survivors from fully participating in the rituals that integrate death into the community of friends and families. In October 2020, seven months after the start of the pandemic, NYU psychiatrist Naomi Simon published a "call to action" paper in *JAMA: The Journal of the American Medical Association* that foretold a grief-related surge in mental health disorders and substance abuse: "The sudden interpersonal loss associated with COVID-19, along with severe social disruption, can easily overwhelm the ways individuals and families cope with bereavement." She and her coauthors called for increased funding for screening, mental health risk assessment, and treatment, including use of the "Prolonged Grief 12" questionnaire to identify surviving family members and friends who are at highest risk for prolonged grief and post-traumatic stress.

People with prolonged grief disorder often feel lonely and lost after someone very close to them has died, as though they've lost a piece of themselves. They can also feel a lost sense of belonging, a loss of their former social definition, after which life itself can feel meaningless. Katherine Shear, a psychiatrist at Columbia University and founding director of the Center for Prolonged Grief, has developed a sixteen-week treatment for prolonged grief disorder that involves cognitive behavioral therapy as well as other approaches to help the bereaved person set personal goals, which can give them a sense of renewed hope and purpose. Achieving these goals usually requires finding people who can fill some of the social roles vacated by the lost loved one. To grieve is to be lonely, and resolving your grief requires attending to your loneliness by making meaningful connections with other people.

Loss of a loved one, like any other trauma, must be integrated into our memories so that we can feel the sadness of our loved one's absence without reexperiencing the initial intense emotional pain of losing them. That can happen only when we tell our story to people we trust and feel close to. If we are too lonely and disconnected from others to tell our story, the debilitating pain of grieving can linger for years, like the pain of any unhealed wound.

In his final radio interview, Sendak recounted some of the losses in his life—his partner of many years, his friends, his mobility due to a heart condition that prevented him from taking the long walks he loved. But he also noted some of the creative benefits of aging. "I'm writing a poem now about a nose," he said. "I always wanted to write a poem about a nose. But, you know, I thought, gee. It's a ludicrous subject. Well, that's why, you know, when I was younger I was afraid of something that didn't make a lot of sense . . . [Now] there's nothing to worry about. It doesn't matter." Among his many losses from aging, Sendak could count a much-welcomed loss of self-consciousness.

He added, "I don't know whether I'll do another book or not. I might. It doesn't matter. I'm a happy old man. But I will cry my way all the way to the grave."

7

Difference

first met Claudia Rankine back in 2006 at the Community of Writers, an annual poetry-writing intensive held each summer in Olympic Valley, California. Claudia was already a well-established poet at the time and had just published a book called *Don't Let Me Be Lonely*, a 169-page meditation in words and images about loneliness, longing, and modern American life. She was one of the five instructors at Olympic Valley that summer, and the workshops she conducted were lively and lighthearted, as was her personal coaching. Her insights about my work that summer increased my confidence in writing poetry, and perhaps just as important, the sense of connection I experienced in reading the work of other poets.

Motivated by the events of 9/11, I had begun reworking some of my old poems and writing new ones. In an attempt to better organize what I was trying to make sense of through poetry, I gathered about fifty of them into a collection. There was only one problem: they weren't as good as I wanted them to be.

What attracted me to the Community of Writers program also terrified me. All the participants, including the teachers, were expected to write a poem each and every day, to read it aloud, share it, and get feedback from others. I wasn't sure I was up for that kind of experience, let alone with complete strangers. But once I got there, I found a warm and diverse environment. My roommate was a young Mexican American poet whose extensive tattoos told the story of his youth in a violent Los Angeles gang. There was a high school teacher, an investment banker, and even another physician, an AIDS researcher I'd known in college. We were all gathered in a beautiful setting with a single purpose, to make poetry together as both a personal and a shared experience.

Claudia's chief contribution to my work involved a poem about my mother. I was struggling with memories of going through my mother's disheveled house following her death. The poem became a litany of unkempt things, like the television that was always on and also always filthy. When I reluctantly showed the poem to Claudia, it was as messy as my mom's house. Fortunately, it wasn't the first poem of mine she'd read. She told me that in each of my poems she saw me telling a story by using poetic form to lay out a series of particulars before taking a surprising turn that would reveal something universal about those particulars. That what made the particulars matter wasn't their relationship to me, but their relevance to others, reminding them of their own experience.

I was surprised and intrigued. What I hadn't told Claudia was how complicated my feelings about my mother were. While there were many things about my mother I admired, there were also things I was ashamed of. That particular poem captured some of them, interwoven with the compassion I felt for the emotional pain my mother experienced as her life unraveled. In recognizing that my shame would be familiar to the reader, I felt less alone and less ashamed. Claudia had pointed out something in my writing that I had never seen myself, and that got me curious about what else I wasn't seeing. It helped me finish what had been a very difficult poem and has informed my writing ever since.

Claudia taught me an important way creative expression is related to human connection. The function of a creative work is to somehow reveal the universal in the personal. Claudia achieves this in her own work. *Don't Let Me Be Lonely* explores the experience of not fitting in, so common in American life. Written as a lyric poem in the first person, the book describes her personal encounters with being subjected to systematic exclusion. "Because the foundations for loneliness begin in the dreamscapes you create," she writes. "Their resemblance to reality reflects disappointment first."

Through the words and images in her book, I absorbed the way she was treated with mindless and casual racist cruelty. I was outraged and saddened, and ashamed. I felt what she had felt. How could this be going on in my country? How could I not have seen it, and now seeing it, how could I look away? It made me feel deeply lonely, too, and for the first time I recognized loneliness as a shared experience that was bigger than the one I was navigating on my own.

Claudia won a MacArthur Foundation "genius" grant in 2016, following the publication of *Citizen: An American Lyric*. This book was about her specific experiences as a Black woman in America, and the essential loneliness of being both a minority and a female in a society dominated by white men. One passage in particular about verbal bullying stood out for me: "Language that feels hurtful is intended to exploit all the ways that you are present. Your alertness, your openness, and your desire to engage actually demand your presence, your looking up, your talking back, and, as insane as it is, saying please."

That is Claudia's perspective on the abject vulnerability of being an outsider, of being marginalized, disempowered, and violated. And, as she points out, the cruel irony of the way our minds make sense of systematic exclusion is that we feel we deserve it, that it's somehow our fault. As a result, it not only wounds us, but shames us, diminishing our sense of what we can be and become. As we withdraw from engaging with others, shame can constrict our lived experience, making it harder to feel confident about our own identity, relevance, and self-worth. We live in a smaller and lonelier world.

This is the experience of "societal loneliness," the second kind of loneliness. Unlike with psychological and existential loneliness, with societal loneliness it is the group that isolates us, through indifference or perhaps outright hostility. Loneliness is inflicted on us through rejection, whether implicit or explicit.

We all experience at one time or another the lonely feeling of difference, of not belonging, of not being part of a group. It inhabits our actual lived experience, as well as our anticipated experience. Imagine having to enter a room filled with people. Are they eager to see you? Are you welcome? Are you safe? Do you feel a sense of belonging? Or are you ignored, disregarded, shunned? Taken to scale, societal loneliness is experienced as a consequence of racism, sexism, homophobia, and transphobia. The larger society has ways of rejecting anyone who is different, whether because of their age, weight, a disability, or simply because in some way they are outside the social norms for attractiveness, speech, dress, or faith. In many cultures, poverty itself is judged as a moral failing or a source of shame, and it is often a source of profound loneliness.

Students in college classes taught by Claudia Rankine have often been assigned an influential essay written in 1989 by Peggy McIntosh, who was then at the Wellesley Centers for Women. The essay coined the phrases "white privilege" and "male privilege" and suggests that both white people and men rarely recognize their privileges as "an invisible package of unearned assets." The paper enumerates forty-six instances of these unearned privileges, including, "I can be late to a meeting without having the lateness reflect on my race," "I can be sure that if I need legal or medical help, my race will not work against me," and "I can expect figurative language and imagery in all of the arts to testify to experiences of my race."

Claudia notes that during class discussions, her students have had little problem coming up with dozens more examples of these privileges, all unearned and typically unacknowledged by those who enjoy them. She went on to write a play called *Help*, in which a single black woman makes her lonely way through a social structure, in Claudia's words, "comprised primarily of white men who ultimately determine all civic possibility."

THE TROUBLE WITH BEING DIFFERENT

My earliest memory of experiencing societal loneliness was when I was seven, after we'd moved from a New Jersey shore town to Pittsburgh. Time spent in those early Pittsburgh days with my parents and sisters had the spirit of eager exploration, especially with my mom rejoining the workforce to supplement my dad's graduate school stipend. We were latchkey kids ahead of the trend, with the complex experience of self-supervision that came with it. Our new neighborhood was a close-knit community, and we were from someplace far away. Some neighbors were warm and welcoming, but many were not. I'll never forget the blank stares, or worse, the utter lack of regard, as if I were invisible. This is the experience of societal loneliness we all have at certain junctions in our lives, and it is usually a transitory experience. The pain is real, but it almost always passes. In a few months, in part because of my parents' efforts to integrate us into Pittsburgh's vibrant Jewish community, I had made new friends. By the time six months had passed, I was no longer seen as the new kid.

The impact of the move was much worse and more lasting for my oldest sister. She had been diagnosed in early childhood with cerebral palsy, which gave her impaired hearing and certain problems with the fine motor skills required for tasks such as handwriting. But no one in our local New Jersey school administration recognized that my sister's problems with speech were related to her hearing loss. Instead, they labeled her "mentally retarded," the term used at the time, and placed her in "special education" classes, where she truly did not belong. Fortunately, my parents weren't at all comfortable with this approach and succeeded in getting my sister more thorough medical and behavioral evaluations, in which the underlying cause of her delayed language and social skill development was eventually recognized and addressed. By the time we made the move to Pittsburgh, she was no longer categorized as mentally retarded but still was not fully mainstreamed into routine classroom activities.

I have a distinct memory of walking alone down the hallway at the end of my first day in second grade at Colfax Elementary School, two blocks from our newly rented duplex. As I passed by one darkened classroom, I saw someone sitting by herself amid the rows of chairs and desks. It was my sister, with her back turned to the door, and I could see that she was sobbing. I stood at the doorway, momentarily frozen with fear and sadness, and then I turned and walked away. When I returned home, I told no one what I'd seen. How could I? I would have needed to explain why I didn't go into that classroom and comfort my sister. My cowardice in that moment is a source of shame that I feel to this day, some sixty years later.

I tell this story because it underlines the pernicious nature of societal loneliness. The shared experience of being in a new school did not strengthen the bond between my sister and me. Instead, when forced to walk among a tribe that saw us as outsiders, we each retreated with fear into our individual corners of loneliness. We were both deep in the grip of societal loneliness—and that intense feeling of not belonging isolated us not only from our classmates at school but from each other.

The problem of being different and the societal loneliness that accompanies such difference cannot be fully understood without appreciating the power that group dynamics exert on all human societies. Academic research on societal loneliness is found most commonly in the field of sociology, which studies how groups function within society, and in the related field of social psychology, which studies how individuals are influenced by and cope with group behaviors and social norms.

One of the fundamental tenets of sociology is that human beings form groups reflexively as a way to increase their odds of survival, and these groups are in part defined by identifying those individuals who *don't* belong. We are all social creatures, and how we define ourselves (what we call our identity) is a combination of who *we* think we are and what *other people* think we are. We form our identities through the stories or narratives we tell ourselves about ourselves. Society, on the other hand, identifies each of us by our outward appearance and by what is known about us broadly, which places each of us in a collective group with others who share those characteristics. In this way, your personal identity is how you perceive yourself, while your social identity is how others perceive you.

In late 2019, as Rebecca Burridge began her transition as a transgender woman at age forty-eight, she felt an urgent desire to be acknowledged as a woman by people who hadn't known her before. "I need strangers," she said. "That's the deal as a trans person. I need people to call me 'Miss' or say, 'Hi, Rebecca.'" She put on a dress, did her hair and makeup, put out all her feminine signals so she could at last connect with other people as her true, authentic self. "Loneliness has always been something pervasive in my life, possibly because I was in the closet," she said. "When you're finally ready to live your life, you need society to help define yourself."

Although Rebecca had the support of her wife and children when she transitioned, their support didn't factor in her need for a new social definition. "My wife is going to call me 'Sweetie.' My kids call me 'Mom' or 'Mama' or whatever. But they don't call me 'Rebecca.'" In her first months of transition, during the 2019 holidays and into early 2020, each uneventful trip to a public restroom felt like a small triumph. It was a thrill to go clothes shopping with her wife and have store associates respond to them as just two female friends talking over their style choices.

Then it suddenly ended in March 2020, as the pandemic curtailed everyone's interactions with strangers. It was a particularly difficult time for Rebecca. "COVID felt like stepping back in the closet," she recalled. "It was pretty devastating." One day, while waiting in her car to pick up her children, Rebecca found herself staving off the pandemic's loneliness by asking Siri, her iPhone's automated assistant, to say her name. "Are you talking to me, Rebecca?" Siri replied. Rebecca recalled, "I had Siri say it over and over again, because it felt so good to hear."

We all have a fundamental need for belonging, and research shows the people who feel a lack of belonging suffer significant consequences.

Typically, each of us adopts the identity of the groups we belong to, which ties us emotionally to these groups and helps form the bedrock of our self-esteem. For example, if you identify yourself as a student, if the feeling of being a student gives you a sense of belonging, you will start to act the way you believe students act. You will conform to the behavioral norms of your group. Studies have found moderate correlations indicating that people's perceptions of their cohesion with a group is associated with lower levels of loneliness, social anxiety, and depression.

We feel bad when we're lonely and we feel good when we belong. That's the way our brains work, as organs of survival, to avoid isolation and to reward cooperation. And just as our brains categorize objects so we can identify them quickly and easily, we also categorize people in groups, so we can quickly and easily navigate our social environment. That's how the brain divides the world into a series of "them" and "us" categories—whether by race, gender, class, or, more harmlessly, by college and professional sports teams. That intense affinity people feel toward their favorite teams and fellow fans (and the animosity they feel toward rival teams and their fans) is a highly profitable and socially benign channeling of the same cognitive processes that fuel prejudice and bigotry.

This is the brain's way of binding us to our own groups and protecting us from other groups. Our brain even distorts our perceptions by heightening our observed similarities with people in our own group, making our differences with members of other groups appear much larger than they are. Stereotyping and prejudice proceed naturally from these cognitive processes because your brain is constantly prompting you to observe members of other groups according to the categories of their social identities before you have a chance to know them as individuals.

Once our brains categorize us as part of a group, we tend to compare that group with other groups. When members of different groups perceive themselves as rivals for social status, they will compete with each other in order for their members to maintain their self-esteem. If a dominant group with power holds a negative view of smaller, less powerful groups—immigrants, people of color, or members of the LGBTQ community—individual members of the dominant group will tend to adopt those prejudicial views. For those subject to prejudice, the experience can be intensely lonely, and worse. It can mean that they are viewed as "other" and everything they do stands out as a reflection of their group identity.

The new society we are constructing post-pandemic gives us the chance to examine the phenomena of difference and societal loneliness in a new light. We can observe how consciously engaging with our differences in an environment of safety and mutual respect can be highly beneficial. It can challenge us to develop empathy, stretch our assumptions, and grow our imaginations.

To illustrate this point, I'll recall how my parents responded to the challenge of helping my oldest sister, Tamar, with the developmental delays that resulted from her cerebral palsy. In that era's relative vacuum of knowledge about cerebral palsy, my parents, who were both scientists, embarked on a series of skill-developing exercises that they hoped would strengthen Tamar's language and motor skills.

It would have been easy for my parents to say each evening to me and my other sister, Naomi, "You kids go play or do your homework. It's time for Tamar's therapy." That would have been a rational and efficient use of everyone's time. In fact, it reflects how children with developmental delays are treated today when they go for specialized therapies or have a therapist visit the house. They get their treatment while their siblings do other things.

But that wasn't at all how my parents handled the helpful activities they devised for Tamar. Instead, they made her evening exercises a fun family activity. To help Tamar develop her manual dexterity, my mother invented a game of using chopsticks to pick up Rice Krispies one by one out of one bowl and drop them into another. At first, none of us were very good at it, so it was something we all learned to do together, right along with Tamar. My parents very wisely understood that if we all participated in Tamar's skill development, she would feel less lonely. They knew that the outside world was not an inviting place for children like her. Within our house, they wanted her to feel fully included and accepted. They wanted to reassure her that she belonged.

I don't recall ever feeling held back by participating in my sister's therapies. From a certain point of view, Tamar's disability brought our family closer together. Because her language development was delayed, my father would lead after-dinner vocabulary drills for all three of his children. He would haul out an old textbook called *Word Wealth* and read new words to us with their definitions. Then we'd attempt to use each new word in a sentence and were expected to remember those words for the next lesson, when we would be tested for recall. With time, and for reasons I still don't fully understand, I fell in love with words. It's very possible that I am a poet today because my relationship with words and their meaning was begun in this very unusual way, intimately associated with my memories of family togetherness and belonging.

My family, as a group, embraced Tamar's difference within the group and did not allow her disability to define her as "other." By reaching across the divide that could have separated us from Tamar, our family became stronger, and our lives were enriched in ways we could not have predicted. Connection to others is particularly valuable when achieving it is difficult enough to force us to grow. That is the underlying aspiration of diversity and multiculturalism, that working to accept differences and make connections across what divides us makes us better and makes the group stronger. Like justice or liberty, it's an unobtainable ideal toward which we must struggle, in the face of doubters who believe groups are strongest when everyone conforms. This is worth remembering as we attempt to reconstruct our torn social fabric. We cannot wish away our differences. But we can reassert the value of engaging with our differences in the name of human connection.

"A COUNTRY WHERE YOU DON'T SPEAK THE LANGUAGE"

For years, strange rumors about Bruce Willis's career had been swirling around Hollywood. Sometime around 2019, the A-list film star had stopped taking acting jobs on major studio productions and instead began appearing in cheaply made action movies that were available only on streaming services and on DVDs sold overseas. Newspaper reports claimed he was making $2 million for each picture, for just a few days of work. In the space of just two years, at least fifteen of these low-quality B movies had been released with his name and likeness on the DVD covers.

The truth finally came out in early 2022. Willis had been suffering from aphasia, a brain condition often related to stroke or traumatic injury, which had diminished his ability to speak and understand written and spoken words. Willis hadn't booked any big movies because he was no longer capable of working for more than a few days at a time. His limited availability forced directors to shoot many scenes with stunt actors and body doubles pretending to be Willis, with their heads turned or their faces obscured. When Willis was on-camera, he needed to receive his lines through a hidden earpiece because he could no longer read and remember scripts. Crew members on one film reported that he had said to them, "I know why you're here, and I know why you're here, but why am I here?"

That March, Willis's family announced he'd be retiring from acting at age sixty-eight. With the announcement, medical experts compared the loneliness of having aphasia to that of living in a foreign country where you don't speak the language. "The general public assumes that if someone doesn't respond, they are intellectually challenged," one speech pathologist told the *Los Angeles Times*. "They are treated like a child, when inside, they are still the same person. It becomes humiliating to be treated that way." Advocates for aphasia treatment expressed hope that the announcement of Willis's condition might help raise public awareness of the condition and reduce the stigma attached to it. Two million Americans have some form of aphasia, and because words so often fail them, their loneliness is something they must suffer in silence.

Some of my very first encounters with the loneliness of difference took place when I was working as a physician treating older people, people with disabilities, and people with both chronic and severe illnesses. These patients often complained of feeling that they no longer fit in, that living with aging, disability, or illness had set them apart from everyone in their world. They would use the language of loneliness as they described their longing for the quality of human connection that their conditions had taken away. Some with diabetes complained that family holiday celebrations were no longer enjoyable, now that they had to check their blood sugar and adjust their insulin dose while everyone else was relaxing and eating whatever they wanted. They felt different, that they no longer fit in, even those who had supportive families. The ones who were overweight also sometimes felt ashamed, feeling that others would judge them for having "eaten their way to diabetes." Their loneliness was their subjective experience, but for some, the discomfort kept them away from the specific activities that could mitigate it, accelerating a cycle of worsening distress.

In Boston in the early 1980s, I also treated some patients who had symptoms of AIDS when it was still a mysterious illness. These were mostly gay young men, and many of them had been utterly abandoned by frightened friends and by family members who hadn't even known that they were gay. In later years, as I started becoming more involved with public health activities, I began to see that race and poverty were among the factors that intensified the feelings of being excluded. Illness, aging, and disabilities were all likely to make you feel even lonelier if you were poor, belonged to a racial minority, or both.

Whether their members are consciously aware of it or not, groups are often desirable because they are exclusive, and people in exclusive groups can have little regard for the feelings of those they marginalize and ostracize. Most people don't do this purposely; fear of strangers has ancient origins and is not always entirely irrational. But whether or not it is conscious or malicious, excluding others will still have the impact of making the excluded people feel less connected. I actually think it's a little more complicated. Yes, excluding others based on group consensus might convey a certain type of exclusiveness and be interpreted as something positive. That said, I think often there is a price to be paid for this exclusion. Whether we are aware of it or not, achieving a sense of connection by excluding others is often revealed as a fragile, temporary, and non-sustainable solution. We're seeing it now as some groups, long accustomed to their ability to exclude others, are finding it less easy or comfortable to do so.

We human beings are very sensitive to being recognized. We notice when we're not being welcomed and accepted, and that lack of recognition directly impacts our sense of connection and belonging. Loneliness arising from the sense of deliberate exclusion by others has significant risk for depression, addiction, or even suicide. Bullying is a classic example, typically in younger people (one in five children experience bullying), but it exists at all ages. When there's a deliberate effort on the part of the bully to undermine the validity, self-confidence, and agency of the bullied person, it puts the health of that bullied person at risk.

At DePaul University, Jaclyn Jensen, an associate professor of management, has been studying the effects of workplace bullying and harassment of overweight workers. She and her associates have found that verbal attacks on such people were usually overt and direct—like the man who "mooed" at his overweight coworker to imply she was a fat cow. "Criticizing someone for their weight may be viewed as unprofessional, yet we live in a society where fat shaming, or humiliating another person for their size, has become culturally normative." Jensen's research showed that 80 percent of victims of such harassment reported depression and anxiety as a result of being bullied, and the vast majority of them grew withdrawn, avoiding interactions with coworkers, declining to speak up at meetings. Not only is it hurtful and destructive for the individual, it's bad for team functioning and learning in any workplace where such behavior is tolerated.

In mid-2021, when companies started calling their white-collar workers to return to their offices, most said they preferred to keep working from home. The strongest resistance to returning to the office came from women and minorities, the groups most often subject to hostile work environments. Members of these groups, to varying degrees, said they experienced the workplace as a minefield of social exclusion and microaggressions.

Sandra McPherson, one of three Black people in an office with eighty workers, recalled the pre-pandemic office environment as one where she was frequently subject to snide remarks about race. "There was always something from my white colleagues that made me feel uncomfortable or offended me," she told *NBC News*. "Some of it was intentional. Most of it was. A little of it was just sort of unconscious. All of it just wears on you." A white peer once said to her, "I thought affirmative action was over. How [did] you get here?" Sandra recalled, "He thought it was funny." Soon after Donald Trump won the 2016 presidential election, she overheard one manager say, "Guess that boat to Africa gonna be full." Then the manager looked at her and snickered.

So when an email arrived from her employer setting an office-return date in ninety days, Sandra felt an unexpected surge of anxiety. After more than a year of working from home, the idea of returning to what she calls "that unnecessary nonsense" left her unable to breathe. She decided she couldn't bear the tension of going back. Instead, she started her own small business on the side, and quit her job weeks before she was due to return to the office.

A 2021 survey by Future Forum, a research consortium sponsored by Slack Technologies, showed that a mere 3 percent of Black professionals working remotely looked forward to a post-pandemic return to the office, compared with 21 percent of white professionals. Just 53 percent of Black workers said they felt "treated fairly at work," while 74 percent of white workers felt that way. And only 54 percent of Black workers said they had a "good or very good" sense of belonging at work, while 70 percent of white professionals said they did.

But if everyone is working in different places, how can managers cultivate feelings of camaraderie and belonging at work? The answer is probably the most surprising finding of this research. For Black, Asian, and Hispanic professionals who were working remotely, this ability to have "location flexibility" *improved* their sense of belonging at work, particularly for Black workers. On the other hand, white professionals on the whole reported a slight decline in feelings of belonging from working remotely.

When *The Huffington Post* reported on these findings, the article cited a Black software engineer who asked to be called Christina. While working from home during the Black Lives Matter protests in the summer of 2020, she felt relieved she did not have to deal with her colleagues' offhand critical comments in person. "We had Zoom meetings," she said, which "made a lot of the discussions around race bearable for the past year."

The challenge for employers is how to deliver on the admirable concept of "strength through diversity." Employers need to support workers' connections with their distinctive personal identities while at the same time nurturing a common workplace culture that makes everyone feel welcome and valued in carrying out the organization's purpose. Larger organizations have provided support for online ERGs, employee resource groups, where people with common identities and interests can communicate and share their experiences. Project Un-Lonely frequently does programs sponsored by ERGs, in which we show selected short films from the UnLonely Film Festival and lead discussions pertaining to the issues surrounding that group's identity.

At the same time, we've also done work on the other side of alleviating workplace loneliness, dealing with the common bond of workplace belonging. During the pandemic, at Northwell Health in New York City, we purpose-built a Creativity Circle program for frontline healthcare workers that engaged with the issue of burnout, led discussion groups about an UnLonely Film Festival short that explored the sharing of emotional exhaustion, and developed handouts offering support for mental and emotional problems, all around the theme that we are all in this pandemic together and will get though it by helping one another.

OUR INTERSECTING IDENTITIES

All of us identify with different groups, and we all have what are called *intersecting* social identities. We identify ourselves most commonly by age, ethnicity, class, religion, gender identity, and sexual orientation, as well as by health condition and physical and mental abilities. These intersecting identities can be a chronic source of inner conflict, social friction, and loneliness when aspects of the different identities are at odds. For example, children who grow up with multiethnic or multiracial identities often suffer from loneliness because they find themselves not fully comfortable and accepted by any of the groups to which they claim membership.

Thema Reed, the New Mexico–born daughter of a Chicano father and Black mother, told an interviewer in 2021, "I've experienced colorism, I've experienced people saying, 'Well, you're not Black and you're not Mexican enough.' I feel really strongly connected to both, but at the same time, sometimes I feel like I belong to neither." When she arrived at Howard University, however, she found such a broad range of ethnic and socioeconomic mixes there that a new world opened up for her. "I had never been in a place where there were so many Black people that looked so many different ways," she said. "I really felt really accepted and loved for the first time." It took a change of geography and social context to help her resolve both her need to belong and her daily experience of being accepted.

Children of immigrants frequently feel torn between the identities their parents brought from overseas and their own experience as Americans. Hyeseung Song, a New York–based visual artist, spent much of her young life trying to satisfy both needs for belonging. Her family moved from South Korea to Texas when Hyeseung was very young, and she grew up in a predominantly white, upper-middle-class suburb of Houston, where she and her two younger siblings were among the few Asian children.

Hyeseung remembers her parents admonishing her and her siblings that they were not Americans. Her challenge was to find ways to fit into American school life without betraying her parents and their Korean culture. "American values are all about individualism and being who you are," she says. "In Korean culture, you serve other people. Your role in a bigger, holistic way is very important."

Her one way to be both Korean and American was to become a superstar student. She had highly conscientious study habits, excellent grades, and many friends. People in the socially precarious condition of being a minority in a larger group can develop special abilities at reading other people's emotions and becoming attuned to subtle social cues. That was Hyeseung. She was highly empathic, very considerate of the needs of others, and always willing to listen to friends talking out their problems. As an outsider, she saw that as her pathway to belonging.

On the inside, though, she felt little connection to this identity she was creating for herself. And while she was a great listener, she was lonely and had no one she could confide in. From an early age she enjoyed drawing, and in her teen years, she engrossed herself in drawing pictures, usually of other people's faces and hands. She almost never drew images of herself.

By high school, the facade began to crack. She grew depressed and isolated. She frequently skipped out on school in the middle of the day, sat alone in a local movie theater, watched the same film twice, and then returned to school to maintain the charade of being a good student. In retrospect, she said, "For me, the mental health piece was that loneliness manifesting in that way." She was grappling with existential loneliness, rooted in her "otherness" as neither Korean nor American.

Hyeseung attended Princeton, hoping she'd left her problems in Houston. She majored in philosophy, thinking it might help her resolve her issues with cultures. But she struggled with her mental health there, too, while keeping up her super-student facade. She went on to Harvard Law School, not because she cared about law, but "to win the love of my parents." After a long period of depression while studying for a PhD in philosophy at Harvard, she attempted suicide with an overdose of pills and woke up in the hospital. She remained an inpatient for weeks afterward and then underwent months of treatment in an outpatient program.

It was then, under psychiatric care, that Hyeseung faced the challenge of integrating her many intersecting identities—the dutiful Korean daughter, the super-student, the lawyer-to-be, the artist. Her many selves, all compartmentalized and competing to be heard, felt to her as though they were drifting apart as her sense of self was disintegrating. "I had this visualization that came to me of everybody out there in the air, and I had to pull everyone back together and celebrate the multiplicity—but also the singularity—of who I am," she said. "Integration was survival. I had to do this, or I would die at twenty-five."

Hyeseung decided she had to leave Harvard and leave academia entirely in order to take up the life of a fine artist. Her parents, who had been so proud of her academic achievements, struggled to understand her choice. It was the first choice she had made that didn't please them. She had to break with them and with the Korean tradition of deference to parents, in order to take hold of her life.

Studies of loneliness show that it is common for first-generation immigrants to experience "stressors that can increase their social isolation, such as language barriers, differences in community, family dynamics, and new relationships that lack depth or history." There are particularly high levels of loneliness found among US immigrants from Latin America, where research suggests there are fewer social ties and lower levels of social integration compared with US-born Latinos.

For individuals who are from immigrant families and are also LGBTQ, the loneliness is compounded by added layers of isolation resulting from stigma, discrimination, and frequent barriers to healthcare. Among the films in season five of the Project UnLonely Film Festival is *Share*, a moving twelve-minute first-person account by filmmaker Tim Chau, depicting a young gay Asian man's difficult decision to come out to his immigrant family. Tim is an Instagram influencer who had despaired about sharing his identity with his family because he had a vivid childhood memory of his father declaring, "If any of you kids are gay, I'm going to kill myself."

This is a case in which intersecting identities led to the phenomenon of intersectionality, when the social disadvantages of two or more overlapping marginalized identities create unique sets of problems for the individual. Intersectionality was defined in 1989 as a legal concept by law professor Kimberlé Crenshaw, who observed that Black women experience racism differently from Black men, and they also experience misogyny differently from white women.

"Intersectionality is a lens through which you can see where power comes and collides, where it interlocks and intersects," Crenshaw said in an interview. "It's not simply that there's a race problem here, a gender problem here, and a class or LBGTQ problem there. Many times that framework erases what happens to people who are subject to all of these things." For example, Black transgender females as a group have by far the highest rates of unemployment, homelessness, suicide, and murder when compared with groups that are either Black *or* female *or* transgender. To be a Black transgender female also means you may be subject to prejudice and rejection from other Black people, other transgender women, and other women, even if you identify with all three groups. For similar reasons, immigrant children who are also LGBTQ face a distinct set of challenges that may cut them off from other immigrant children, while their immigrant identity may cut them off from the LGBTQ community.

Young people with intersectional identities of all kinds must always make the lonely estimation of how much of their orientation to express, how many of their individual needs and preferences can be satisfied at the risk of judgment, marginalization, and rejection. That depth of isolation can also bring about a sense of shame and self-recrimination that is common among very lonely people: "I've brought this on myself" and "There is something wrong with me." When your own family rejects who you are, finding your way back from that level of loneliness is hard to do without building trusting relationships and having intimate conversations about your struggles. Common in the LGBTQ community is the acknowledged imperative for developing a "found family" or a "family of choice" who will fulfill each person's need to be fully seen and fully appreciated for their whole selves.

Whether you are LGBTQ or not, a found family can make it easier to put some distance between yourself and any negative assessments from your family of origin that may leave you feeling cast out and marginalized. Merely recognizing the need for a found family opens the door for seeking closer connections with those people in your life who make you feel seen, witnessed, and heard. These are the people much more likely to recognize and appreciate the aspects of your identity that give your life meaning. Because of the pain caused by marginalization, we can better begin to appreciate our need for authentic relationships that are built on respect, mutual acceptance, and a shared desire to be connected.

COLLEGE INTERVENTIONS

The need to find one's own "tribe" of kindred spirits can be particularly urgent on college campuses each fall, as freshmen arrive unmoored from familiar surroundings in a new social environment. I remember my own freshman year at college when I felt the need to fit in on a campus where I knew no one and lacked both the confidence and the skills to do it. I grew withdrawn, but eventually found connection with a few peers at a local center for the practice of a Japanese form of Buddhism called Nichiren Shoshu, which involved long meditative sessions of chanting a single Japanese phrase over and over again. On anxious sleepless nights, I would chant the devotional incantation "Namu Myōhō Renge Kyō" until sleep could find me. That sect also had group prayer meetings I attended, and although unfamiliar with the prayers and the rituals, I had a place to go, a place where I felt welcome in a way I didn't feel in the more typical campus settings. It was temporary, a Band-Aid of sorts, but it got me over the worst of it. I still have the prayer beads I held and rubbed together as I chanted, a souvenir of that lonely period in my life.

The pandemic years have brought with them an epidemic of loneliness, especially among people ages eighteen to twenty-four, who were already notorious as the loneliest adult demographic. Inspired by our positive experiences with Creativity Circles, we developed a single-session, one-hour workshop called Colors and Connection. It features the same three modalities of mindfulness meditation, creative exercises, and shared conversations as Creativity Circles, but the hour is focused on the simple exploration of moods and emotions as expressed by color. We were able to pilot several of these workshops in Chicago and Boston in 2021, thanks to a charitable donation from essie, L'Oréal's nail polish brand. We made Colors and Connection available online to campuses across the country the following year.

A Colors and Connection workshop involves a group of twelve to fifteen students and a facilitator, who distributes oil-pastel crayons and six-inch cardstock squares and leads a brief opening discussion. After several minutes of guided meditation in which the group is asked to imagine colors associated with emotions like stress or calm, they are then asked to bring to their mind's eye the colors evoked when they allow themselves to experience various emotions associated with recalled or imagined experiences, and everyone goes to work on their piece of creative making. Each participant is asked to divide their paper square into four window-like panels and use color in each panel to express the emotions evoked when recollecting a meaningful and memorable engagement with a person, a place, and an experience in the past. For the fourth panel, the participants are asked to use color to express their hope for the future.

After twenty minutes of coloring, the participants pair up and spend about ten minutes talking about their four windowpanes and the story behind the colorful images. A guided group discussion follows, with particular emphasis on how it felt to share stories and feelings in this creative way. At the conclusion of the session, participants place their artworks on the floor or on a posterboard so they can appreciate every contribution as a single mosaic reflecting each individual's effort as a collaborative and connecting experience.

No different from the children who made art in the aftermath of 9/11, participants in the Colors and Connection workshops can connect intimately with each other by responding to a simple request: "Tell me about your picture." When Diana Shaari, then a Harvard sophomore, volunteered to put on a Colors and Connection workshop during finals week in fall 2021, more than sixty students signed up for the available twenty-five places. After the workshop, she recalled, "Everyone was so calm afterwards, they were commenting how relaxed they felt. Their mood was better. Some said they need to do this every month." When I personally participated in a Colors and Connection group in 2022 at the Harvard T. H. Chan School of Public Health, during that spring semester when we were still getting used to being in classes face-to-face, the student I was paired with, Victor Yu, said, "I do not really know much about art, so I was somewhat nervous at first. However, I loved the atmosphere and people communicating without much stress. This was one of my best experiences at the school all year."

CALLING OUT AND CALLING IN

Historically, most religious groups have devised methods of organizing the social rejection of individuals whose behavior is deemed threatening to the group. Leaders of the Catholic Church would declare people with heretical beliefs to be "anathemas" and force them from the community of faith. To this day, social shunning is how the Amish enforce their church rules and preserve their faith and way of life. If an Amish congregation unanimously votes to shun an individual for violating the Church's strict rules on daily living, everyone agrees to exclude that individual from all social activities. They cite a biblical basis for shunning in 2 Thessalonians 3:14 ("And if any man obey not our word by this epistle, note that man, and have no company with him, that he may be ashamed.").

Today the reach of social media makes it possible for someone to be shunned or canceled online—which is a kind of social shunning at scale. The function of canceling is really no different from that of Amish shunning. It's how groups enforce cultural standards of behavior.

The #MeToo movement began among women in show business in 2017 after an exposé about the abusive behavior of movie producer Harvey Weinstein went public. Actress Alyssa Milano simply tweeted to her millions of followers, "If you've been sexually harassed or assaulted write 'me too' as a reply to this tweet." Within two days, more than a million Twitter users had reposted the hashtag #metoo, and within a year scores of high-profile American men in entertainment, government, education, and other fields had lost their jobs. Big names like Woody Allen, Charlie Rose, and comedian Louis C.K. lost their agents and lost access to production money for their projects. *Today Show* host Matt Lauer was fired, and the heads of Amazon Studios and Pixar Animation Studios had to step down. Many lesser names also became untouchable in their industries, all because no one wanted to risk the backlash on social media from being associated with them.

A comprehensive 2018 report by *The New York Times* concluded that in a single year, #MeToo had "brought down" 201 powerful men, almost half of whom had been replaced in their roles by women. Social media, it's been noted, can function in this way as an instrument of accountability and social justice. It's a leveler that gives power to the bullied over their bullies. In fact, when Western governments issued harsh sanctions against Russia in 2022 to punish the Kremlin for invading Ukraine, thousands of international companies voluntarily canceled Russia. Although some industries were required by governmental sanctions to withdraw from Russia, most of them (including McDonald's, which had franchises in Russia) decided it would be best to shed the reputational risk of having anything to do with a country that had launched an attack on its peaceful neighbor.

The backlash against cancel culture started after some celebrities were subject to condemnation on social media for their comments about race, religion, and LGBTQ issues. Most incidences of cancellation on these issues were attempts to boycott authors and entertainers caught making racial or ethnic slurs or airing unpopular political viewpoints. When author J. K. Rowling voiced some skepticism about transgender issues, many of her fans rose up against her and complained of her insensitivity, especially as a bestselling author writing about the adventures of a once-lonely little boy who had been raised to be someone he was not.

In 2020 comedian and former *America's Got Talent* TV host Nick Cannon was fired from his contract with Viacom after he made clumsy remarks on his podcast that repeated classic antisemitic tropes about the power of "Zionists" and "the Rothschilds." Cannon apologized profusely that he never intended to cause anyone pain, but he also admitted that apologies weren't good enough. He invited Rabbi Abraham Cooper of the Simon Wiesenthal Center as a guest on his podcast the next day.

"I am asking to be corrected from your community, give me books, teach me, I am an empty vessel, an empty broken vessel," he said. "Teach me, fix me, lead me."

Cannon said he'd like to see cancel culture replaced by "counsel culture." As an alternative to shunning, counsel culture is all about curiosity and conversation. Shunning deploys loneliness as a weapon, while curiosity and conversation are two of the most reliable countermeasures for alleviating loneliness.

Loretta Ross, who teaches at Smith College, recognizes that it is tempting for some people who have been victimized to use their history to bully the bullies of this world. In an interview she cited the danger of "claiming that, well, I am a rape survivor, so I get a right to hurt people. 'I've been hurt myself' kind of approach. And they want to silence sometimes and dominate others." The trouble with that approach, she says, is that a victim can hang on to the identity of being a victim, believing that victimizing others will protect them. Recall how recovery from trauma entails telling a story about your identity so that the trauma no longer has a grip on you. "Sometimes," Ross said, "they wrap that victimhood mantle so securely around themselves, that they've yet to form an identity that is not based on their trauma and victimization."

Loretta has become an advocate for a counsel culture approach to even the vilest hate speech. As opposed to "calling out" people to be shunned, she advocates "calling in" and discussing the source of hurtful speech. The trouble with calling people out, Loretta says, is that people stop talking to each other. The fear of being targeted prevents conversations, and she knows all about the power of conversation. When she was just twenty-five, she taught Black feminist theory in a prison program for men who had raped and murdered women. In the 1980s, she also worked with Ku Klux Klan members and white supremacists as part of a civil rights initiative led by Reverend C. T. Vivian, who told her, "When you ask people to give up hate, then you need to be there for them when they do."

A typical calling-in conversation might be what Loretta calls the Uncle Frank strategy. Uncle Frank at the Thanksgiving table says something objectionable and hurtful about race, ethnicity, or gender. You respond by telling Uncle Frank everything you love about him. Then you say, "Uncle Frank, help me understand how such a good man that I know you are, a kind man, would have those kinds of words coming out of his mouth. Tell me how I am supposed to reconcile the good Uncle Frank with mean Uncle Frank. How does that work for you? But mostly, how am I supposed to deal with you, when I'm looking at the man I could love versus the man who scares me?" When you do this, she says, you help Uncle Frank build his kindness muscle, because you know he doesn't really want you to have a low opinion of him.

Loretta's talk recorded at TEDx Monterey has been viewed over two million times. It is a stirring and inspiring personal testimony to the power of connection to overcome the pain and loneliness of difference. In this talk she quotes a fellow feminist leader, Dázon Dixon Diallo, who claims that the practice of "calling in" is as fundamental to human rights in the digital age as nonviolence was in the early days of the civil rights movement. Calling in, Loretta said, represents "a new way to understand how to truly achieve justice. It's not a matter of what we do, but how we do it."

We can't sustainably address our loneliness by making others lonelier. But in a world that grows more diverse every day, difference is destined to keep pushing us apart, with our needs for group belonging continually challenging what I also believe is our deep desire for broader human connection.

8

Modernity's Divide

In Alaska's Katmai National Park and Preserve, October 2021 began with Fat Bear Week, an annual online event in which people all over the world watch through the park's live nature cameras as dozens of hungry brown bears gather to pluck migrating sockeye salmon out of the Brooks River rapids. Visitors to the Fat Bear Week website can cast votes for their favorite bears, in a tournament format akin to college basketball's March Madness, until one bear is crowned as that year's champion. The 2021 winner was Otis, a slow-moving aging bear who naps a lot and is distinguished by a patch of blond fur on his left shoulder. Otis's appeal to online voters was his placid demeanor and great skill at fishing. Unlike the younger bears, who were seen comically fumbling with their wriggling prey, old Otis conserved his energy as he stared at the rushing waters and patiently waited for the right moment to reach in and scoop a salmon into his mouth.

Managing this annual competition is a seventy-year-old native New Yorker named Naomi Boak, a seasonal park ranger who employs her decades of professional media experience to help promote Fat Bear Week worldwide. Naomi believes we get a kind of vicarious thrill from watching the giant bears gorge themselves in preparation for winter hibernation. As she told one interviewer, "They get to do something and be healthy that we don't get to do, and that is be fat."

I've known Naomi for many years, and the last place I ever thought she'd spend her seventieth birthday was in the wilds of Alaska. Hers is a story of finding one's passion from a place of loneliness. And it's a story that could have happened only in a 24-7 world connected by the internet.

After her husband passed away in 2010, Naomi moved back to Manhattan from Minnesota and lived alone, working as an independent TV producer. Sometime in 2014, she discovered the live-streamed bear cams maintained by the Katmai Conservancy and Explore.org, which operates a network of nature cams all over the world. On the Katmai bear cam web page, a global online community sprouted through its message board, populated by bear fans fascinated by the daily antics of the beautiful and majestic creatures. Naomi joined the online conversations, sharing observations and insights about bear behavior and the personalities of individual bears. The message board visitors also discussed witnessing aspects of survival not found in Disney films. Through the bear cam lenses, they could see some bears struggling and suffering through illness, injury, and old age.

During this time, Naomi was suffering from autonomic nerve system damage and painful arthritis in her hips. She remembers it as a lonely and stressful time, as her illnesses and treatments made it difficult to find new work, and her income suffered. One day, almost as an aside, she posted to the Katmai message board some of the details of her health struggles. The board responded with an outpouring of supportive comments and promises of prayers from Naomi's Katmai friends. Even though she knew most of them only by their clever message board nicknames, the shared affection for Katmai's bears had knitted them into a community. With a few message board members who'd faced similar health challenges, Naomi's exchanges about her treatments were more detailed and intimate than what she shared with anyone else in her life. The anonymity of the message board gave her the space to be herself among people with whom she already shared a special bond. After she underwent hip replacement surgery in 2017, the first person to wish her well was Juergen, a bear cam lover from Stuttgart. On days when Naomi returned home from a taxing session of rehab, she would log in to the Katmai site, where she could watch the bears and where her special support community awaited to learn how she was doing.

By 2019, when Naomi was sixty-seven, her health was restored, but her career as an independent TV producer had not recovered. On a whim, she replied to a "seasonal media ranger" job posting she spotted on the Katmai Conservancy Facebook page. Ten days later, on May 14, 2019, she was offered the job, and ten days after that, Naomi was going through her orientation, hiking along the Brooks River trails she had previously seen only online. For each of the next three years, she wrote and coproduced Fat Bear Week, hosting live weekly educational broadcasts for millions of bear cam viewers around the world. "It is thrilling, invigorating, and healing to be with all the bears all the time," she said. As she moved into her seventies, Naomi became fully involved and increasingly socially connected through a new passion, years after most people retire.

Around the same time of Fat Bear Week 2021, four thousand miles away in Florida, Maureen McNamara decided to take a plane to Dallas for a special event at the site where President Kennedy was assassinated in 1963. There she joined hundreds of other QAnon conspiracy theorists, led by a man who claimed that Kennedy's son, John F. Kennedy Jr., had faked his death in a 1999 plane crash. Everyone gathered on Elm Street had been promised that on November 2, JFK Jr. would reveal himself to them at 12:29 p.m., the exact time of his father's assassination. The returned Kennedy, who would be fifty-eight, would then announce his plan to run for vice president in 2024 on a ticket headed by Donald Trump.

For more than sixteen hours, Maureen and hundreds of other believers stood waiting beside a busy thoroughfare in Dallas, calling their spot their "promised land." As 12:29 p.m. came and went, the group's leader continued to insist that JFK Jr. could appear at any moment. When evening arrived, the leader had news. The Rolling Stones were in Dallas that night for an outdoor concert. This was a sign, the leader said, that JFK Jr. would reveal himself during the show. The group abandoned Elm Street and traveled to the concert site, where they bought three-hundred-dollar tickets. Maureen went along, even though it was too cold and rainy for an outdoor concert, and she never cared for the Rolling Stones, anyway. When the concert ended, with still no sign of young Kennedy, many of the cult members spoke excitedly of returning to Elm Street the following morning to continue their vigil.

By then Maureen had run out of money and patience. She left the group and flew home to Florida, where she began reaching out to the media to denounce the cult's leader, fifty-eight-year-old Michael Brian Protzman. Under the username Negative48, Protzman had emerged a year earlier on QAnon online message boards and quickly built a following of more than a hundred thousand on the online messaging app Telegram. Through videos his followers find mesmerizing, Protzman spouted antisemitic conspiracy theories and claimed his contacts within the Kennedy family and Trump's inner circle had assured him they were working in secret to destroy a global cabal of Satanic pedophiles. Protzman, who previously had been a self-employed demolition contractor in Washington State, also urged his followers to buy his investment products, which promised big returns by speculating on foreign currency prices.

Maureen struggled to explain to reporters how she'd been taken in by such a character. She told how Negative48's messages had first caught her attention, but when she tried to discuss it with friends and family, they began to shun her. As Maureen grew more isolated, her commitment to the cult and its stories deepened. More and more of her social involvement was confined to Negative48's online followers. By the time she decided to join the Dallas event, she was lonely and craving physical connection with her new online friends.

"What drew me in was an opportunity to be with like-minded people," she explained. "Because everybody's story in this movement is that we've lost friends. . . . We've lost family, we've lost credibility, we've been isolated, we've been lonely and we've been called lots of different names, 'crazy' among them." She ended up friendless and in debt.

Two stories of online connection, two very different outcomes. Together, they illustrate how difficult it is to assess the modern world's impact on loneliness. Loneliness, after all, is a purely personal, subjective experience, while modernity is a universal, objective reality. Modernity's impact on loneliness can only be measured by each individual's unique experience of modern life.

In that narrow sense, the digital technologies that define today's modernity are no different from any other tool that can be either used or abused. "We are imprisoned by our technology only when we use it in naïve and uncreative ways," nature writer Giles Slade has observed, pointing out the utility of high-tech hiking and fishing gear. "We can use any new technology to support and foster human relationships and our relationship to nature itself."

While that's true, it's also true that these digital tools are uniquely powerful in how they can produce extreme outcomes quickly and at scale, for better and for worse. Our world is at once highly connected and uniquely disconnected by our modern culture of online all the time, and the resulting effects of connection and disconnection are rapidly accelerating in opposite directions.

Modernity has always been a force for social disruption, going back to the Renaissance and the Enlightenment. In simple terms, modernity extols the ideals of individual freedom and progress, and challenges the rigid class systems and religion-bound customs found in traditional societies. The US Declaration of Independence was a declaration of modernity, with its assertion of every individual's right to "Life, Liberty and the pursuit of Happiness."

Today's modernity, however, feels very different from the relatively slow and mechanical modernity of previous centuries. Our accelerated, digitally mediated reality suggests we've moved beyond modernity into something utterly new. One popular term for our times is "late modernity." Another is "liquid modernity," coined by the late Polish-born philosopher Zygmunt Bauman, who claimed that the primacy of the digital over the mechanical (and of software over hardware) has introduced a uniquely high degree of fluidity to daily life.

In Bauman's thinking, all our essential social constructs—work, love, individualism, community—have been unmoored and atomized in our new liquid state of being. Modernity's promise has always been to grant each person the responsibility to define their own social self, as a departure from traditional societies where each individual was confined by the gender, religious faith, and social rank they were born with. The digital tools of liquid modernity magnify this modern responsibility for self-definition, offering each of us almost boundless freedom to choose how we create and connect, and with whom. Freedom of choice is the paramount value in liquid modernity, but that freedom has proved to be a double-edged sword.

For example, Bauman described social media platforms as "very useful, they provide pleasure, but they are a trap." Online networks are not really communities, he said, because a community is something you belong to, while an online network belongs to you. With your network, he said, "You feel in control. You can add friends if you wish, you can delete them if you wish. You are in control of the important people to whom you relate. People feel a little better as a result, because loneliness, abandonment, is the great fear in our individualist age."

The trouble is that the more hours you spend communicating with people in your online network, the more you risk losing social skills like tolerance and patience, which are required to sensibly interact with people in your physical community—at work, at the store, on the street. Said Bauman, "Most people use social media not to unite, not to open their horizons wider, but on the contrary, to cut themselves a comfort zone where the only sounds they hear are the echoes of their own voice, where the only things they see are the reflections of their own face."

Each individual in today's society is free to choose their preferred methods and depths of connection with others, unconstrained by social conventions and expectations. If your temperament is suited to this extreme degree of freedom, you will likely find unprecedented opportunities for self-expression, connection, and flourishing. But today's lack of structure and custom in social relations can be very difficult for anyone whose temperament craves certainty and security. For these people, the chore of creating their own identity can make them feel inadequate, anxious, and lonely.

Also, the fast-paced, ever-changing world of liquid modernity is more likely to be enticing if you are young, healthy, and educated and have resources. If you're older and poor, if you have limited employment prospects, if you're struggling with your health, if you have depression or an anxiety disorder, today's modernity may look remote, chaotic, arbitrary, unfeeling, isolating, and alienating. Modernity's divide is a loneliness divide. It often delivers emotional pain to those who are least equipped to deal with it. What's more, the loneliness territory of modernity is the one terrain on which all other loneliness territories coexist. For the traumatized, for the ill, for the aging, and for those with any kind of social difference, modernity's loneliness is a force multiplier.

Traditional society's ties of connection—to religious faith, to marriage, to gender roles, to career paths—have never been weaker. People who in the past were temperamentally content to follow the herd are now at risk of feeling abandoned and isolated. They may have a vague sense that the herd has abandoned them, when in fact it's now up to all of us to find our own herd, to develop our own networks of people with shared assumptions and values. Online we have freedom of choice to follow our unbounded curiosity and seek connection wherever we may find it. For some, their path of curiosity leads to fat, hungry bears in Alaska. For others, their curiosity takes them to bizarre cults in Texas.

What happens to community and social cohesion when individual choice is held up as the paramount value? And what are the unintended consequences and social hazards that result from technology's immense unfettered power to both elevate and isolate? Modernity leaves us untethered and free to be creative, to build stronger, deeper, and more meaningful ties of our own choosing, ones that reflect and project our unique forms of self-expression and sense of wonder. But in order to make the most of these vast opportunities, we must also recognize the new challenges and responsibilities thrust upon us. It takes new skills to steer along this knife-edge of possibility and peril, and to recognize that individualism is not a recipe for isolation. Pursuing your personal dreams in the intimate company of kindred spirits is both more fulfilling and more effective, which is not always clear in a culture that celebrates drive, determination, and self-reliance as essential requirements for success.

THE UBIQUITOUS SMARTPHONE

One day in New York back in 2019, I was waiting for the next train to arrive at the Broadway and Lafayette subway platform when a middle-aged woman approached me, cell phone in hand.

"Do you know," she said to me, "you're the only person at this station who's not on a device?" Her name was Margaret, and she was a Midwesterner visiting New York for the first time. Margaret had been taking pictures to record her first-ever subway ride and was struck by the image of dozens of self-absorbed New Yorkers staring down at their phones—and a single man, me, looking down the tunnel to see if the train was coming.

Margaret and I started talking, and as we shared our stories about where we were from and where we were going, it occurred to me that I was in no particular hurry that day. It turned out that she was thinking of running the New York marathon wearing a David Bowie costume and was scouting the city to get a better feel for it and to connect with some NYC-based runners she knew, also Bowie fans. I told her about my own marathon experience as a spectator in Boston's famed run in 2013 marked by a lethal bomb explosion and how the community responded with a variety of concerts and music events to share our grief and recover from our collective trauma. Although accidental, a non-digital encounter within the liquid stream of modernity revealed a solidly engaging reference point that connected us through a shared story. We left the subway and found a nearby coffee shop so we could continue our conversation. Although no deep or enduring friendship emerged, I thought of her during the next New York City Marathon and mentally cheered her on. She had become part of a world I felt more connected to.

I would never suggest that before smartphones, New York's subway platforms were convivial places awash in friendly chatter. If you'd visited that same Broadway and Lafayette subway station forty years earlier, you would have seen a crowd with heads similarly bowed in silence, reading books, newspapers, and magazines. What's different is the intensity of attention paid to our smartphones. Printed reading material informs you about the world outside yourself. Your smartphone informs you about you. There's something particularly addictive and self-centered about the phone, and how it faithfully feeds our egotistical impulse to check for the latest email, the latest tweet, the latest social media mention.

In the spirit of full disclosure, I'm rarely far from my phone. It was a total fluke that Margaret spotted me as the only person on the subway platform without one. Like a lot of people, I'm a compulsive text-and-email checker. I was an early adopter of email-capable mobile phones in 1999 when the BlackBerry came along.

In the history of the world, there has never been such a wide range of inputs we can hook into our brains on demand. It's not something they were designed to deal with. We are all guinea pigs in a massive experiment about what would happen if billions of ordinary humans could hold in their hands access to just about everyone in the world and all the world's information—and all the worst, most exploitive misinformation, too.

I've come to believe that the phone itself is not the problem, nor is it just FOMO—fear of missing out—that drives this addiction. I think the smartphone and the continual attention it demands have fed a gnawing sense of urgency that we must stimulate our brain cortices throughout each day. The smartphone forces us to confront this dilemma of liquid late modernity—whether there is anything natural or desirable about having focused, purposeful activities for every waking moment of our lives. Instead, the phone has become an enabler of impatience with being alone with our thoughts. We have trouble being bored.

In 2013, researchers at the University of Virginia led by social psychologist Timothy Wilson decided to find out just how impatient we've become. "So we started out just kind of by the seat of our pants, trying stuff to see how easy it was for people to entertain themselves with their own thoughts," Wilson told *The Atlantic* in 2014. "With the expectation, to be honest, that it wouldn't be that hard. We kind of thought, well, we have this huge brain that's stocked full of pleasant memories and has the ability to generate fantasies, and surely it can't be that hard to spend a few minutes enjoying yourself with your thoughts. And we just kept doing study after study, finding that—for many people anyway—not so much."

Across the eleven experiments, most test subjects did not enjoy spending six to fifteen minutes in a room by themselves with nothing to do but think. Even when prompted to occupy themselves with pleasant memories, the test subjects did not enjoy the experience of idle boredom. One found a pen and used the time to write a to-do list. Another fashioned an origami figure out of an instruction sheet accidentally left behind. In one experiment, the subjects were wired to give themselves safe but painful electric shocks during their time alone (and were offered money for not shocking themselves). About one-quarter of the women and two-thirds of the men chose to break their boredom by shocking themselves at least once. Wilson's team concluded: "Most people seem to prefer to be doing something rather than nothing, even if that something is negative."

Each year the US Bureau of Labor Statistics surveys how Americans spend their time, and in 2019 about 82 percent of adult respondents reported they spent no time at all "relaxing or thinking" in the previous twenty-four hours. It's as though most of us have lost any sense of the importance of collecting our thoughts or daydreaming. As a result, we're missing out on the considerable benefits of "wasting time"—taking a random walk of our imagination through the landscapes of recent experiences, allowing us to make sense of them as well as to calibrate our thinking for the future opportunities those thoughts may reveal.

Alan Lightman, a world-class physicist who is also an MIT professor of the practice of the humanities, gave a talk on the campus in 2018 and confessed that he's terrible at wasting time. "I rarely goof off," he said. "I rarely follow a path that I think does not lead to some profitable ending. I rarely waste time." The title of the talk was "In Praise of Wasting Time: How the Rush and Heave of Modern Life Is Destroying Our Inner Selves."

Lightman said that his creative activities suffer when he's busy because creativity thrives on unstructured time. He cited as examples

Gustav Mahler, Carl Jung, and Gertrude Stein among the many creative geniuses who were known to waste hours at a time taking long, solitary walks in nature. Without such opportunities for reflection, Lightman said, "We're losing our ability to know who we are and what's important to us." Interestingly, Lightman's engagement with his inner self led him to an unanticipated experience of deep human connection. On a trip to Cambodia, he and his daughter somewhat unexpectedly became very involved in helping to build a school in a rural village. In an interview about his experience, he said, "We ate meals with them. We participated in ceremonies with them. We got really heavily involved. We really felt like we were becoming part of their community. . . . We were making connections of human beings to human beings. It's a very very different experience than just mailing a check."

Making time for thought and relaxing is an interesting matter for adult minds to consider, but when it comes to children's minds, deprivation of downtime is a serious mental health matter. The growing rates of loneliness, anxiety, and depression among younger people in developed nations (the so-called digital natives who have never known a world without the internet) suggest that we are not adapting well to this new reality.

In his talk, Lightman made mention of research that found creativity has been declining among schoolchildren in recent decades. Psychologist Kyung Hee Kim of the College of William & Mary studied three hundred thousand creativity tests taken since the 1970s and found that since 1990, children have been less imaginative, less humorous, and less capable of producing unique and unusual ideas. Kim suspects that the rise of standardized testing in the schools and the No Child Left Behind Act passed by Congress in 2001 have contributed to the decline in creativity scores. When her study was published, she asked in one interview, "If we just focus on . . . No Child Left Behind—testing, testing, testing—then how can creative students survive?" Kim noted that even as SAT scores and intelligence scores have been increasing in recent years, scores on the widely used Torrance Tests of Creative Thinking have been going down. It suggests that children are getting better at remembering rote answers taught to them and worse at coming up with creative responses of their own. Her work has also shown that creative thinking declines in adulthood, as our practical minds become more concerned with right and wrong answers.

It may be a coincidence that as creativity scores have dropped and school testing pressure has increased, the rates of depression and suicide among teenagers have been climbing since at least 2011. Jean M. Twenge, a psychologist who has spent thirty years researching generational differences, says there was an abrupt shift in reported teen behaviors and emotional states starting in 2012 that represented a sharper break in the data than any previous change going back to the 1930s. The source of these changes, she believes, is the dominant role of the smartphone in young people's lives. The year 2012 marked a tipping point at which smartphone adoption in the US population surpassed 50 percent.

In the decade preceding the pandemic, teenagers were already spending less time going out and socializing with each other than any previous generation of teens. After-school hours instead were more commonly spent at home, engaged with texting and social media on their phones. "The number of teens who get together with their friends nearly every day dropped by more than 40 percent from 2000 to 2015," Twenge wrote in *The Atlantic* in 2017. She declared that studies had made a clear connection between smartphone usage and distressed mental states: "Teens who visit social-networking sites every day but see their friends in person less frequently are the most likely to agree with the statements 'A lot of times I feel lonely,' 'I often feel left out of things,' and 'I often wish I had more good friends.'"

Limiting social media usage, on the other hand, has been associated with improved mental states. One experiment published in 2018 showed that when a group of University of Pennsylvania undergraduates limited their use of Facebook, Instagram, and Snapchat to ten minutes per platform per day, after three weeks they showed significantly reduced levels of loneliness and depression when compared with a control group that continued unrestricted social media use. Perhaps what's even more interesting about this study is that *both* groups showed significant decreases in measured levels of anxiety and FOMO. It appears that even if you don't set a strict time limit on your social media use, there is a benefit to self-monitoring and being mindful of your social media usage. The paper's authors concluded: "Our findings strongly suggest that limiting social media use to approximately 30 minutes per day may lead to significant improvement in well-being."

These study authors are offering sound advice, but it flies in the face of the powerful business model of all social media, which aims to maximize each user's hours of engagement with its app. Social media, like most media, profits by delivering audience attention to advertisers. The special appeal of social media is its personalized and interactive nature, which allows it to grab your attention and hold on for hours at a time. Sophisticated algorithms work around the clock to deliver you the kind of content most likely to command your personal attention—which can be very helpful in most contexts, but very destructive in others.

My friend Rakesh Khurana, a sociologist, an author, and dean of Harvard College, told me he is troubled by the performative aspects of social media, in which "how you present yourself is not necessarily how you actually feel." The risk is that young people become hooked on getting positive reactions from social media's "hive mind," which can affect one's sense of self-efficacy and self-worth.

"You can find yourself constantly trying to please the hive and becoming more other-directed than inner-directed," Rakesh said. "The external judgments of others can matter more to you than your own internal judgment."

Performative social media postings can also foster pernicious social comparison effects that lead some people to think they are superior and others inferior. Seeing vivid images and friends' comments following a party you weren't told about can leave you feeling rejected and unworthy. Rakesh said, "People on social media who are lonely tonight may feel they are the only ones not having a good time."

In the early morning hours of January 4, 2015, a Wisconsin high school senior named Christopher Dawley shot and killed himself in his bedroom. His family found him with his hunting rifle in one hand and his blood-spattered smartphone still on and glowing in his other hand. "He was so addicted to it that even his last moments of his life were about posting on social media," Christopher's mother recalled years later. In the months before he killed himself, the young man had become sleep-deprived and obsessed with his body image. Christopher was addicted to Instagram in particular, staying up until three a.m. exchanging messages that sometimes included nude selfies.

The Dawley family has since become one of a growing number of families who have sued Snap (Snapchat's parent company) and Meta (parent company of Instagram and Facebook) for ignoring their own research showing how the addictive design of their platforms was damaging the mental health of young people. In 2022, one law firm filed eight lawsuits against Meta claiming defective design, failure to warn, fraud, and negligence that led its plaintiffs to eating disorders, sleep-lessness, attempted suicides, and actual suicides. "These applications could have been designed to minimize potential harm, but instead, a decision was made to aggressively addict adolescents in the name of corporate profits," said Andy Birchfield, a principal at Beasley Allen.

Leaked documents from Meta show that the company's internal researchers had done a "teen mental health deep dive" on Instagram data and discovered 32 percent of teen girls said that "when they feel bad about their bodies, Instagram made them feel worse." Teens blamed Instagram for increased anxiety and depression. "This reaction was unprompted and consistent across all groups." Among teens with thoughts of suicide, 13 percent of British users and 6 percent of US users traced their ideations to Instagram.

Instagram's researchers discovered the app was causing problems for users that weren't found with Snapchat, TikTok, and other social media. "Social comparison is worse on Instagram," they reported, pointing to Instagram's algorithm-driven Explore page, which delivers glamorous content that sparks negative feelings of social comparison in young women. The researchers concluded that "aspects of Instagram exacerbate each other to create a perfect storm."

Studies have since shown there are developmental windows in young lives when they are particularly vulnerable to destructive social media habits. For young men social media has the most negative effects at ages fourteen to fifteen and again at nineteen. For females, the most vulnerable ages are eleven to thirteen and then again at nineteen.

Emma Lembke was just twelve when she joined Instagram, and over time she found herself on the app six hours a day, "just mindlessly scrolling, absorbing all these unrealistic body standards." She developed anxiety and eating disorders, but she couldn't quit social media. "It just became this horrific loop of going on these apps, specifically

Instagram," she told *The New York Times*. "[I was] feeling worse about myself, but feeling as though I could not stop scrolling because it has this weird power over me."

In 2020, while still in high school in Mobile, Alabama, Emma launched the Log Off movement as an online space for conversation about social media. Two years later, as a freshman at Washington University in St. Louis, she and another college student founded Tech(nically) Politics, in order to push for legislation that will regulate Big Tech. The group supports congressional passage of the Kids Internet Design and Safety Act (KIDS Act), which would create new protections for online users under age sixteen, banning many of the addictive "auto-play" settings, push alerts, "like" buttons, follower counts, and badges that reward time spent on the apps. Prominent members of the tech industry see the need for regulation. "I think that you do it exactly the same way that you regulated the cigarette industry," Marc Benioff, CEO of the software company Salesforce, said back in 2018. "Technology has addictive qualities that we have to address, and . . . product designers are working to make those products more addictive and we need to rein that back."

Meanwhile, Emma still struggles with generalized anxiety disorder, and she still uses Instagram. She's developed some strategies for controlling its effect on her. She switches her phone to the grayscale setting sometimes, so that the content is in black and white. She uses apps like Screentime Genie and HabitLab to help her cut back on time spent online. "It creates a level of friction between you and addictive technology," she says.

With new regulations and raised awareness about social media, we might be able to ensure that the smartphone remains our servant and not our master. Apps have proven to be just as useful in granting us peace of mind as they are at pilfering it. An influential study led by

Emily K. Lindsay at the University of Pittsburgh found that mindfulness training and monitoring through a smartphone app can be highly useful in reducing loneliness and increasing social contacts. Researchers recruited 153 adults with moderate to high levels of loneliness and introduced them to a variety of fourteen-lesson interventions in the specific mindfulness skills of monitoring one's present-moment experiences and doing so *with an orientation of acceptance.*

The results were remarkable and encouraging. Measures of daily loneliness dropped by 22 percent, and people averaged two additional interactions each day with one more person per day. For lonely people, the difference of just one extra contact each day can be enormous, and daily practice of making those contacts can become pleasurable and self-reinforcing.

For someone with elevated levels of loneliness, practicing an orientation of acceptance toward such encounters can break the cycle of loneliness in which self-judgment can lead people to isolate themselves further. Feelings of loneliness don't necessarily mean you need more friends, and gaining mindful recognition and deeper appreciation of the friends you already have might be more effective in reducing your painful feelings of loneliness than seeking more. After all, loneliness is defined as a subjective gap between the level of human connection you have and the level you feel you need. Mindfulness meditation could enhance your sense of self-sufficiency and help calm your self-judgment and anxiety to the point where you recognize that your needs for connection are relatively modest and easily met.

During the first year of the pandemic, there were millions of downloads of mindfulness meditation apps, with Calm, Headspace, and Meditopia leading the way. Before the smartphone arrived, access to this kind of training wasn't really available without going to a therapist or joining a meditation group. The infinite scalability and potent brain engagement of smartphone apps guarantee the smartphone's status as a uniquely powerful vehicle for both the ills and opportunities of our age.

MODERNITY'S CONSTRAINTS

On that particular morning in 2019 when Margaret the Midwestern tourist caught me not looking at my phone, it was one of the rare days that I didn't have a flight to catch. Right up until the first week of the pandemic, in early 2020, I was taking three or four airplane trips a week between Boston, New York, and other places, giving talks and having meetings about a variety of public health projects in addition to my growing focus on loneliness, the arts, and healing.

The pandemic's travel restrictions did me a favor of sorts. They forced me to stop and reflect on why my life had become such a spinning hamster wheel of activity. I recognized how I had drifted away from a lot of healthy habits I valued, how I had begun to lose track of my purpose, my reasons for pursuing this cause. Staying home gave me a chance to learn about myself and consider how I want to organize my remaining years on the planet. I think this was true for a lot of people, judging by the reports of how many millions have either chosen to retire, quit their jobs, or resisted returning to the commuting grind of five days a week in the office. I don't see myself ever returning to my old three-or-four-flights-a-week schedule.

There is some substance to the fear that years of social distancing have made us lonelier, more isolated, and dependent on our communication technologies for connection. But that's not the whole story. My experience is that social distancing achieved a number of things, as well. It's begun many much-needed conversations about loneliness. It's also awakened us to our need to see people smile, to hug and be hugged. And finally, it's opened us up to Zoom and other videoconferencing apps as a second-best option for meeting in person. I've heard all the complaints about "Zoom fatigue" turning people into Zoombies by the end of the day. But consider that all your videoconference meetings had instead been done over the phone, leaning with one ear into a jumbled void of disembodied voices. What kind of hell would that have been?

Social distancing also showed us all what we miss by not having direct contact with each other. It's given us a chance to do better now that we're aware of what matters most. Arthur C. Brooks, an author who teaches leadership at Harvard Business School, explored this pragmatic and optimistic approach to the pandemic's challenges in a *Washington Post* article, "How Social Distancing Could Ultimately Teach Us How to Be Less Lonely." After talking to several psychologists on the subject of human connection, he defined two specific hazards of social distancing and mask-wearing that would tend to make us feel lonely: we'd miss seeing people's facial expressions, particularly their smiles, and we'd miss feeling the physical stimulation of human contact. Brooks then devised two practical countermeasures. To help us cope with the loss of seeing faces, we should pay special attention to people's eyes when speaking with them. To compensate for our general loss of physical contact, we should make sure we give extra hugs to the people closest to us.

"Make a house rule that everyone gets a 20-second hug every two hours," he wrote. "And if you live alone but have a pet, maybe make a practice, on the hour, of taking a break to pet the dog or cat or even the hamster." He expressed the hope that if we learned these habits and made them routine, we'd emerge from social distancing better off than before: "less glued to social media, making eye contact with others and freely hugging our friends and family."

I think it would be very beneficial to apply this same curious and practical approach to each of the problems modernity has generated in our lives. Let's face it: Modernity's genie is out of the bottle. There's no going back to the way things were before. Constant change is the new reality as modernity keeps inventing new temptations that will push us apart. Our response must be to keep taking note of what's being lost in the turmoil and reimagine how to remain connected with one another despite the change. Use the new tools granted to us in which human connection is enhanced (as we discovered when our Successful Aging program was forced to move to Zoom), and learn to draw some creative and more appealing boundaries when the risk of becoming isolated is too great.

It's easy to overlook the benefits of having some limitations and constraints on our freedoms in a culture that worships freedom of choice. Constraints are good. They help us focus our thoughts and spare us the fatigue and cognitive overload of choice paralysis. As a poet, I have a particularly privileged view on the use of constraints to encourage the flow of creativity. The fourteen-line sonnet, a favored form of Shakespeare's, has a very restrictive set of rules for rhyming and meter, resulting in countless gems of English literature. Haiku, one of my own favorite poetic forms, limits the writer to three lines in a pattern of five, seven, and five syllables, which is so simple and fun to work with that we often use it in our Creativity Circle exercises. Rigid frameworks, as T. S. Eliot once remarked, create richer ideas by taxing the imagination. "Given total freedom," he said, "the work is likely to sprawl."

Could a haiku a day keep the doctor away, so to speak? I don't know. I can't say for certain that replacing time spent online with time spent in creative "time wasting" will make you less anxious and more connected. But I do know that ten minutes writing a haiku is likely to be time better spent than ten minutes doom scrolling your Instagram feed.

OUR FRAGMENTED FOUNDATIONS

"Love and work," Freud wrote, "are the cornerstones of our humanness." Today those cornerstones rest on shifting sands. Some would say both are sinking in quicksand. We can see modernity's profound effects on love and work most vividly in the spread of online dating apps and the rising numbers of "gig economy" jobs. In each case, modernity grants us vast new freedoms while saddling us with unforeseen risks of anxiety and loneliness.

Online dating has been a tremendously positive experience for millions of people. Surveys have shown that approximately three in ten US adults have used an online dating app and 12 percent of adults have been in a committed relationship or married someone met through online dating. With those who are LGBTQ, the numbers are higher. Just about half have used one of the sites, and one in five have had a relationship with or married someone they met online.

Online dating, however, is a lot like everything else technology touches. It's the best of times for some people and it's the worst of times for others. About 45 percent of dating app users feel frustrated by the experience, and especially women under the age of thirty-five: about 60 percent have experienced harassing behavior of some sort, either by being contacted after they said they weren't interested or by receiving unwanted sexually explicit messages and images.

Many people join dating sites for casual relationships, while others are looking for soulmates to spend their lives with. But to the people running dating apps, the most important relationship is the one you have with the app itself, because that's their source of revenue. A third of people who subscribe to dating apps have never gone on a date with anyone through the apps. A survey of users of Tinder, one of the most popular "hookup" apps, revealed that 70 percent of users had never met any of their Tinder contacts in real life, and 44 percent used the app for what they called "confidence-building procrastination."

When writer Nancy Jo Sales interviewed Jonathan Badeen, one of Tinder's cofounders, he explained to her the innate excitement of the swipe-right, swipe-left process of sorting profiles. "It kinda works like a slot machine," he told her. "You're excited to see who the next person is—or excited to see, did I get the match? It's a nice little rush." The comparison with slot machines is accurate because both foster tiny rushes of pleasurable dopamine, followed by a mild crash that demands more dopamine. The reward center in our brain releases dopamine in response to pleasurable experiences so that we will remember the experience and feel motivated to repeat it. Dopamine itself is not addictive, but it supports addictive behaviors by strengthening memories of past pleasures. In the case of dating apps, this cycle of addiction is built into the rapid number of pleasurable stimuli a user can swipe through every minute, prompting users to spend more time on the app and encouraging them to subscribe to higher-priced premium services.

Sales noted that some people spend ten hours or more every week on dating apps, and wondered whether the apps are actually contributing to an increase in loneliness. She cited studies showing that young people today are having less sex than those of earlier generations, and asked, "If we're getting some sort of satisfaction from merely swiping, then what do we need to go on dates for? Why do we need to have sex? What do we need other people for, when we've got this absorbing little app at our fingertips?" Dating apps are so addictive for some people that one survey showed that 13 percent of users have opened a dating app to check out other people's profiles while out on a date.

Tinder's usage exploded in late March 2020, as pandemic quarantines and social-distancing recommendations first took hold around the United States. With bars and restaurants closed indefinitely, dating apps became a way of meeting new people and forming online relationships. The trouble is that even before the pandemic, a lot of dating app users were texting with people they admitted in surveys they had no intention of ever meeting. The apps can become a way of flirting from a safe distance, which is deceptive if the person on the other end of the conversation is looking for a meaningful relationship— as half of all dating app users claim. Dating coach and author Jess McCann cautions, "Just texting back and forth is not going to make you feel any less lonely because there is no human-to-human contact. While that can keep you busy for a couple of hours, it's not going to feed your soul."

There are critics who complain that dating app technologies are destructive in many other ways, particularly their emphasis on looks. The algorithms behind the apps have a way of intensifying discrimination or "formalizing prejudice," as one writer put it. Black women, Asian men, and short men of all ethnicities get significantly fewer matches, studies have shown. Though many who have found their spouses through online dating claim that they never would have met any other way, it's also true that when given so many choices of potential mates, people can become exceedingly picky.

This ambivalence toward technology is shared by workers in the app-driven gig economy. An extensive 2021 study by Pew Research Center found that about one-fifth of US adults have earned money from an online gig platform—usually delivery apps like Grubhub and DoorDash or ride-hailing apps like Uber and Lyft. Most workers say they love the flexible scheduling and extra money gig work makes available to them, compared with the alternative of getting a second job with rigid work hours. Most also think they are paid fairly, and nine out of ten of those who do gig jobs full time say they love the independence.

At the same time, significant numbers of gig workers say they feel lonelier, less happy, and less in control of their lives than other workers. Compared with workers in traditional jobs, Pew found that gig workers are twice as likely to report frequently feeling signs of loneliness, and they're 50 percent more likely to experience feelings of helplessness. Younger workers are often treated rudely by customers, and young women say they are frequently subjected to unwanted sexual advances. Making deliveries and picking up riders at night often feels dangerous; many gig workers have been victims of violence.

The algorithms on dating apps are set to keep users involved with the apps. The algorithms on gig platforms are set to make workers compete with each other and drive down each other's pay rates. It's called "gamification," but there's little in the way of fun and games in how it works. In the Pew study, fewer than half of all gig workers said they understand how their pay is calculated, thanks to algorithms that pay more when the demand is high and less when demand is low. Temporary labor shortages give drivers a boost in income that disappears as more drivers join the company.

With both dating apps and gig work platforms, it's important to be aware of their social and emotional hazards as you use them. In each case, digitization has turned love and work into vast fluid gamified marketplaces, and as with all games, there are rewards for winning and pain in losing. Everyone who interacts with these apps needs to be aware of their power to alternately gratify and frustrate your most intimate emotional needs. Both of them to some degree put your sense of human connection at risk.

A subtle fact about online dating apps is that they give heterosexual women more power in mate selection than perhaps they have ever had in human history. It wasn't that long ago that because women were discriminated against in the workplace, they needed to marry at a young age just to get out of their parents' house. Today, most women are economically independent and don't need to marry whatever boy they were dating in high school. Online dating apps provide women of all ages many more potential mates than they ever would have been able to consider in decades past. For many men, on the other hand, the competition online is more than they can handle. Online dating opens them up to more rejection than they would ever have had to deal with in decades past.

One result of this development is the growth of an online movement of angry, lonely, woman-hating men who call themselves "incels," which is short for "involuntary celibates." Incels have created a sort of ideological belief system spawned on chat sites like Reddit and 4chan; it maintains that dating apps and social media have distorted the "sexual marketplace value" of women so that women no longer need to date men like them—average or below average in looks. Researchers who have studied incel online forums say that the discourse is "characterized by anti-feminism, endorsing violence against women, removal of women's rights, self-loathing, and racism." Men espousing incel beliefs have been responsible for a mass shooting in 2014 that killed six people in Southern California and a motor vehicle attack on a crowd of pedestrians in 2018 that left eleven people dead in Toronto.

In January 2021, a Reddit user named Ben started a new sub-

Reddit topic area called Incel Exit. For the first time, there was a place within the incel culture for discussion of how to escape its dark grip. In an interview with *Vice*, Ben said he'd been inspired to start Incel Exit after reading another topic area called Incel Tears, where postings make fun of incels and advocate various ways of bullying them. "It didn't sit well with me," he said. It made him see the need for a forum where lonely young men who want to leave the incel community could have discussions without fear of being bullied.

The excerpts *Vice* published from Incel Exit show the evidence of young men's need for connection and identity all being turned into a place of hate, fear, and isolation online. One wrote, "On the forums, you do feel a sense of community and a weird sense of empowerment. It's validating. It's not a place for critical thinking, it's an echo chamber where people get their fears confirmed." Another wrote, "I started posting about how I was frustrated with women and feeling sad and lonely. The focus on the way people look was relieving, because it made you feel like there's no use worrying about it—you have an explanation for why you are in the situation you are." Incel Exit helped this user abandon the incel online forums for good. "I desperately needed positive energy at that time," he wrote. "I don't believe I have no potential anymore. I'm hopeful now."

COLLATERAL DAMAGE

The era of marrying the boy or girl next door and receiving a gold watch upon retirement is long gone, but it's evident that not everyone is prepared for the new social reality emerging in its place. All of liquid modernity's powerful new tools for connection leave it to each of us to navigate for better or worse, and it can be an enormous burden of personal responsibility because of the capacity for their misuse and abuse.

But while these responsibilities are borne by each individual in their own lives, the pain of growing loneliness in this emerging society is shared by everyone, in countless ways. Loneliness is contagious, and its negative effects are shaping the world we live in. We are all connected, so when any one of us suffers, we are all diminished. We all feel the pain of the loneliness of others, in one way or another. To borrow a phrase from the civil rights movement, none of us are free until all of us are free.

Back in 2012, as I was making some of my first explorations into the nature of loneliness, a young man shot and killed twenty-six students and staff members at an elementary school in Sandy Hook, Connecticut, before turning his gun on himself. The media characterized the shooter, twenty-year-old Adam Lanza, as a loner with mental illness. I was so horrified by the details of the shooting that I recall asking myself, "What kind of mental illness could this young man have had?" Initial reports showed no evidence he was hearing voices that told him to kill, or that he was in a dissociative mental state. The more I looked into Adam Lanza's circumstances, what I saw instead was the familiar pattern of chronic loneliness: vulnerability feeding anxiety, which led to isolation and distorted social cognition. The course of Adam's young life was defined by marginalization, alienation, and anger—culminating in horrific acts of mass murder and suicide.

The people who suffer from psychological or societal loneliness—who feel they are on the outside looking in on the wonders this world offers—will develop a sense of vulnerability that leads to anxiety, which tells them to retreat and isolate themselves. For many, the story ends with a sad decline into self-destruction, most commonly through drugs and alcohol. For others, however, mostly men, this isolation and alienation produces rage—and then sometimes unspeakable violence.

Whenever an act of senseless violence shocks our conscience, we tend to blame mental illness as the root cause, or we dehumanize the killer by calling him a monster. But mass shootings are rational, premeditated acts. Mass shooters know what they are doing, and they know it's wrong. They plan carefully and conceal their plans from anyone who might try to stop them. If we can't imagine how someone could do such a thing, it's because we've never suffered from distorted social cognition so profound that murder and suicide appear to be a reasoned and desirable course of action. Mass shooters feel their own emotional pain so intensely, they have no empathy for their victims. Planning mass murder gives them a feeling of power so strong that it relieves their emotional pain. And so the unthinkable becomes for them a rational set of choices.

Adam Lanza's young life was one that descended slowly into a spiral of loneliness and social isolation. As a teenager he resisted treatment for various anxiety disorders, and after his parents divorced he lived alone with his mother, who tried to connect with him by sharing her interest in guns and going to shooting ranges with him. As Adam's isolation grew, he rarely left his room and limited his communication with his mother to text messages. His only connection to the outside was through violent games like *World of Warcraft* and an online community of fellow gamers.

On the weekday morning he chose to die in infamy, Adam got up and destroyed the hard drive of his computer. Then he went to his mother's gun safe, took out her Bushmaster rifle, entered her bedroom while she was sleeping, and shot her four times in the head. Next he slipped on a multi-pocket utility vest, put on sunglasses, and put in earplugs. He got into his mother's car with the rifle, a Glock pistol, and thirty ammunition clips, and drove to Sandy Hook Elementary School, where he had attended school years earlier. He shot his way through a glass panel next to the school's locked doors and within five minutes had killed twenty-six children, teachers, and school staff members before turning his pistol on himself.

The numbers of mass shootings have been climbing for decades in concert with rising rates of loneliness. Those who have studied the phenomenon say that most of these shooters are desperately lonely young men plagued by depression and anxiety and trapped in compulsive behaviors. They commonly study other mass shooters and identify with them, gaining a sense of comfort and social definition—here is someone who felt the way they do.

"There's this really consistent pathway," says Jillian Peterson, a criminologist and coauthor of *The Violence Project: How to Stop a Mass Shooting Epidemic*. "Early childhood trauma seems to be the foundation, whether violence in the home, sexual assault, parental suicides, extreme bullying. Then you see the build toward hopelessness, despair, isolation, self-loathing, oftentimes rejection from peers." At some point, there is a change in behavior that represents a red flag. It could be a suicide attempt. From there, the self-hate might turn outward, she says. "They start asking themselves, 'Whose fault is this?' Is it a racial group, or women, or a religious group, or is it my classmates?"

Peterson says the danger of thinking of mass shooters as evil or as monsters is that then we don't recognize a red flag when we see one. She points out that the eighteen-year-old white supremacist who shot and killed ten Black people in a Buffalo supermarket in 2022 had told his high school teacher he was going to commit a murder-suicide after graduation. "People aren't used to thinking that this kind of thing could be real because the people who do mass shootings are evil, psychopathic monsters and this is a kid in my class."

In February 2018, shortly after a nineteen-year-old man had shot and killed seventeen children and teachers in a high school in Parkland, Florida, a thirty-nine-year-old Denver-area married father of two named Aaron Stark wrote a heartfelt letter to his local TV news station that began, "I was almost a school shooter." His letter explained how as a child he'd been abused by his parents in a violent, chaotic household, and in high school he was bullied for being smart, for being fat, and because his dirty clothes smelled. He was depressed and suicidal, and when his parents kicked him out of the house, he felt at age seventeen he had nothing left to lose. The letter concluded: "I wrote this because my wife and daughter kept saying how they could not understand what could make someone do this. Sadly, I can. This is a hard conversation to have, but we must have it."

In 2022, Aaron appeared on CNN in the aftermath of yet another school shooting, and he described in detail why, as a teenager in 1996, he didn't become a mass murderer. It was because someone had shown him kindness.

At the time he was homeless and sleeping in a shed in the backyard of a friend he admits he'd lied to and stolen from. He was ready to die. He'd given away most of his belongings. He'd made arrangements with a gang member to get a weapon, and he was mulling whether he'd shoot up the school or a mall food court. Then his friend came out and invited him inside, where he took a much-needed shower. Aaron's friend served him a meal, and together they watched a movie.

"At the time I didn't even feel human," Aaron said. "I felt like I was just a ball of destruction waiting to explode. And I had someone who looked through all that and saw me as a person in pain, and just a kid crying out for help. And it literally saved my life and changed my whole world. That was the most powerful thing that ever happened to me."

Aaron believes that we need to remove the stigma of talking about the pain that makes men grow isolated and become capable of horrible things. The key, he says with great eloquence, is to "love the ones you feel deserve it the least, because they need it the most. It'll help you just as much as it helps them." Only a small sliver of potential shooters actually follows through, he says. There are many more young men who are like he was at age sixteen, who are desperate for human connection.

"If you see someone who's in that spot, who feels like they're worthless, show them that they matter," he told CNN in 2022. "Bring them into your fold, treat them like a friend. Simple friendship is what stopped me from committing a horrible atrocity and you never know what a simple hello might stop the next person from doing."

Modernity is inexorably challenging us to redefine our relationships with society and with one another as it exacts a rising and unsustainable toll on our spirits, on our very souls. The contagion of loneliness is real and spreading. Creativity is falling while anxiety and loneliness are rising. Young children are killing themselves at a rate never seen before, and the number of mass shootings continues to escalate. These trends are like alarm bells, warning each of us to take personal precautions, to reclaim our brains from modernity's seductive attractions and diversions, and to embrace the essence of our humanity. If we can accept that, then we can be motivated to find creative new forms and contexts for human connection. It's a skill we pick up easily once we learn to value it, because we are all hardwired for connection.

CAN THE FUTURE BE AWESOME?

When Jeff Bezos launched the first of his space tourism efforts with Blue Origin's suborbital capsule *New Shepard* in 2021, his brilliant marketing people invited ninety-year-old William Shatner—*Star Trek*'s original Captain Kirk—to come along for the ten-minute ride sixty-six miles above the Earth.

Video cameras recorded the landing of *New Shepard* as it parachuted to the surface of the Utah desert in a cloud of dust. Bezos greeted the aging but fit Shatner emerging from the capsule. Bezos was elated that the mission was a success and couldn't wait to pop open a bottle of champagne and celebrate.

Shatner's mood minutes after landing was very different. The normally loquacious actor was at a loss for words. He made eye contact with Bezos (who looked impatient to start partying) and finally said, "You have done something . . . what you've given me is the most profound experience I can imagine. I am so filled with emotion about what just happened. It's extraordinary. I hope I never recover from this. I hope that I can maintain what I feel now, I don't want to lose it."

I had to laugh when I saw the video. It was a laugh of recognition. Shatner was having an absolutely classic reaction to an *awe* experience. His words were so clumsy, you could tell he wasn't just acting out a script he'd prepared in his head. His senses and cognition had been overwhelmed, leaving him literally speechless.

So much of this book has been about how traumatic experiences can isolate us and make us lonely, because they deny us the capacity to tell our story. The awe experience is the flip side of the traumatic experience. Both command our full attention and arouse intense, hard-to-define emotions. But unlike the traumatic experience of injury and threat, we feel awe when our emotions are stirred to their utmost in a safe and controlled context. That's what William Shatner experienced aboard *New Shepard*.

The first effect of an awe experience is to provide momentary relief from our petty egotistical concerns. Awe experiences give us goose bumps, and when we have goose bumps, any anxieties about holiday plans or back and shoulder pain recede from our awareness. Awe commands our attention, and like creative expression or any other intensely focused activity, it engages with our imagination and pulls us out of ourselves.

In descriptions of awe experiences, from natural phenomena to spiritual revelations, the same sentence crops up again and again: "I felt so small." Awe activates awareness of this "small self," a self in which the ego shrinks in the presence of something much larger than oneself. Way back in 1902, William James described experiences of wonder and religious rapture as having this "unifying" effect, in which "the sand and grit of the selfhood incline to disappear, and tenderness to rule." This may be the most genuine type of humility we will ever experience, one that can lend depth of meaning to our very existence. Philosophy professor Helen De Cruz claims, "Awe increases our tolerance for uncertainty and opens our receptivity to new and unusual ideas," which is central to all creativity and all imagination. Awe stretches the imagination and opens the door to new realms of creativity because nothing new can be created that isn't imagined first. The boxer Muhammad Ali, also a poet, observed that "a man with no imagination has no wings." This from a fighter who claimed to "float like a butterfly, sting like a bee."

Feelings of awe also have a useful social function. Just as the experience of loneliness prompts us to make connections with others, studies have shown that awe experiences reduce selfishness and promote generosity. One study of fifteen hundred people across the United States showed that those who reported experiencing more awe in their lives tended to be more generous to strangers. The relationship between awe and generosity is subtle yet profound. The same experimenters, in another study, had one set of people look up at giant two-hundred-foot eucalyptus trees on the UC Berkeley campus and another set of people look at the facade of the science building. Then the experimenters "accidentally" dropped a handful of pens. The people who'd been looking at the trees were far more likely to bend down and help pick up the pens.

The implication is that we need awe like we need creativity and conversation, as a steady diet of experiences that keep us connected in a world of centrifugal forces moving us apart. We know cognitively that we are all interdependent on this planet, but we need to *feel* our smallness in new and interesting ways that command our attention, or else our attention is apt to settle into worry about our immediate concerns, accompanied by doom scrolling on social media.

In 2019, during New York's celebrations to mark the fiftieth anniversary of the *Apollo 11* lunar landing, children's writer Oliver Jeffers created scale models of the Earth and moon on the High Line park in Manhattan, with two spheres set two hundred feet apart to represent the approximate distance to scale. On the globe, he painted all the nation-state borders, but to highlight their imagined nature, Jeffers replaced each country's name with the phrase "People live here." The moon was marked with another phrase: "No one lives here."

Walking from that globe to the moon, dozens of steps away, you could turn back and see the smallness of Earth. It put things into a certain perspective and offered a sense of the stark isolation of space. This is the farthest vantage point from which human eyes have witnessed, for themselves, our own Earth, and the visual angle it takes up is the same. To venture farther—to Mars, say—you'd have to walk at least six miles, a point from which the Earth would be invisible, and its concerns insignificant. Jeffers said, "This is the beautiful, fragile drama of civilization. We are the actors and spectators of a cosmic play that means the world to us here but means nothing anywhere else."

When William Shatner landed back on Earth, he was so excited about the experience, he expressed a desperate and unrealistic desire to share it. "Everybody in the world needs to do this," he said. "Everybody in the world needs to see. It was unbelievable. Unbelievable. I mean, the little things, the weightlessness. But to see the blue color go whip by, and now you're staring into blackness. That's the thing. The covering of blue is this sheet, this blanket, this comforter of blue that we have around. We think, 'Oh, that's blue sky.' And there's something you shoot through, and all of a sudden, as though you whip a sheet off you when you're asleep, and you're looking into blackness, into black ugliness. And you look down. There's the blue down there and the black up there. And there is mother and Earth and comfort." The experience, he said, had left him with a more profound connection to our tiny planet.

Of course, not everyone can afford a three-hundred-thousand-dollar ticket to ride aboard Jeff Bezos's rocket ship, but just about everyone can have the same awe experience, thanks to the burgeoning field of virtual reality technologies. Immersive experiences provided through virtual reality (VR) headsets are expected to be commonplace by 2030 for work, school, and shopping. Shipments of VR headsets now rival the sales of new gaming consoles.

Whether you're wearing a VR headset or going up in a rocket, your brain will interpret the sights, sounds, and sensations very similarly, because our brains understand the world only through our senses. That's why psychologists have used VR exposure therapies—sometimes combined with psychedelics like MDMA—to treat social anxiety and anxiety disorders such as claustrophobia, fear of driving, fear of heights, and fear of flying. The same exposure therapy is being used to treat war veterans for PTSD by placing them on virtual battlefields, so that in a physically safe environment, they can reexperience their emotional reactions and integrate them into a trauma story. It appears that VR's ability to induce health-enhancing brain states or block health-impairing ones is only going to expand. A small 2022 experiment with thirty-four hand-surgery patients found that the seventeen who spent the hour-long surgery wearing VR headsets that took them through guided meditations up mountainsides and through verdant forests required much less anesthetic and recovered more rapidly post-surgery. Why shouldn't VR's ability to alter brain response to perceived scenarios be applied to loneliness, particularly for those most impacted? I think it's only a matter of time.

Not everyone can climb Mount Everest, take a gondola through Venice, hike through the Amazon jungle, stroll on the surface of Mars, or take a rocket into space. But soon everyone will have access to those experiences, either at home or at commercial venues of some sort. The technology already exists, and soon it will be ubiquitous, like (dare I say it?) smartphones. As liquid modernity and all its technologies continue to spin us away from our connections with one another, we in our loneliness must keep trying to balance the ledger and keep exploring how modernity's magical technologies can bring us together and deliver awe-inspired connecting experiences.

Staring out into the vast cosmos from our tiny floating orb, we remember that in the grand scheme of things, our small anxieties are ripples on the ocean. As lonely as the vacuum of our galaxy is, we can recognize our home planet with its billions of beating hearts, creative spirits, and boundless dreams as the least lonely place in the universe.

9

A Call to Connect

As you turn to this final chapter, here are five things I hope you'll take to heart:

1. If you're lonely, it's not your fault.

2. Loneliness is essential to everyone's humanity. Like thirst or cold, it signals your need for relief. Like fear or pain, loneliness can be useful because it alerts you to a problem.

3. Loneliness is subjective. Only you can determine how much intimate human connection you need. Increasing the depth and breadth of your social connections is just one way to address your feelings of loneliness. You can also reexamine your assumptions and expectations regarding social connection. You may be surprised

to learn you need less of certain types of connection than you thought.

4. Creative activities and art appreciation are effective at quelling feelings of loneliness, *even when you are alone*, possibly because our brains have shared pathways for both art and social connection.

5. Modern life presents relentless challenges to the health of the human mind, body, and spirit. In countless ways, modernity tempts us to isolate from one another even as it offers wonderful tools for creativity and connection that we can use to take back our brains and reclaim our souls.

In order to deal effectively with your loneliness, I'd suggest you first consider where you would locate yourself in the Pyramid of Vulnerability for loneliness. If you recognize yourself in the stories of people who are extremely lonely and are suffering life-damaging consequences as a result, I strongly recommend you seek professional help. As you assess your situation, remember that loneliness tends to distort social cognition. It can make you mistrustful of others and wary of asking for help when you need it most. It will take your intellect—the power of your rational mind—to acknowledge your need for guidance to escape the trap of loneliness. Rationally, you have the ability to accept that loneliness is not your fault. With proper guidance, you are capable of releasing yourself from its downward spiral.

Perhaps you see yourself in the middle tier of the pyramid. You often feel lonely but typically remain connected enough to avoid the devastating effects of the loneliness spiral. But a recent experience has left you feeling lonelier than ever. Maybe you've had a bad breakup, you're dealing with a serious illness, or you're grieving the loss of a parent or a spouse. When reading about the territories of loneliness, consider how many you have visited. Which ones have you passed through, and which ones may have become your permanent place of residence? Did one or more of the territories speak loudly to you, perhaps because of an unresolved childhood trauma, a chronic illness, or maybe an ongoing issue with workplace bullying? Could it be that you judge yourself too harshly for feeling lonely in these circumstances? Could it be that the stigma of feeling lonely has prompted you to avoid the issues that are bothering you the most?

If you are struggling with loneliness in this way, I'd suggest you try creating your very own personal Project UnLonely. First, consider seeking new social connections within whatever territory stirs your deepest feelings of loneliness and disconnection. Whether the territory is trauma, illness, aging, or difference, there are communities of people whose lives have brought them to the same terrain and who are looking to connect. Sharing your story in a support group relevant to your territory of loneliness and conversing with others who have had similar experiences will likely make you feel less alone, while you'll also enjoy a "helper's high" from being of service.

There are no support groups specifically designated for loneliness because support groups of all kinds address our fundamental need for connection. This is why 12-step programs, Weight Watchers, and many other support group structures have spread wherever there are people in shared distress and seeking connection. In any support group, the ability to speak of your experience in a room where everyone shares some aspect of that need responds to our very human need to be seen, heard, and acknowledged.

I would never discount the pain and suffering that your loneliness has caused you, but if you can recognize your pain as a signal, then your loneliness can be a gift. It can lead you to find precious human connection with those who share your source of distress and are willing to hear and accept your story. The one great thing common to all the loneliness territories is the wide-open space they offer for building communities of connection. At the edge of every loneliness territory, there is a vast frontier where new settlers can create and connect.

Modernity, the fifth territory, presents problems we all share. I'd suggest that everyone's Project UnLonely would benefit by learning from the example of Naomi Boak, who followed her passion for grizzly bears all the way to Alaska. Identify one of your most passionate interests, that thing in your life that moves you the most, and seek intimate human connection in that area. You are much more likely to feel seen and known though conversations with those who share your specific passion. I sincerely believe that the stresses and strains of modernity have made these kinds of conversations absolutely essential to our mental, emotional, and physical well-being.

Meanwhile, consider making space in your day for mindfulness activities of some sort. See how it feels to meditate in the morning, set a daily limit on your time in front of computer and smartphone screens, and avoid scrolling social media before bed. Try carving out some cherished moments outside your endless checklist of obligations to waste some time by taking a walk. By consciously balancing the levels of solitude and connection in your daily life, you might find it's not such a heavy lift to take back your brain and reclaim your soul from modernity's grip.

All of the above are positive, healthy habits that everyone should try to adopt and develop. If you find that you are at the base of the

Pyramid of Vulnerability and are occasionally lonely, like most people, you would benefit by recognizing the nature of your loneliness when you feel it. How much of your loneliness is psychological? How much is societal? How much is existential? Try not to dismiss the signals you're receiving, but instead try to listen more carefully and interpret them. Can you take a moment to be curious about your loneliness signal? Can you identify its source? Can you explore it by making something, in whatever expressive medium you prefer? Try to draw the feeling or to write something. Can you call someone you trust and have a conversation about your feeling? By putting a name to your feelings of loneliness and following through with appropriate action, you can be among the lucky few who experience the gifts that loneliness offers.

If you gain nothing else from reading this book, I hope you will come away from it possessed by the conviction that your habits of personal creative expression are just as important to your health and well-being as your diet, exercise, and sleep. Art is a medicine that requires no prescription. There is no co-pay required for creating and conversing. Creative expression is a tonic to be imbibed freely and often, without any side effect except the chance to connect more deeply with the humanity you share with the rest of the world.

There is one thing I've been struck by in the participant feedback from our creative programs: rarely does someone feel lonelier afterward. The programs impact some people more profoundly than others, but as far as I can tell, there is very little downside from participating. So my advice is that while I can't guarantee that creating and conversing will resolve your specific problems with loneliness, I'm confident that doing so is unlikely to make you feel worse—and will probably be highly enjoyable and beneficial.

SEEKING THE "HELPER'S HIGH"

If the topic of loneliness really resonates with you and you'd like to share the message of this book with others, there are any number of things you can do in your community to promote awareness, foster connection, and have fun doing it. One simple step is to organize a viewing of one of the videos from the UnLonely Film Festival and have a group conversation afterward. Think of it as a book club but with the added benefit of enjoying the creative content all together, at the same time.

There are ways to engage with community programs that offer opportunities for people to spend meaningful time together, building the skills and confidence to maintain a sense of connection. Most communities have volunteer programs for outreach to elderly and disabled adults who are most at risk of social isolation. Adult volunteers are also needed to contribute their skills and talents to after-school programs that address the growing problem of adolescent loneliness. The force of human connection is so powerful that it doesn't take that much to make a huge difference in the life of someone who may be deeply lonely. And, perhaps not surprisingly, reaching out to connect with those who most need it naturally increases our own sense of belonging and human connection.

Some of our Project UnLonely programs, like Colors and Connection, were designed so that they can be run without any formal training in the arts or psychotherapy. You can organize a Colors and Connection session with friends and acquaintances just by registering at artandhealing.org and downloading the instructional materials. If you're unsure of your skills in facilitating such an event, we have videos that offer helpful coaching on techniques that have worked best with this program.

An evening of Colors and Connection can be engaging and fun, almost like a parlor game. Perhaps there are people within your circle of friends and acquaintances who are lonely and resistant to connecting. Inviting them to participate in an evening of Colors and Connection may be a more attractive option than simply inviting them for dinner. A lonely person with social anxiety may avoid the unstructured human contact of a party but may react completely differently to the opportunity to connect with others through creative expression. That's especially true within a group where they already feel some level of familiarity and safety.

The experience of running such a program can be emotionally rewarding for you as well as your participants. At each stage, everyone is involved in the process of stepping back from everyday life and stimulating the creative expression areas of our brains for no other reason than the simple fun of it. Art making is inherently fun, which is why children do it all the time. No one has ever had to bribe kids to draw or do finger painting. Given the materials and the opportunity, they just jump in and enjoy the process.

Another way to contribute to the UnLonely cause is to raise awareness of our programs among local community groups that already do programming for vulnerable populations: aging agencies, chronic illness support groups, mental health groups, caregiving groups. Perhaps you have personal connections with your local college or university and could bring Project UnLonely and its programs to the attention of the student health office. If you did, you'd be doing something meaningful to support one of our country's loneliest demographics.

Reach out to Project UnLonely and enlist yourself as one of our UnLonely Ambassadors. The impact of your involvement could go far beyond the hours that you might devote to running a single workshop, and who knows—maybe along the way you'll be able to recruit other UnLonely Ambassadors, too. Your ambassadorial activities need have no bounds!

THE PUBLIC HEALTH CHALLENGE

When we launched Project UnLonely in 2016, we set as our three main goals to raise awareness, reduce stigma, and produce scalable programs. It's a three-pronged approach that is typical among public health initiatives. For example, the public health problem of hunger is being addressed through each of these three prongs by Feeding America, a nonprofit network of 200 food banks and 60,000 food pantries that provides 6.6 billion meals each year. With the mission of "an America where no one is hungry," Feeding America's local affiliates reach 43 million people annually—1 in 7 Americans, including 12 million children.

What if the cause of loneliness had the same kind of national network represented in every city and town, rallying around the banner of "an America where no one is lonely"? What if it were part of a global network dedicated to a world where no one is lonely? Imagine how such a network could advance the common understanding of loneliness as a physiological signal—no different than hunger—of an essential human need. That the ache of loneliness exists to protect us, not torture us. That it is central to our humanity and nothing to be ashamed of, no more than the parched feeling in our throats when we are thirsty.

What a wonderful UnLonely world that would be.

Stage One: Raise Awareness, Reduce Stigma

The students in my public health course on loneliness are assigned team projects to design innovative public health interventions for loneliness. Most students are surprised when I tell them that the novelty and thoughtfulness of their program designs account for only about 20 percent of their grades. The rest of each grade is based on how well the teams have anticipated the difficulties of attracting participants to their programs and all the other potential obstacles to their programs' effectiveness.

Even the best program designs in public health will fail if the program sponsors aren't prepared to deal with public reactions that don't go as expected. Look at how COVID spread so quickly in the pandemic's first year, despite the proven effectiveness of social distancing and mask wearing. Then, after a full year of vaccine availability, more than one-third of American adults remained unvaccinated and hospital ICUs remained crowded with COVID patients. Studies showed that vaccinated people were 90 percent less likely to die from the virus, but many millions still refused to get the shots for a wide variety of social, political, and religious reasons.

Any public campaign about loneliness faces similar obstacles in public acceptance. At first blush, it would be reasonable to assume that an "It's OK to be lonely sometimes" promotional campaign would help reduce the stigma of loneliness. However, such a message, while potentially attractive to most people, risks making the most vulnerable people feel even lonelier. Dealing with such an emotional topic is far more complicated than designing awareness campaigns for less-emotional public health measures, like using seat belts. Deeply lonely people are usually repelled by public messaging about loneliness, because many believe their loneliness is a hopeless situation for which they shoulder most of the blame. Presumably helpful messages actually remind them of their pain and perhaps a sense of inadequacy. Still others are so deeply traumatized by loneliness that they are triggered by being told there might be another way. Public outreach for loneliness requires empathy and compassion for how the individuals most in need of the message are among those most resistant to tuning in.

Instead, I think an effective awareness campaign around loneliness would be aimed at making people intrigued and curious about the subject. It needs to be organized around stories that demystify loneliness and promote our ability to navigate it. The objective would be to encourage people to look below the surface and see other possibilities. Campaigns could build on positive themes and prompt shared social engagement and purpose-driven activities, like walks for community connection.

Artistically inspired messaging about embracing the pleasures of connection enjoys the added advantage of igniting the imagination. Creative images, words, and music that resonate with our innate yearning to connect are more likely to overcome the psychological resistance of shame or stigma. Creative expression can short-circuit the brain's impulse to look away.

A coordinated international campaign, perhaps partnered with the World Health Organization, already a global leader in arts and health, could involve the thousands of existing organizations in the performing, visual, and language arts in an international campaign supporting creative connection. It's worth noting that we live in a celebrity culture, and most celebrities are highly creative people. Many of them might enjoy contributing to a public campaign that celebrates the vital importance of the creative path to connection. The biggest stars in music, film, and TV are all intimately familiar with the loneliness and disconnection rampant in the entertainment industry. Imagine the impact of dozens of immensely popular celebrities contributing their personal stories of loneliness and creative connection.

Let's involve Silicon Valley, too, in promoting ways to harness the power of digital technologies to promote healthy connections. What would it take to create a digital marketplace that rewards innovators and investors for creating loneliness solutions at scale? Let's put the big tech companies on the spot and challenge them to put their algorithms to work optimizing for human connection, while breaking their feedback loops for hate speech and exploitation. The FDA keeps toxic substances from poisoning our food and medications. Maybe we need a similar regulatory agency to prevent toxic algorithms from poisoning the minds and spirits of millions of young people.

The stakes are incredibly high. As social media algorithms grow increasingly sophisticated, the idea of "taking back your brain" is at risk of falling victim to the powerful profit motive in monopolizing your precious attention. We already see among the most vulnerable how social media contributes to distorted social cognition and leads to loneliness, depression, suicidality, and violence. Public health messaging urging you to curtail your time with your smartphone can't possibly overcome the power of social media's profit motive. If we as a society surrender control over our attention to an unbridled tech-world marketplace, I fear we face a cascade of crises—degraded levels of civility, impeded economic productivity, and the permanent loss of our democratic virtues.

Stage Two: Celebrate Examples That Change Lives

In 2016, the Montreal Museum of Fine Arts became the first museum anywhere to hire a full-time art therapist and open a studio, or an atelier, for art therapy that includes a medical consultation room. Primary care doctors in Quebec can now prescribe visits to the museum for patients they think will benefit from a connection with art. The museum has reinterpreted its role in Montreal as a "therapeutic, restorative and healing device."

The arts community has a tremendous role to play in promoting the link between creativity and connection. Artists, art therapists, art museums, performance venues, art galleries, arts philanthropists, and art collectors, along with leaders in the field of arts and health, all need to champion the role of the arts as a collective force for connection in a society that is leaving people isolated and alienated—and act on it. After all, why should the field of medicine (or society at large, for that matter) believe in the value of the arts to health and well-being if those most deeply engaged in the arts don't believe and act on it first and foremost?

The departments in visual, language, and performing arts at schools and colleges are particularly important to this effort, due to the epidemic of loneliness among young adults. I see an opportunity for colleges and universities, with their concentrated communities of faculty, staff, alumni, and students, to serve as laboratories to test new public health approaches to loneliness.

"We live in an interdependent world," said Rakesh Khurana, dean of Harvard College. "Rather than seeing our interdependence as a source of fear, how do we make it a source of comfort and strength?" He envisions how colleges could move in this direction by creating leadership opportunities for students outside the classroom, perhaps in natural settings, where they could engage with our society's complexities and embrace a vision of interdependence and shared destiny. "Building that into education feels like a great opportunity," he said.

Higher education should have an especially keen interest in loneliness because of the association between loneliness and suicidal ideation, and the fact that suicide is now the second leading cause of death among college-aged students. If today's young people could become a rising generation with a new take on loneliness, asserting that there is nothing unusual or shameful about it, that would be a hopeful sign of progress, one that could set a positive example for succeeding generations.

None of this will be easy to do. The Montreal museum's example has yet to be replicated elsewhere, perhaps due to the difficulty of implementing it. Just to put the medical prescription program in place took more than five years. However, building on that success, the MMFA also convened a committee of medical experts and art therapists to sponsor original research on the connection between the arts and healing. The committee has more than a dozen clinical trials underway, studying the effects of art on patients suffering from eating disorders, breast cancer, epilepsy, mental illness, and Alzheimer's disease. If the most prominent art museum in every major city were to make a similar commitment to such research, we might see exponential growth in our understanding of all the connections between creative expression, art appreciation, and public health.

Stage Three: The Project UnLonely Moon Shot

When the US government made it a priority to send astronauts to the moon, the effort involved coordinating a vast array of resources that touched nearly every sector of society. A Project UnLonely Moon Shot would do the same. With deaths of despair and chronic illnesses driving down US life expectancy to its lowest level in twenty-five years, the time to act is now.

We need to develop a coordinated national public health campaign to address loneliness, fortified by government incentives, encouraged by marketplace rewards, and led by the three institutional sectors in our society simultaneously responsible for people's well-being and whose bottom lines also stand to benefit: healthcare organizations, large employers, and universities and colleges.

All three have leadership roles to play in the four pillars of execution in public health: education, screening, intervention, and continual improvement. With this systems-oriented approach, the Project UnLonely Moon Shot would lend support and focus to all the good work on loneliness already being done in all four of these areas.

The Project UnLonely Moon Shot, however, must be carried out with the recognition that all of these institutions are bound by processes and procedures that frequently isolate people and exacerbate loneliness among the most vulnerable. The healthcare and education systems often do more harm than good for people who don't fit within their data-driven protocols. We've seen it with long COVID patients, whose ailments had no diagnostic codes for doctors to punch in. We've seen it with suicides among college students who could not find a place for themselves on campus. As Paul LeBlanc points out in his book *Broken*, our social systems must reclaim the human values around which they were founded and put humanity and care at the center of their decision-making. By developing a focus on reducing loneliness, these institutions could recover their original purpose.

1. EDUCATION

We have a loneliness literacy problem that is holding us back. Many struggle to identify what loneliness is, let alone its inherent risk. Healthcare professionals and teams must educate patients about risks of loneliness, while also orienting them to the steps required to treat loneliness as a comorbid condition for chronic and major illnesses, much as they do stress, smoking, and being overweight. Large employers should educate workers and frontline management about the health risks of loneliness and emphasize the health benefits of connection and belonging, while also offering a variety of programs to foster and maintain connection and community at work. Colleges and universities should embrace sustained educational efforts to sensitize students, faculty, and staff (especially those in leadership positions) to the danger signs of loneliness and isolation, so that the people who need support get it in a timely manner.

2. SCREENING

You can't manage what you can't measure. It begins with finding out who's lonely and analyzing the extent of each person's loneliness. There are many conceptual models for screening people at risk for becoming chronically lonely, but they are not in widespread use and are rarely tailored to specific populations, which is when they are likely to deliver the most benefit. Employers should screen for loneliness and social isolation during annual health risk assessments. Healthcare providers should offer screenings as part of any hospital admission workup, as well as during patient assessments in an ambulatory care setting. They should also identify behaviors, conditions, and circumstances, such as adverse childhood events, that increase vulnerability to loneliness and isolation. Insurers can develop claims-based proxy measures that quantify loneliness and social isolation burdens, and include screening in direct member engagement through case management and population health support programs.

Imagine if Medicare mandated a simple screening survey to detect loneliness as part of the "Welcome to Medicare" initial visit for which all Medicare beneficiaries are invited. Additionally, Medicare could recommend loneliness screening for their annual wellness visit. Those visits are supposed to screen for mental health and lifestyle risk factors, so screening for loneliness can easily be added. In a similar way, educational institutions must develop mechanisms to screen students for loneliness, while also alerting teachers and administrators to the urgency of the problem so that screening is embraced as vital to the success of their shared educational mission.

Insurance carriers are well positioned also, with an ability to integrate a member-directed loneliness assessment with an offer of screening guidance and analytic support to those who deliver care on the front lines. The most influential US health providers, especially those who also have integrated provider payment capabilities, including Kaiser Permanente and the Department of Veterans Affairs, need to keep experimenting with more accurate screening measures for loneliness and innovative interventions. When our largest and most influential players in the healthcare field seize the initiative, others will follow, especially if payment models provide economic incentives to do it effectively. There are moral incentives, too, as the social consensus grows that loneliness as a health risk simply can't be ignored. We've seen this before with both smoking cessation and drunk-driving reduction. Community-based groups and religious organizations rely on healthcare leaders to set the agenda in nearly all preventive health education and screening, and are then well positioned to spread the word, amplifying engagement and benefit.

To gain maximum value from loneliness screening, we will need a national standard survey questionnaire, just as depression screening has the PHQ-9 form and anxiety screening has the GAD-7. The current loneliness screening tools themselves are in need of careful review and need to be adapted to high-risk scenarios in which lonely people may need immediate attention. The Penn State project I've contributed to, the Multidimensional Loneliness and Social Connection Scale (MLASC Scale), might prove extremely useful with its ability to flexibly assess up to ten different dimensions of loneliness and social connection. Each of the ten four-question batteries can be used alone, linked with other loneliness questionnaires, or added as a module to a survey on, say, pregnancy, mental health, or a workplace annual burnout review, all with the intention of probing for specific kinds of loneliness that can be addressed in targeted ways.

On average we know that loneliness increases the risk for illness, but with more and better data we can refine our methods for identifying those at the highest risk and for determining the strategies and tactics most effective in mitigating that risk. Insurers, large employers, and educators have leadership roles to play here. Insurers need to expand their data collection to include loneliness measurements in all annual member health surveys, health risk appraisals, and any other health risk data collecting that they do. Employers should combine loneliness assessments made through their medical claims data and employee survey results with all their other data on employee illness, medical utilization, disability claims, and employee performance and retention. Educators should similarly combine the data from student loneliness surveys with their existing data from student health services and behavioral and physical health impairment, as well as various measures of student success (academic performance or dropout rates).

Larger employers and large universities should be leading the way for better screening and innovative interventions. That's because many are big enough to be self-insured, which means that improving the health of their populations in these ways can directly and quickly impact their financial bottom lines. These big companies and institutions have the capacity and infrastructure in place to identify best practices for screening and support that we all can learn from and duplicate. It all starts with better data, which would show these large organizations where help is needed most, and where improved care and resources would most likely reduce suffering and serious health impairment in their respective populations. Expanded access to this data will also assist in the rapidly emerging scientific research in neurophysiology, psychology, and health services delivery to help us arrive at new insights to better design the programs and initiatives that can address loneliness and its burdens.

3. INTERVENTION

I once was asked by a reporter to describe what would spell success for the Foundation for Art & Healing. I told him it would look something like this: When you go to your doctor, you'll be asked whether there is a creative activity that is important to you. If you don't have regular habits of creative expression, your care team may prescribe a solution, just as they might recommend cutting back on coffee or getting in some exercise each day.

As noted earlier, "social prescribing" of this kind is already common in the UK, and research has shown that patients are more likely to try such activities when they are part of a primary care prescription. The question is whether US primary care providers will take on this additional task when the field is already stretched so thin. Government programs like Veterans Affairs, Medicare, and Medicaid (along with the commercial insurers who account for a third of all US health-care spending) need to set adequate reimbursement structures that encourage loneliness screening and interventions as a part of prevention and wellness measures. Payment models for primary care need to be adjusted to reflect the long-term cost benefits of social prescribing. The Togetherness programs for seniors at SCAN Health Plan are just one example of how medical costs can be reduced sustainably through thoughtful investments in human connection. We need many more.

4. CONTINUAL IMPROVEMENT

As I'm constantly reminding my public health students, the design of every public health program must include a baked-in cycle of measurement, analysis, and program adjustment. We approach the public health problem of loneliness by acting on what we know, while knowing that we need to know more. Sustained progress in addressing loneliness at scale will only be achieved when our major social systems and institutions move from being concerned bystanders to becoming fully engaged stakeholders.

Loneliness brought on by the pandemic has inspired the US government to make its first substantive public health investment on the issue. The Administration for Community Living within the US Department of Health and Human Services (HHS) has launched Commit to Connect, a user-friendly online system that can connects anyone to community-based programs and resources for loneliness, based on their individual needs, interests, and abilities. The project would be the first online tool that provides access to resources and contacts in every city and county in the nation. It's the first stage in what HHS promises will be a public-private campaign that could reach "up to 10 million socially-isolated older adults, people with disabilities, and veterans."

For the first time ever, all the organizations with a common interest in loneliness will be able to connect with one another. What they do with this tremendous opportunity remains to be seen.

In the meantime, how much longer must we wait before we begin to take on the vital mission of healing an increasingly divided and disconnected society? I don't think it will be long. I don't think we have long. As a society, we must heed the loneliness epidemic as a signal that we are creating conditions that are unsustainable for normal social development and well-being. We need to have the clarity, courage, and conviction to engage in both personal and collective action.

THE SCIENCE AND POETRY OF LONELINESS

Can we really accomplish all this? Can we make a more connected world?

The scientist part of my brain says, "Absolutely!" From a public health perspective, systems thinking suggests that the powerful PDCA approach (plan, do, check, act) can untangle and solve even the thorniest problem, from rising sea levels to worldwide food redistribution. Systems thinking can define desired outcomes through an arsenal of grids, frameworks, and expanding arrays of fish-bone diagrams and multilayered dependency tables. It can test the ranges of possibilities through Monte Carlo computer simulations and advanced AI applications. My scientist brain knows that we can use all these tools to create theoretical operating models, evaluate them, and optimize them toward solving the problem of loneliness as a threat to human health. And with our newly found shared sense of connection, additional public health improvements would follow. With that shared sense that we are "all in this together," we would be motivated and empowered to address many other global problems, like climate change, poverty, and inequality.

Then the poet in me laughs and says, "Get a grip."

No blueprint for action born of trillions of calculations will ever produce an unlonely world. Such a blueprint may be necessary, but it would never be close to sufficient. Loneliness has far too tenacious a grip on our psyches and our spirits to succumb to rational analysis and orchestrated program activities if viewed solely as a health problem. The realms of loneliness and connection encompass as many different realities as there are people on the planet. I doubt that those diverse realities, with all their profound and troubling nuances, can ever be reduced to a set of equations, much less reliably used.

To make the world unlonely, we must also rely on our imaginations. We must imagine an unlonely world as a real possibility. "Anything you can imagine is real," as Picasso once said. Einstein also paid due respect to the power of imagination when he observed, "Logic will get you from A to B. Imagination will get you everywhere."

The poet in me imagines a different world, a world of connection and creativity. I can imagine a world where kids entering their school building pick up art supplies at the door instead of going through a metal detector. A world where every morning when they come into school, they spend the first twenty minutes doing mindfulness exercises; the next twenty making sense of their thoughts, with access to construction paper, crayons, sparkles, glue, magazine photo cutouts, anything that invites their imaginations to collide with opportunities to create; and then twenty minutes sharing the work and talking about it. That hour will offer a daily opportunity for mental relief from social media, while allowing the kids to make sense of the lava flows of experiences, thoughts, and feelings that constantly course through them.

Let's think about whether schoolkids are the only ones who might want to begin their day with mindfulness, creative making, and sharing. How about the rest of us giving ourselves the gift of that set-aside time to be mindful, to make, and to connect? Maybe creatively connecting starts the night before with a notepad next to every pillow. And by the side of each bed is also a pen or pencil, and a light that's easy to turn on so that if you wake up in the middle of a dream-filled night, you can put something down on this paper: first the words, then the lines, then the connection of lines into the paragraphs or poems that allow us to sense and say who we are. By doing so, you can attempt to answer the questions the painter Paul Gauguin inscribed in his 1897 masterpiece: *Where Do We Come From? What Are We? Where Are We Going?* We can establish through our curious investigations what could possibly matter and what makes sense to us. And then how do we share that with others? How do we capture those fleeting thoughts, those sometimes-disturbing feelings, those sometimes-inspiring feelings? Can we share them as messages in a bottle cast into the seas of our shared experiences, where they can wash up on a shore to be found by someone else, closing the electric circuit of human connection?

Maybe we take weekly walks in our neighborhoods, or beyond our neighborhoods in more remote areas of natural beauty. These are walks in which we have no obligation other than to pay attention. Maybe we take photographs. Maybe we come back and put the photographs on a table in front of us and pick the one or two that we love the most that vibrate within us for some strange, hard to decipher, and hard to completely know reason. And we put those special photographs into action as "gifts of connection" and share them with others, inviting them to share back.

There are already many places and ways to do this. We don't need to build new social media channels, community centers, places of worship, or town squares. We can use the ones we have, but maybe in different and more purposeful ways—ways that detoxify modernity's constant streaming of our personal accomplishments into constructions designed not to connect us, but to promote and curate a personal brand. Instead, maybe it's a more deliberate and humanizing activity powered by an eagerness to authentically connect with someone else. A chance to just say, "Here's a meaningful photo I took or a few words that matter to me. I want to share it with you. Here's what I have to say about it and what it means to me." Think of Neruda's pinecone. If someone offered it to you, what would you share back?

Let's keep going! How about starting drum circles after school or work? How about if every institution that brings us together with shared purpose to learn or make things invited people to let the rhythms of the day turn into the rhythms of a bigger story? To let the magic of a small drum, held between our knees, bring forth the vibratory resonance that moves through our bodies even as it moves through the air that separates us, becoming shared medicine that connects and heals us?

In the world that I imagine there's a garden in every neighborhood, and in that community garden there are benches where people who don't know each other sit and have conversations. There are no algorithms to curate those conversations, just a simple prompt: "What's on your mind?" or "What lit you up today?" And the only requirement is mutual respect and recognizing that in our speaking and listening we are caring for each other and the planet. The gardens and parks are already there, and park benches are not that expensive. And I don't think these opportunities would be that difficult to bring into being. Let's try it and see!

As a medical doctor, I don't find it hard to imagine ways we can change what a hospital experience includes. Maybe the check-in process offers you some art supplies in addition to your plastic bracelet and awkward garment. And with those art supplies, the hospital staff invites patients to tell their stories and put those stories up on the walls of their rooms. Maybe once in a while throw in some shared art making with the clinical team that comes on morning rounds as a way to better communicate, reduce burnout, and heal.

How about regular conversations between older adults and younger people, organized by a coalition of community groups? Easy to organize on Zoom, these would be opportunities for simple conversations to share thoughts and feelings and tell our stories. Sometimes, in addition to the conversations, people could share works of visual art or writing done earlier that day. We don't have to keep it virtual. We can take conversations into the community, setting up "connection cafés," open tables to sit around and chat, with art supplies available for those interested in using them. If this came to pass, we would all have a place to begin our day with a meaningful conversation instead of loneliness. Connection conversations could be organized in parks, in municipal gardens, or inside in libraries, museums, and community centers—anywhere human beings can enjoy being side by side in sharing their past, present, and hopes for the future with each other.

We can have conversations in pairs or as groups. Imagine a wonderful army of docents, like those who guide us through art museums, to guide us through the natural world in all the ways we encounter it, who can welcome, educate, inform, support, and enable the exploration of ourselves and each other, embroidering our experiences with personal perspectives shared, received, and savored.

We can explore beyond visual arts and into the world of culinary arts, sharing what we eat and drink in ways that recall the way we sat around ancient campfires in times long past. An opportunity to fortify ourselves with stories in the same vital way we are nourished by the food that strengthens our bodies.

Sometimes there are special circumstances we can also share, perhaps grieving a loss but also celebrating something generative, like births or marriages. At these threshold moments, so much is in play as we move from one defining life circumstance to another. What if in our connection cafés we could recall and share memories of the past while also imagining our future possibilities, recognizing both as no less a part of who we are than our musculoskeletal, cardiovascular, and digestive systems? And in those times of precious reflection, maybe we could ask some essential questions and share the answers. Who did I love and lose? What was it about them that I cherished most and most admired? That most challenged me, most encouraged me, most supported me? What does the pain of not having this person by my side look like? Feel like? How can I share that with you? How can I somehow be that missed and longed-for presence in the world and fill the empty space? How can I not be lonely, even with this empty space inside me? What would fill that empty space? What would it sound like, smell like, taste like? If the empty space had a name, what would that name be? If you wanted to send a bouquet of flowers to the empty space to brighten it up, what would you use for an address?

As far-reaching as all these activities may sound, there is little I've described that doesn't already exist in some form somewhere. The issue is: What would it take to move these bold and sometimes brash experiments forward into accepted parts of mainstream culture? How can they transform from stray oddball curiosities into interlocking elements in a rich worldwide tapestry of culture and connection?

My scientist brain insists that all these good ideas require rigorous study and validated data so that they can be scaled into common practice reinforced by public policies. My scientist brain has a point, of course, but I am also sure that studies and data will not be sufficient. They may not even be necessary. Culture, after all, predates scientific research by tens of thousands of years. Shaping culture, therefore, is not dependent on science or research. The better question to ask is how we can uplift our culture, from its most humble foundations to its loftiest aspirations.

If we want to inhabit a more connected world, we should pursue that goal with persistence, kindness, and patience. Celebrating and sharing that journey though the marriage of dreaming and doing matters more than arriving at the desired destination. Each of us, after all, is granted only so many years on this tiny parcel as it spins through an infinite universe. There may not be a more meaningful way to spend our time remaining than in the deliberate, passionate, committed pursuit of human connection.

ACKNOWLEDGMENTS

As with the making of many of my poems, the opportunity to make this book began with a sense that there was something important that was missing, a demanding crater or insistent divide needing and longing to be filled or bridged. To get it done I knew I might need to develop new skills or sharpen buried ones, but what the heck, it was January 2020 and I was excited to get started. Two months later, the world was in lockdown and Project UnLonely, except for its online activities, had ground to a halt.

To my great good fortune, despite the COVID pandemic's upending influences, I was kept mentally and spiritually afloat by the kindness and generosity of others. In addition to the many, many people whose enthusiasm, skills, wisdom, commiseration, and humor accompanied me through the inevitable ups and downs, many who made this book possible had long departed from this world and offered support from the uncanny realm. To all these first responders, I am indebted.

In the birthing of this book amid the COVID-era tumult, a few heartfelt shout-outs. For his tenacious insistence that this book was a possibility despite all the unanticipated challenges, a special bouquet of roses to my agent Will Lippincott of Aevitas. There is no one who is more responsible for this book being a reality than him. Since the making of a book is a team sport, how lucky I was in having an abundance of remarkable and inspiring teammates. Leading that long and cherished lineup is my editor at Penguin Random House's Avery imprint, Caroline Sutton, whose enduring belief in the book, warm friendship, and patient guidance never flagged. Appreciative kudos to Megan Newman, Lindsay Gordon, Farin Schlussel, Casey Maloney, Lillian Ball, Viviana Moreno, Sara Johnson, Lota Erinne, Caroline Johnson, and Laura Corless at Avery, whose peerless skills were vital in getting this book into the hands of all those who might benefit. A standing ovation of praise for Noel Weyrich, my indefatigable word-smithing collaborator and coach whose unmatched book-crafting acumen comes paired with ready humor and infinite patience. Those diligent efforts to make sure the right words made it to these pages were aided and abetted with caring support by a host of others, including Shannon O'Neill, Bradley Riew, Colleen Wouters, Carl Spector, John Zweig, Suzie Becker, Jessa Gamble, and Kathy Kiely. A grateful hat-tip to all!

For getting this book from dream to done, a small cottage on the banks of the New Meadows River in West Bath, Maine, was my pandemic sanctuary. I am indebted to my Birch Point neighbors whose cheer and charm got me through the darkest of COVID times, especially Donna and Paul McCole next door and their adult kids Becca and Marc; Bill and Sally Haggett down at the end of the road; and Karen Budd and Tim Swann in Brunswick, the next town over. I was also lucky to get to know bike whisperer and primary care doc Mark Wheeler, a jewel of a human being who walks the walk of deep commitment to community through his championing of group bike rides for connecting people. And for joining me on those magnificent rides, a horn-toot of thanks to Rob Copeland, Judy McGuire, Janet Watkinson, Linda Trapp, Rob Varney, Moe Bisson, Tim Brokaw, and Mary-Jane Riley. There are no finer riding companions anywhere. Heading back to Brookline, MA, a lifelong hug to Patty Maher and Michael Wessels for almost four decades of love and tolerance and for allowing me to be part of their family, living "just upstairs" in the venerable wood-frame Victorian we shared. Continuing with Boston's neighborly embrace, boundless gratitude to my college classmate Carl Spector and his wife, Marilu Swett, for keeping me pandemic-sane when not ensconced in Maine through weekly pod dining and the occasional hand-wringing about the impossibility of an entire book project, followed by Lemon Zinger tea and homemade desserts. Finally, untethered to any fixed geography and for many decades of love and care, a big hug for my friend Maureen Gill, clinician, maker, dreamer, empath, and problem solver who brightens any room she enters.

A book like this only matters if it has readers attentive, unafraid, and ready to dig in. For taking loneliness out of the closet from a public health perspective, there is no one who has done more than Vivek H. Murthy, our nineteenth and twenty-first Surgeon General. When Dr. Murthy interviewed me for his own book on loneliness that came out in April 2020, he told me his goal was to make it easier for practitioners like me to push ahead with ways to address it. That is exactly what his book did and what his ongoing focus on the enduring need for human connection continues to do.

For me, understanding loneliness began with exploring its scientific underpinnings. I was fortunate to have some of the field's most esteemed scholars share their research and wisdom with me directly, along with an open and curious receptivity for my idea that the arts could connect us. For that gift, there will always be special places in my heart for John Cacioppo and his wife and research partner Stephanie Cacioppo, both intrepid pioneers in the field of social neuroscience related to loneliness. Deepest thanks also to the preeminent scientists Julianne Holt-Lunstad and Louise Hawkley, who shared their wisdom generously and often and without whose seminal contributions loneliness would be far less well understood.

For my orientation that science matters and for having some easy facility with it, a deep gratitude to all those responsible. First, lavish credit and thanks to my parents, Sidney and Deana, both research chemists. They often brought their enthusiasm for science home, sharing details of lab experiments around the family's dinner table before taking me and my sisters, Naomi and Tamar, out for ice cream on the boardwalk or to the beach at Asbury Park to dig for imaginary buried treasure. My sisters and I never found the buried treasure, but their sisterly love for me, their little brother, made up for that and still does. I can't imagine a world without the treasure of my beloved sisters in it.

Following my mom and dad, I was fortunate to be influenced by a steady and encouraging stream of remarkable and lauded scientists, including Tom Spiro, my chemistry thesis adviser at Princeton, and Darcy Wilson at Penn Med and Woods Hole. Moving from science to medicine, Donald Martin at Penn Med, a virtuoso at both, encouraged my transition from lab bench to bedside with grace and humor. At Boston's Beth Israel hospital, the small boat of my early years in clinical medicine pitched and yawed. I survived in large part thanks to the generous caring, kindness, and mentoring of a compassionate few, especially Matthew Budd, a brilliant and empathetic physician and innovator who had the bold idea of putting patients at the center of their own healing. Matt showed me how I could be at the center of my own healing, too, as I hope this book does for others.

As my professional wingspan and "field of view" expanded from science and medicine to include the practice of public health, I was guided and inspired by some remarkable faculty members at the Harvard T. H. Chan School of Public Health, including Richard Monson, Nancy Kane, Nancy Turnbull, David Hemenway, Michelle Williams, Arnie Epstein, Howard Koh, Jeff Levin-Scherz, and Tyler Vander-Weele. Also Joe Kvedar, telehealth pioneer, who was never more than an email away to help with some of the earliest courses on digital health taught anywhere. On the Harvard Medical School side of my work life, deep thanks to longtime friend and "once upon a time" fellow medical resident Russ Phillips, who leads the Center for Primary Care at Harvard Medical School, for the timely opportunity to imagine addressing loneliness in primary care. And for my HMS Global Health and Social Medicine colleagues David Jones, Allan Brandt, and Arthur Kleinman, whose support and encouragement for my exploration of the power of creative expression to address loneliness made me feel less lonely, a grateful bow.

Over time, my engagement with science and medicine, and even public health, became the sound of one hand clapping unless the arts were there to provide the other hand. For flinging open wide the gates to the kingdoms of imagination, creativity, and the arts and for making sure I knew I was welcome there, I owe an illimitable debt to the poet Galway Kinnell and the photographer Emmet Gowin. Their kindness and inspiration were the silver linings in the often dark and lonely cloud of my college years.

Through Galway's influence I was intrigued and humbled by poetry's possibilities and couldn't let go. I came eventually to also study with, be indebted to, and be inspired by Denise Levertov, Bob Hass, Brenda Hillman, Sharon Olds, Edward Hirsch, Lucie Brock-Broido, Catherine Barnett, Deborah Landau, Claudia Rankine, Mark Doty, Terrance Hayes, Toi Derricotte, Matthew Zapruder, Naomi Shihab Nye, Rafael Campo, Marie Howe, and Jane Hirshfield, met through the Community of Writers in Olympic Valley, California, or at the Creative Writing Program at NYU, or simply out and about in the world. And to tie a last grateful bow around my good fortune to study poetry at NYU, I offer a fond salute to my fellow MFA students, and especially to M'Bilia Meekers, Mallory Imler Powell, Ocean Vuong, Jessica Modi, and Holly Mitchell, who only rarely seemed to notice that I was over twice their age.

For my love of photography, I offer another deep thanks to Emmet Gowin and offer him a hearty embrace and a firm handshake for his saying the word *beautiful* in his slow Virginia style so it rang in my ears as if I'd never heard the word before. A gush of gratitude, too, for his pointing me toward Robert Frank, Walker Evans, Frederick Sommer, Diane Arbus, Cindy Sherman, Nan Goldin, Larry Fink, Garry Winogrand, Lee Friedlander, and Ralph Eugene Meatyard, and for reassuring me a few weeks before college graduation that it didn't matter whether I studied medicine or art and that it would lead to the same place. How could he have known?

The intertwining of my interests in arts and medicine led to the creation of the Foundation for Art & Healing in 2003. It would not have been possible without founding board members Jonathan Cohen and Les Gosule. A heartfelt hug to both, with love left over for the incomparable Bill T. Jones, who got the foundation launched with a 2004 arts and health talk in San Francisco, and for the late Richard Rockefeller, whom I turned to for guidance in 2011 when I had the idea that the arts could be a powerful antidote to disconnection. Over potent coffee in Portland, Maine, Richard and I debated whether the arts or psychedelics offered more hope in reducing loneliness. At the time, we scored the debate a draw, thinking time would tell. I still think it will.

For sticking with me through the thick and thin of the nonprofit world, my deep and abiding appreciation goes to past directors of the

Foundation for Art & Healing, the mother ship of Project UnLonely: Deborah Obalil, Michael Monson, Laurel Pickering, Rose Higgins, and Bob Gabbay; as well as to directors currently serving, including Robert Murphy, John Zweig, Marc Lieberstein, Niyum Gandhi, Michael Sturmer, Marco Diaz, Arnell Hinkel, David Shulkin, and board cochairs Myrna Chao and Cindy Elkins. Special thanks to FAH Inner Circle members, resolute supporters who go the extra mile, including Lee Shapiro, Glen Tullman, Marlis and Kjartan Jansen, Rachel Kohler, Alex and Doug Drane, Julia Spicer, Barry Weiss and Laurie Alpert, George Vradenburg, John Chao, Steven and Ruth Ryave, and Norbert Goldfield. And lastly, an ever-enduring wellspring of admiration and thanks to our inspiring, passionate, and deeply committed staff members, past and current, without whom there would be no Project UnLonely. Those stalwarts include Vivian James, Stephanie Pruitt Gaines, Katie Doyle, Bradley Riew, Brendan Creamer, Jennifer Weiss, Amy Powers, Bradley Woody, Frank Spiro, Amy Poueymirou, Louisa Hudson, Lee Colaluca, Jennifer Martin, Dana Osterling, Holly Mohr, Pauline Himics, and Jessica Liu.

Like much that operates at the intersection of dreaming and doing, Project UnLonely would move at a snail's pace without the contributions of our many treasured advisers, ambassadors, friends, and spirit guides. That remarkably diverse assembly includes Renée Fleming, Cyndi Lauper, Eileen Rockefeller Growald, Joanna "JoJo" Noëlle Levesque, Kate Snow, Dean Ornish, Sherry Turkle, Phil Imperial, Veronique Boissonnas, Atul Gawande, Tom Insel, Paula Poundstone, Michael Pollan, Laurie Anderson, Bjorn Amelan, Arianna Huffington, Sachin Jain, Patrick Kennedy, Rakesh Khurana, Jack Kornfield, Susan Cohn Rockefeller, Joan Snyder, Ashish Jha, Mark D. Smith, Steven Safyer, Andrew Dreyfus, Michael Weintraub, Anne Avidon, Tom Morrison, Assaf Morag, Robert Hort, Jennifer Hastings, Christie

Blish, Susan Walker, Jack Taylor, Deborah and Derek Van Eck, Josh Smyth, Harlan Krumholz, Rita Redberg, Robert Mittman, Jill Rosenthal, Lisa Marsh Ryerson, Emily Allen, Paolo Narciso, Ken Plumlee, Jason Molony, Susan Piver, Trudy Goodman, Lauren Thermos, Tobi Abramson, Beth Finkel, Charlotte Yeh, Mitchell Elkind, Leo Asen, Joanne Silberner, Howie Frumkin, Cathryn Gunther, Paul Sheils, Lindsay Katt, Marion Nestle, Lillie Shockney, Hyeseung Song, Tomer Ben-Kiki, Ofer Leidner, Brian O'Neill, Tom Lundquist, Chris Johnson, Bill Rutter, Matt Sanders, Henry Loubet, Vic Strecher, Ji Lee, Robert Lynch, Mark Kramer, Gus and Arlette Kayafas, Tali Lennox, Carla Perissinotto, Kristin Russell, Ellie Friedman, Lisa Wong, Susan Pories, Leah Kane, Tonya Hong-sermeier, Toby Nelson, Ken and Jill Michielsen, Irene S. Nesbit, Peter Klosowicz, Maureen Shea, Lisa Hahn, Doug and Sheila Smith, Leah Binder, Michelle Probert, Peter Hayes, Marc McDonald, Ron Marks, Laura Epstein Schlatter, George Monteleone, Felice Dublon, Joseph Behen, Drew Holzapfel, Mark Meridy, Briana Hilfer, Ira Nash, Neal Sofian, Wendy Everett, Rachel Warren, Chris Chamberlin, Laura Tufariello, Candace Sherman, Patricia Flynn, Kathryn Haslanger, Gregg Nevola, Barbara Lewis, Mary Schinhofen, Matthew Holt, Amir and Ronit Kishon, Kerry Tremaine and Barbara Ramsey, Ellen Friedman, Jane Stafford, Marty Walsh, Debra Charlesworth, Claire Levitt, Garen, Shari, and Brandon Staglin, Noelle Serper, Paul Le-Blanc, Fred Foulkes, Renee Panda, Carol Levine, Bill Reynolds, Mary Abbott Hess, Terry Fulmer, Miriam Freimer, Barbara Mittleman, Julie Pfitzinger, Marshall Votta, Steve Cohan, James Cohan, Earl Steinberg, Jeremy Brody, Jane Brody, Warren Browner, Lew Sandy, Steve Akers, Bob Galvin, Jeffrey Flier, Robin Strongin, Joe Tallman and Liz Snowden, Lois Drapin, Patricia Leitch, Rushika Fernando-pulle, Andy Ellner, David Blumenthal, Julie Murchinson, Margaret

Laws, Helene and Ralph Ellison, Harvey Fineberg, Brad Fluegel, Norman Stein, Sophie Pauze, Kristin Gill, Joe Coughlin, Michael Cantor, Mark Wenneker, David Howes, Steve Amendo, Jonathan Harvey, Teague Morris, Tamlin Connel Kinnan, Dexter Shurney, Vicki Shepard, Kate Cunningham, Tom Williams, Steve Kahane, Kevin and Nella O'Grady, Erinn White, Ido and Roy Schoenberg, Jack Rowe, Donna Healy, Ted Rybeck, Donato Tramuto, Matt Stover, Joel Beetsch, Jo Anne and Jamie Loundy, Kate Walsh, Mary Michael, David Brailer, Jeri Rosenberg, Lisa Suennen, and Pamela Carson.

At its core, the foundation's work to be a bridge between art and medicine builds on the vision, efforts, and incredible accomplishments of a diverse community of artists, healers, researchers, community leaders, and others who fully understand and embrace the idea that the arts can be a powerful force for health and well-being. This outstanding group of people, many far better known for success in other fields, are the tribe I am honored to work among. They include John Zweig, Deborah Obalil, Moira McGuire, Jill Sonke, Ping Ho, Girija Kaimal, Robbie McCauley, Edythe Hughes, Mary Hambleton, Marco Donner, Mia Allen, Agnieszka Miter, Neal Slavin, Alyson Maier Lokuta, Margery Pabst Steinmetz, Jason and Gillian Schuler, Charles Marmar, Harris Allen, Lewis Kazis, Bill O'Brien, Sunil Iyengar, Melissa Walker, Joel Katz, Suzanne Koven, Marete Wester, Greg Weintraub, Evan Horwitz, Sam Pressler, Mara Walker, Susan Magsamen, Annie Brewster, Mike Paseornek, Germaul Barnes, Chris Bailey, Roman Baca, Ted Chapin, Alan Siegel, Vivien Marcow Speiser, Phil Speiser, Naj Wikoff, Sally Taylor, Brynna Bloomfield, Danielle Ofri, Alexandra Beller, Catherine Cabeen, Joan Snyder, Matthew Sullivan, Jill Medvedow, Blossom Benedict, Joy Voeth, My Södergren, Lashaun Dale, Claire Pentecost, Alex Stark, Arlene Wanetick, Shana Ruggenberg, Stephanie Paseornek, Meghan O'Rourke, Jon Adler, Dawn

McGuire, Robin Farr, David Ehlert, Meg Stafford, Haleh Liza Gafori, Dabney Hailey, Heather Stuckey, Erica Curtis, and Dave Schroeder. You all rock!

Lastly, I appreciate beyond measure the many people who through interviews and conversations contributed directly to the material in this book. I bow my head with respect for the wisdom of their insights and the courage to share it. Responsibility for any shortfalls in bringing their invaluable contributions forward in beneficial ways rests with me alone.

———————————⬭———————————

JEREMY NOBEL
January 5, 2023

NOTES

1: The Loneliness Crisis

4. **For a wide variety of reasons:** M. É. Czeisler et al., "Mental Health, Substance Use, and Suicidal Ideation During the COVID-19 Pandemic—United States, June 24–30, 2020," *Morbidity and Mortality Weekly Report* 69, no. 32 (2020): 1049–57, http://dx.doi.org/10.15585/mmwr.mm6932a1.

4. **It's been well publicized:** Julianne Holt-Lunstad, Timothy B. Smith, and J. Bradley Layton, "Social Relationships and Mortality Risk: A Meta-analytic Review," *PLoS Medicine* 7, no. 7 (2010): e1000316, https://doi.org/10.1371/journal.pmed.1000316.

4. **Social isolation and loneliness are increasingly recognized:** Holt-Lunstad, Smith, and Layton, "Social Relationships and Mortality Risk"; Sarvada Chandra Tiwari, "Loneliness: A Disease?," *Indian Journal of Psychiatry* 55, no. 4 (October–December 2013), https://www.ncbi.nlm.nih.gov/pmc/articles/PMC3890922.

5. **Studies in the US, UK, Australia:** Daniel L. Surkalim et al., "The Prevalence of Loneliness Across 113 Countries: Systematic Review and Meta-analysis," *BMJ* 376 (2022): e067068, https://doi.org/10.1136/bmj-2021-067068.

5. **Among middle-aged white working-class Americans:** Deidre McPhillips, "US Life Expectancy Lowest in Decades After Dropping Nearly a Full Year in 2021," CNN, August 31, 2022, https://www.cnn.com/2022/08/31/health/life-expectancy-declines-2021/index.html.

5. **Psychologists studying this phenomenon:** William E. Copeland et al., "Associations of Despair with Suicidality and Substance Misuse Among Young Adults," *JAMA Network Open* 3, no. 6 (2020): e208627, https://doi.org/10.1001/jamanetworkopen.2020.8627.

5. **A 2018 study by Cigna revealed:** Alexa Lardieri, "Study: Many Americans Report Feeling Lonely, Younger Generations More So," *U.S. News*, May 1, 2018, https://www.usnews.com/news/health-care-news/articles/2018-05-01/study-many-americans-report-feeling-lonely-younger-generations-more-so.

5. **Status and power, by the way:** Thomas J. Saporito, "It's Time to Acknowledge CEO Loneliness," *Harvard Business Review*, February 15, 2012, https://hbr.org/2012/02/its-time-to-acknowledge-ceo-lo.; Lauren Vogel, "Medicine Is One of the Loneliest Professions," *Canadian Medical Association Journal* 190, no. 31 (2018): E946, https://doi.org/10.1503/cmaj.109-5640.

13. **The late social neuroscientist John Cacioppo:** John T. Cacioppo, Stephanie Cacioppo, and Dorret I. Boomsma, "Evolutionary Mechanisms for Loneliness," *Cognition and Emotion* 28, no. 1 (2013): 3–21, https://doi.org/10.1080/02699931.2013.837379.

13. **Gavin de Becker's bestselling *The Gift of Fear*:** Gavin de Becker, *The Gift of Fear: Survival Signals That Protect Us from Violence* (Boston: Little, Brown & Co., 1997).

14. **Kendall Palladino, today the director of spiritual care:** Kendall Palladino, "Mother Teresa Saw Loneliness as Leprosy of the West," *News-Times*, April 17, 2004, https://www.newstimes.com/news/article/mother-teresa-saw-loneliness-as-leprosy-of-the-250607.php.

15. **An internal Facebook document obtained by *MIT Technology Review*:** Karen Hao, "Troll Farms Reached 140 Million Americans a Month on Facebook before 2020 Election, Internal Report Shows," *MIT Technology Review*, September 16, 2021, https://www.technologyreview.com/2021/09/16/1035851/facebook-troll-farms-report-us-2020-election.

16. **Andrew Bosworth, chief technology officer:** Kelsey Vlamis, "Facebook Executive Blames 'Individual Humans' for the Spread of Misinformation, Saying They Choose What to Believe and What to Share," *Business Insider*, December 12, 2021, https://www.businessinsider.com/facebook-executive-blames-people-for-the-spread-of-misinformation-2021-12.

2: The Power of Creative Expression

20. **"Children and artists have ready access to the imagination":** Robin F. Goodman, Andrea Henderson Fahnestock, and Debbie Almontaser, *The Day Our World Changed: Children's Art of 9/11* (New York: Harry N. Abrams, 2002).

22. **The field of art therapy:** Nadine van Westrhenen and Elzette Fritz, "Creative Arts Therapy as Treatment for Child Trauma: An Overview," *Arts in Psychotherapy* 41, no. 5 (2014): 527–34, https://doi.org/10.1016/j.aip.2014.10.004.

27. **In 2015, a groundbreaking study:** Julianne Holt-Lunstad et al., "Loneliness and Social Isolation as Risk Factors for Mortality: A Meta-analytic Review." *Perspectives on Psychological Science* 10, no. 2 (2015): 227–37, https://doi.org /10.1177/1745691614568352.

31. **The poet Pablo Neruda:** Pablo Neruda, "Childhood and Poetry," in *Neruda and Vallejo: Selected Poems*, trans. Robert Bly, John Knoepfle, and James Wright (Boston: Beacon Press, 1993).

31. **The link between art and social connection:** Janneke E. P. van Leeuwen et al., "More Than Meets the Eye: Art Engages the Social Brain." *Frontiers in Neuroscience* 16 (February 25, 2022): 738865, https://doi.org/10.3389/fnins.2022 .738865.

32. **Back in 2002, I learned:** Goodman, Fahnestock, and Almontaser, *The Day Our World Changed*.

3: Our Loneliness Heritage

36. **And when Henry David Thoreau was asked:** Henry David Thoreau, *Walden*, (1854; Project Gutenberg, 2021), https://www.gutenberg.org/files/205/205-h /205-h.htm.

38. **"I don't feel very much like Pooh today":** A. A. Milne and Ernest H. Shepard, *Winnie-the-Pooh* (New York: Alfred A. Knopf, 2022).

42. **"a lonely speck":** "Carl Sagan Quote," LibQuotes, accessed January 5, 2023, https://libquotes.com/carl-sagan/quote/lbm2k1q.

42. **"He who has a why":** Friedrich Wilhelm Nietzsche, "Maxims and Arrows," in *Twilight of the Idols; and, the Anti-Christ*, trans. R. J. Hollingdale (London: Penguin Books, 2003).

47. **In the early 1990s:** John T. Cacioppo, Stephanie Cacioppo, and Dorret I. Boomsma, "Evolutionary Mechanisms for Loneliness," *Cognition and Emotion* 28, no. 1 (2013): 3–21, https://doi.org/10.1080/02699931.2013.837379.

48. **associated with the evolution:** Alexandra Rosati, "Food for Thought: Was Cooking a Pivotal Step in Human Evolution?," *Scientific American*, February 26, 2018, https://www.scientificamerican.com/article/food-for-thought-was -cooking-a-pivotal-step-in-human-evolution.

49. **John's book *Loneliness*:** John T. Cacioppo and William Patrick, *Loneliness: Human Nature and the Need for Social Connection* (New York: W. W. Norton & Company, 2009).

49. **John reasoned that this is why:** Cacioppo and Patrick, *Loneliness*, 48–49.

50. **Your loneliness isn't just your problem:** John T. Cacioppo, James H. Fowler, and Nicholas A. Christakis, "Alone in the Crowd: The Structure and

Spread of Loneliness in a Large Social Network," *Journal of Personality and Social Psychology* 97, no. 6 (2009): 977–91, https://doi.org/10.1037/a0016076.

51. **Tocqueville noted that Americans:** Alexis de Tocqueville, "Of Individualism in Democratic Countries," in *Democracy in America*, vol. 2 (1835; Project Gutenberg, 2013), https://www.gutenberg.org/files/816/816-h/816-h.htm.

51. **Durkheim formed a theory:** Émile Durkheim, *Suicide: A Study in Sociology* (Oxford: Routledge, 2002).

52. **Princeton professors Anne Case and Angus Deaton:** Anne Case and Angus Deaton, *Deaths of Despair and the Future of Capitalism* (Princeton, NJ: Princeton University Press, 2020).

53. **An apocryphal story about Ernest Hemingway:** David Mikkelson, "Did Ernest Hemingway Write a Six-Word Story to Win a Bet?" Snopes.com, October 29, 2008, https://www.snopes.com/fact-check/hemingway-baby-shoes.

56. **One psychological view of curiosity:** George Loewenstein, "The Psychology of Curiosity: A Review and Reinterpretation," *Psychological Bulletin* 116, no. 1 (1994): 75–98, https://doi.org/10.1037/0033-2909.116.1.75.

57. **Daniel Kahneman, the Nobel Prize–winning psychologist:** Daniel Kahneman, *Thinking, Fast and Slow* (New York: Farrar, Straus and Giroux, 2011).

62. **Psychologist Arthur Aron claims:** Daniel Jones, "The 36 Questions That Lead to Love," *New York Times*, January 9, 2015, https://www.nytimes.com/2015/01/09/style/no-37-big-wedding-or-small.html.

4: Trauma

70. **Phil Klay, a former US Marine:** Phil Klay, *Redeployment* (New York: Penguin Group US, 2014).

71. **Albert Szent-Györgyi, the Hungarian biochemist:** Leon N. Cooper and Sorin Instrail, "Mental Experience and the Turing Test: This Double Face Is the Face of Mathematics," Brown University, accessed January 5, 2023, https://www.brown.edu/Research/Istrail_Lab/resources/Cooper-Istrail012912FINAL.pdf.

73. **Bessel van der Kolk, a psychiatrist:** Bessel van der Kolk, *The Body Keeps the Score: Brain, Mind, and Body in the Healing of Trauma* (New York: Penguin Books, 2015).

74. **"Confusion and mutism are routine":** van der Kolk, *The Body Keeps the Score*.

74. **On average, approximately one-fifth of PTSD sufferers:** Zac E. Imel et al., "Meta-analysis of Dropout in Treatments for Posttraumatic Stress Disorder," *Journal of Consulting and Clinical Psychology* 81, no. 3 (2013): 394–404, https://doi.org/10.1037/a0031474.

74. **Since 2017, the FDA has acknowledged:** Allison A. Feduccia et al., "Breakthrough for Trauma Treatment: Safety and Efficacy of MDMA-Assisted Psychotherapy Compared to Paroxetine and Sertraline," *Frontiers in Psychiatry* 10 (2019): 650, https://www.ncbi.nlm.nih.gov/pmc/articles/PMC6751381/.

75. **"Finally, these invisible wounds":** Melissa Walker, "Unmasking the Invisible Wounds of War," filmed November 2015 in Palm Springs, CA, TEDMED video, 10:06, https://www.tedmed.com/talks/show?id=526823.

75. **In a TED talk she gave:** Walker, "Unmasking the Invisible Wounds of War."

79. **A landmark 1998 survey:** "About the CDC-Kaiser ACE Sudy," Centers for Disease Control and Prevention, last updated April 6, 2021, https://www.cdc.gov/violenceprevention/aces/about.html.

79. **In 1988, when Harvard Medical School researcher:** Judith Herman, *Trauma and Recovery: The Aftermath of Violence—from Domestic Abuse to Political Terror* (New York: Basic Books, 1997).

83. **The role of loneliness in the diagnosis:** A. P. DePrince, A. T. Chu, and A. S. Pineda, "Links Between Specific Posttrauma Appraisals and Three Forms of Trauma-Related Distress," *Psychological Trauma: Theory, Research, Practice, and Policy* 3, no. 4 (2011): 430–41, https://doi.org/10.1037/a0021576.

83. **Another study, published in 2019:** Yael Dagan and Joel Yager, "Addressing Loneliness in Complex PTSD," *Journal of Nervous and Mental Disease* 207, no. 6 (2019): 433–39, https://doi.org/10.1097/nmd.0000000000000992.

84. **"When intimate and relational loneliness":** Dagan and Yager, "Addressing Loneliness in Complex PTSD."

88. **The global pandemic that began:** Richard Weissbourd et al., "Loneliness in America: How the Pandemic Has Deepened an Epidemic of Loneliness and What We Can Do About It," Making Caring Common Project, February 2021, https://mcc.gse.harvard.edu/reports/loneliness-in-america.

89. **A survey of two thousand people in the UK:** Katie Camero, "Loneliness vs. Solitude: Study Finds Early COVID Isolation Was Positive for Many," McClatchy DC, last updated November 2, 2021, https://www.mcclatchydc.com/news/coronavirus/article255455446.html

5: Illness

92. **When Linda Topf's multiple sclerosis gradually robbed her:** Linda Noble Topf and Hal Zina Bennett, *You Are Not Your Illness: Seven Principles for Meeting the Challenge* (New York: Simon & Schuster, 1995).

93. **"Illness is the night-side of life":** Susan Sontag, *Illness as Metaphor: AIDS and Its Metaphors* (New York: Penguin Books, 1991).

93. **"Ruins, for me, are the beginning"**: "Anselm Kiefer Quotes," BrainyQuote, accessed October 18, 2022, https://www.brainyquote.com/quotes/anselm_kiefer_505220.

97. **As much as 90 percent**: National Center for Chronic Disease Prevention and Health Promotion, "Health and Economic Costs of Chronic Diseases," Centers for Disease Control and Prevention, last updated September 8, 2022, https://www.cdc.gov/chronicdisease/about/costs/index.htm.

97. **Healthcare spending in 2021 totaled $4.3 trillion**: "National Health Expenditure Data: Historical," Centers for Medicare and Medicaid Services, last updated December 15, 2022, https://www.cms.gov/Research-Statistics-Data-and-Systems/Statistics-Trends-and-Reports/NationalHealthExpendData/NationalHealthAccountsHistorical.

97. **The cardiovascular ailments of heart disease and stroke**: "Cardiovascular Diseases," World Health Organization, accessed October 20, 2022, https://www.who.int/health-topics/cardiovascular-diseases#tab=tab_1.

97. **Many of the well-known physiological effects**: Christian Hakulinen et al., "Social Isolation and Loneliness as Risk Factors for Myocardial Infarction, Stroke and Mortality: UK Biobank Cohort Study of 479,054 Men and Women," *Heart* 104, no. 18 (September 2018): 1536–42, https://pubmed.ncbi.nlm.nih.gov/29588329.

98. **A 2015 study of gene expression**: Steven W. Cole et al., "Myeloid Differentiation Architecture of Leukocyte Transcriptome Dynamics in Perceived Social Isolation," *Proceedings of the National Academy of Sciences* 112, no. 49 (2015): 15142–47, https://doi.org/10.1073/pnas.1514249112.

98. **In 2018, the American Heart Association**: Sheila M. Manemann et al., "Perceived Social Isolation and Outcomes in Patients with Heart Failure," *Journal of the American Heart Association* 7, no. 11 (2018): e008069, https://doi.org/10.1161/jaha.117.008069.

98. **A statement by the chair of the writing group**: American Heart Association, "Social Isolation and Loneliness Increase the Risk of Death from Heart Attack, Stroke," *ScienceDaily*, August 4, 2022, https://www.sciencedaily.com/releases/2022/08/220804102547.htm.

99. **(Patient-Reported Outcomes Measurement Information System)**: "Patient-Reported Outcomes Measurement Information System (PROMIS)," National Institute on Aging, accessed January 5, 2023, https://www.nia.nih.gov/research/resource/patient-reported-outcomes-measurement-information-system-promis.

99. **The PROMIS social isolation short form**: "PROMIS Short Form—Social Isolation 4a—Version 2.0," LOINC, accessed January 5, 2023, https://loinc.org/76801-0.

99. **The study's senior author, Lila Rutten:** "The Dangers of a Lonely Heart," American Heart Associaton News, May 23, 2018, https://www.heart.org/en /news/2018/05/29/the-dangers-of-a-lonely-heart.

100. **The famously cynical George Bernard Shaw:** "The Universal Regard for Money Is the One Hopeful Fact in Our Civilization," Quotefancy, accessed October 18, 2022, https://quotefancy.com/quote/812397/george-bernard-shaw -the-universal-regard-for-money-is-the-one-hopeful-fact-in-our.

100. **This economic argument:** David Frank, "The High Price of Social Isolation," AARP, November 29, 2017, https://www.aarp.org/health/medicare-insurance /info-2017/isolation-higher-medicare-fd.html.

100. **CareMore Health, a division of Anthem:** "CareMore Health Announces New Outcomes Data from First-of-Its-Kind Togetherness Program," Business Wire, December 18, 2018, https://www.businesswire.com/news/home/2018 1218005059/en/CareMore-Health-Announces-New-Outcomes-Data-from -First-of-its-Kind-Togetherness-Program.

101. **Psychotherapist Alisa Robinson describes:** Alisa Robinson, *The Loneliness Cure: How to Gain Connection and Fulfillment in a World of Isolation* (Los Gatos, CA: Smashwords, 2013).

102. **Mental Health America, a national advocacy group:** I learned these facts about Mental Health America from Patrick Hendry, who was MHA vice president of peer advocacy, supports, and services in 2021. He participated in an FAH webinar panel discussion of the film: Stefanie Abel Horowitz, Katy Wright-Mead, Patrick Hendry, and Jeremy Nobel, "Filmmaker Connect Series: Sometimes I Think About Dying," Project UnLonely and the Foundation for Art & Healing, webinar, streamed live on March 5, 2021, 56:29, https:// www.artandhealing.org/filmmaker-connect-series-sometimes-i-think-about -dying.

103. **More than thirty years ago, Dr. Matthew Budd:** Matthew has been a colleague of mine for many years. For more on this subject, I highly recommend his book: Matthew Budd and Larry Rothstein, *You Are What You Say: A Harvard Doctor's Six-Step Proven Program for Transforming Stress Through the Power of Language* (New York: Crown, 2000).

105. **"His scores for obsessions":** Thomas R. Insel, *Healing: Our Path from Mental Illness to Mental Health* (New York: Penguin Press, 2022).

107. **Other outcome measures:** US Department of Health and Human Services, "Measuring Healthy Days," Centers for Disease Control and Prevention, November 2000, https://www.cdc.gov/hrqol/pdfs/mhd.pdf.

110. **In its November 21, 1953 edition:** Helen Furnas, "I've Got the Lonesomest Disease!," *Saturday Evening Post*, November 21, 1953.

111. **Such "lonesome" diseases are categorized:** "Rare Diseases at FDA," US Food

and Drug Administration, last modified September 21, 2022, https://www
.fda.gov/patients/rare-diseases-fda.

111. **Patrick James Lynch was a twenty-one-year-old:** Yitzi Weiner, "Social Impact
Heroes: Why & How Patrick James Lynch of 'Believe Limited' Decided to
Change Our World," *Authority Magazine*, October 21, 2020, https://medium
.com/authority-magazine/social-impact-heroes-why-how-patrick-james
-lynch-of-believe-limited-decided-to-change-our-862bb52d703a.

113. **Drawing on their personal experiences:** Mary Chapman, "'Hemophilia: The
Musical' Lets Teens Confront Their Illness, and Educate Others, via Song,"
Hemophilia News Today, November 21, 2018, https://hemophilianewstoday
.com/2018/11/21/hemophilia-the-musical-lets-teens-confront-illness-educate
-others-via-song.

113. **I worry now about the loneliness experienced:** "Nearly One in Five American
Adults Who Have Had COVID-19 Still Have 'Long Covid,'" Centers for
Disease Control and Prevention, June 22, 2022, https://www.cdc.gov/nchs
/pressroom/nchs_press_releases/2022/20220622.htm.

113. **As a result, people with long COVID:** "Nearly One in Five American Adults
Who Have Had COVID-19.'"

114. **Until October 2021:** Leah J. McGrath et al., "Use of the Postacute Sequelae
of COVID-19 Diagnosis Code in Routine Clinical Practice in the US," *JAMA
Network Open* 5, no. 10 (2022): e2235089, https://jamanetwork.com/journals
/jamanetworkopen/fullarticle/2797042.

6: Aging

119. **Marinella Beretta's neighbors:** Clément Vérité, "An Italian Woman, 70, Found
Dead at Home 2 Years Later," *Newsendip*, February 8, 2022, https://www
.newsendip.com/marinella-beretta-an-italian-woman-found-at-home-2-years
-after-her-death.

120. **"What happened to Marinella Beretta":** Hada Messia, Sharon Braithwaite,
and Hannah Ryan, "Body of 70-Year-Old Italian Woman Found Sitting in
Chair, Two Years after Her Death," CNN, February 9, 2022, https://www.cnn
.com/2022/02/09/europe/italian-woman-two-years-dead-intl-scli/index.html.

120. **There had been a similar hue and cry:** Richard C. Keller, *Fatal Isolation: The Devastating Paris Heat Wave of 2003* (Chicago: University of Chicago Press, 2015).

120. **While the French government scrambled:** Keller, *Fatal Isolation*.

121. **Carla Perissinotto, a geriatrician:** "The Epidemic of Loneliness," Aspen
Ideas, June 25, 2017, https://www.aspenideas.org/sessions/the-epidemic-of
-loneliness.

121. **As author Philip Roth wrote:** "Everyman Quotes," Goodreads, accessed October 20, 2022, https://www.goodreads.com/work/quotes/14069-everyman.

124. **A 2012 study led by Carla Perissinotto:** Carla M. Perissinotto, Irena Stijacic Cenzer, and Kenneth E. Covinsky, "Loneliness in Older Persons: A Predictor of Functional Decline and Death," *Archives of Internal Medicine* 172, no. 14 (2012): 1078–84, https://jamanetwork.com/journals/jamainternalmedicine /fullarticle/1188033.

125. **A health and retirement survey:** A. Sutin et al., "Loneliness and Risk of Dementia," *Innovation in Aging* 2, suppl. 1 (2018): 966–97, https://doi.org /10.1093/geroni/igy031.3581.

125. **After a heat wave killed:** Jan C. Semenza et al., "Heat-Related Deaths During the July 1995 Heat Wave in Chicago," *New England Journal of Medicine* 335, no. 2 (1996): 84–90, https://doi.org/10.1056/nejm199607113350203.

126. **"Chicago's Latinos," Klinenberg explained:** "Dying Alone: An Interview with Eric Klinenberg," University of Chicago, 2002, https://press.uchicago.edu /Misc/Chicago/443213in.html.

126. **In his book *Heat Wave*:** Eric Klinenberg, *Heat Wave: A Social Autopsy of Disaster in Chicago* (Chicago: University of Chicago Press, 2015).

126. **The heat wave itself:** "Dying Alone."

126. **In 1999, another heat wave struck:** "Dying Alone."

127. **When the COVID-19 pandemic struck:** "Reflecting on Chicago's 1995 Heat Wave, COVID-19, and Housing Inequity," Elevate, July 14, 2020, https:// www.elevatenp.org/climate/blog-chicago-1995-heat-wave.

127. **In the United Kingdom:** Kate Jopling, *Promising Approaches Revisited: Effective Action on Loneliness in Later Life*, Campaign to End Loneliness, October 2020, https://www.campaigntoendloneliness.org/wp-content/uploads/Promising _Approaches_Revisited_FULL_REPORT.pdf.

128. **In 2017, CareMore:** Robin Caruso, "CareMore's Togetherness Program Addresses a Symptom of Living with Chronic Illness: Loneliness," *American Journal of Managed Care* (August 15, 2018), https://www.ajmc.com/view/caremores -togetherness-program-addresses-a-symptom-of-living-with-chronic-illness -loneliness.

128. **The greatest impact:** Sumathi Reddy, "The Goal: Longer Life with Less Loneliness," *Wall Street Journal*, April 28, 2018, https://www.wsj.com/articles/the -goal-longer-life-with-less-loneliness-1524913200.

129. **The aim of SCAN's Togetherness programs:** Anuja Vaidya, "SCAN Health's New Program to Tackle Senior Isolation Focuses on Connections with Peers," *MedCity News*, June 3, 2021, https://medcitynews.com/2021/06/scan-healths -new-program-to-tackle-senior-isolation-focuses-on-connections-with-peers.

129. **In 2017, SCAN sponsored a survey:** "SCAN's National Research Uncovers Solutions for Seniors Battling Isolation and Loneliness," Scan Health Plan, accessed October 20, 2022, https://www.scanhealthplan.com/about-scan/press -room/october-2017/scans-national-research-uncovers-solutions-for-seniors -battling-isolation-and-loneliness?scan_state=CA&.

139. **The CDC study of 1995 Chicago heat wave fatalities:** Semenza et al., "Heat-Related Deaths During the July 1995 Heat Wave in Chicago."

141. **Mickey had appeared in 1991:** "Forever Young: Music and Aging." Hearing Before the Special Committee on Aging, 102nd Cong. 102-9 (1991), https://www .aging.senate.gov/imo/media/doc/publications/811991.pdf.

141. **Oliver Sacks also testified at that hearing:** *Forever Young.*

142. **One early noteworthy example:** "The MoMA Alzheimer's Project," Museum of Modern Art, accessed October 20, 2022, https://www.moma.org/visit /accessibility/meetme.

142. **Then there is TimeSlips:** "Our Mission," TimeSlips, accessed October 20, 2022, https://www.timeslips.org.

143. **Studies of TimeSlips programs in nursing homes:** "What's the Latest on Why and How Creativity Works?," TimeSlips, accessed October 20, 2022, https:// www.timeslips.org/impact/research.

143. **A TimeSlips program offered:** Andrea Loizeau, Yvonne Kündig, and Sandra Oppikofer, "'Awakened Art Stories'—Rediscovering Pictures by Persons Living with Dementia Utilising TimeSlips: A Pilot Study," *Geriatric Mental Health Care* 3, no. 2 (2015): 13–20, https://doi.org/10.1016/j.gmhc.2015.10.001.

145. **Research shows that caregivers:** Christina R. Victor et al., "The Prevalence and Predictors of Loneliness in Caregivers of People with Dementia: Findings from the IDEAL Programme," *Aging & Mental Health* 25, no. 7 (2020): 1232–8, https://doi.org/10.1080/13607863.2020.1753014.

145. **Studies have also shown:** Christina M. Marini et al., "Marital Quality, Loneliness, and Depressive Symptoms Later in Life: The Moderating Role of Own and Spousal Functional Limitations," *Research in Human Development* 17, no. 4 (2020): 211–34, https://www.ncbi.nlm.nih.gov/pmc/articles/PMC8261617.

145. **Even in loving marriages:** Sherri L. Lavela and Nazneen Ather, "Psychological Health in Older Adult Spousal Caregivers of Older Adults," *Chronic Illness* 6, no. 1 (March 2010): 67–80, https://pubmed.ncbi.nlm.nih.gov/20308352.

146. **My colleague at Harvard, Arthur Kleinman:** Arthur Kleinman, *The Soul of Care: The Moral Education of a Husband and a Doctor* (New York: Penguin Books, 2020).

147. **Children's book author Maurice Sendak:** "Maurice Sendak: On Life, Death and Children's Lit," interview by Terry Gross, *Fresh Air*, NPR, December 29, 2011, https://www.npr.org/transcripts/144077273.

147. **In 2021, the American Psychiatric Association:** Ellen Barry, "How Long Should It Take to Grieve? Psychiatry Has Come Up with an Answer," *New York Times*, March 18, 2022, https://www.nytimes.com/2022/03/18/health /prolonged-grief-disorder.html.

147. **"If you've recently lost someone":** "APA Offers Tips for Understanding Prolonged Grief Disorder," American Psychiatric Association, accessed October 20, 2022, https://psychiatry.org/news-room/news-releases/apa-offers-tips-for -understanding-prolonged-grief.

148. **These are feelings that might be common:** Kristin L Szuhany et al., "Prolonged Grief Disorder: Course, Diagnosis, Assessment, and Treatment," *Focus* 19, no. 2 (2021): 161–72, https://doi.org/10.1176/appi.focus.20200052.

148. **It is estimated that as much:** Alison McCook, "Why Scientists Think the COVID Era Could Cause More Prolonged Grief," PBS, April 7, 2022, https:// www.pbs.org/newshour/health/why-scientists-think-the-covid-era-could -cause-more-prolonged-grief.

148. **By some estimates:** Lucy Lloyd, "A Silent Epidemic of Grief," University of Cambridge, accessed October 20, 2022, https://www.cam.ac.uk/stories /bereavement.

148. **In October 2020:** Naomi M. Simon, Glenn N. Saxe, and Charles R. Marmar, "Mental Health Disorders Related to COVID-19-Related Deaths," *JAMA* 324, no. 15 (2020): 1493–94, https://doi.org/10.1001/jama.2020.19632.

149. **Katherine Shear, a psychiatrist at Columbia:** Sharon Tregaskis, "When Time Doesn't Heal," *Columbia Medicine*, December 15, 2016, https://www.columbia medicinemagazine.org/features/fall-2016/when-time-doesnt-heal.

149. **In his final radio interview:** "Maurice Sendak: On Life, Death and Children's Lit."

7: Difference

153. *Don't Let Me Be Lonely* **explores the universal experience:** Claudia Rankine, *Don't Let Me Be Lonely: An American Lyric* (Minneapolis: Graywolf Press, 2004).

153. **Claudia won a MacArthur Foundation:** Claudia Rankine, *Citizen: An American Lyric* (Minneapolis: Graywolf Press, 2014).

154. **Students in college classes taught:** Peggy McIntosh, "White Privilege: Unpacking the Invisible Knapsack," *Peace and Freedom*, July/August 1989, https:// psychology.umbc.edu/wp-content/uploads/sites/57/2016/10/White-Privilege _McIntosh-1989.pdf.

155. **She went on to write a play:** Elizabeth Foster, "Claudia Rankine's Play *Help* at the Shed," Front Row Center, March 25, 2022, https://thefrontrowcenter.com /2022/03/claudia-rankines-play-help-at-the-shed.

162. **The truth finally came out in early 2022:** Meg James and Amy Kaufman, "Concerns About Bruce Willis' Declining Cognitive State Swirled Around Sets in Recent Years," *Los Angeles Times*, March 30, 2022, https://www.latimes .com/entertainment-arts/movies/story/2022-03-30/bruce-willis-aphasia -memory-loss-cognitive-disorder.

163. **That March, Willis's family:** Laura J. Nelson, Thomas Curwen, and Emily Baumgaertner, "Bruce Willis' Aphasia Battle: Living in a Country Where You Don't Speak the Language," *Los Angeles Times*, April 1, 2022, https://www .latimes.com/california/story/2022-04-01/bruce-willis-what-is-aphasia -symptoms-diagnosis-severity-treatment-caregivers.

165. **At DePaul University, Jaclyn Jensen:** Robin Florzak, "Scholar Studies Weight-Based Bullying at Work," Driehaus College of Business, DePaul University, March 5, 2018, https://business.depaul.edu/news-events/Pages/201803/jaclyn -jensen-workplace-harassment-research-depaul.aspx.

165. **Jensen's research showed that 80 percent:** Florzak, "Scholar Studies Weight-Based Bullying at Work."

166. **Sandra McPherson, one of three:** Curtis Bunn, "Why Most Black Office Workers Are Dreading the Return to Offices." *NBC News*, July 29, 2021, https://www.nbcnews.com/news/nbcblk/black-office-workers-are-dreading -return-offices-rcna1539.

166. **A 2021 survey by Future Forum:** Bunn, "Why Most Black Office Workers."

167. **On the other hand, white professionals:** "Winning the 'War for Talent' in the Post-Pandemic World," Future Forum by Slack, June 2021, https://futureforum .com/wp-content/uploads/2021/06/Future-Forum-Pulse-Whitepaper-June -2021-1.pdf.

167. **When *The Huffington Post* reported on these findings:** Monica Torres, "Office Culture Is So Unwelcoming to Black Employees, They Don't Want to Go Back," *HuffPost*, June 17, 2021, https://www.huffpost.com/entry/black -workers-prefer-remote-work-racist-office_1_60c8f805e4b0f7e7ccf59fa1.

168. **Thema Reed, the New Mexico–born daughter:** Vox First Person, "The Loneliness of Being Mixed Race in America," Vox, January 18, 2021, https://www .vox.com/first-person/21734156/kamala-harris-mixed-race-biracial-multi racial.

171. **Studies of loneliness show:** "Loneliness and Social Isolation Linked to Serious Health Conditions," Centers for Disease Control and Prevention, last modified September 7, 2022, https://tools.cdc.gov/medialibrary/index.aspx?mediaType =eCard&displayName=eCards#/media/id/406617.

171. **There are particularly high levels of loneliness:** Vox First Person, "The Loneliness of Being Mixed Race in America."

171. **For individuals who are from immigrant families:** Tim Chau, "Filmmaker

Connect Series: *Share*," Foundation for Art & Healing, https://www.artand
healing.org/filmmaker-connect-series-share.

171. **This is a case in which intersecting identities:** Kimberlé Crenshaw, "Mapping
the Margins: Intersectionality, Identity Politics, and Violence Against Women
of Color," *Stanford Law Review* 43, no. 6 (1991): 1241–99, https://doi.org
/10.2307/1229039.

171. **"Intersectionality is a lens":** "Kimberlé Crenshaw on Intersectionality, More
than Two Decades Later," Columbia Law School, June 8, 2017, https://www
.law.columbia.edu/news/archive/kimberle-crenshaw-intersectionality-more
-two-decades-later.

175. **Leaders of the Catholic Church:** *Encyclopædia Britannica*, s.v. "excommunica-
tion," last modified May 25, 2022, https://www.britannica.com/topic/excom
munication.

175. **To this day, social shunning is how:** "Why Do the Amish Practice Shunning?,"
Amish America, accessed October 20, 2022, https://amishamerica.com/why
-do-the-amish-practice-shunning.

176. **The #MeToo movement began:** Jodi Kantor and Megan Twohey, "How to
Measure the Impact of #MeToo?," *New York Times*, October 3, 2022, https://
www.nytimes.com/interactive/2022/10/03/us/me-too-five-years.html.

176. **A comprehensive 2018 report:** Audrey Carlsen et al., "#MeToo Brought down
201 Powerful Men. Nearly Half of Their Replacements Are Women," *New
York Times*, October 29, 2018, https://www.nytimes.com/interactive/2018/10
/23/us/metoo-replacements.html.

176. **In fact, when Western governments:** Natasha Turak, "Goodbye, American
Soft Power: McDonald's Exiting Russia After 32 Years Is the End of an Era,"
CNBC, May 25, 2022, https://www.cnbc.com/2022/05/20/mcdonalds-exiting
-russia-after-32-years-is-the-end-of-an-era.html.

177. **When author J. K. Rowling:** Christopher Luu, "The 'Harry Potter' Fandom
Officially Canceled J. K. Rowling," *InStyle*, July 2, 2020, https://www.instyle
.com/celebrity/harry-potter-fansites-no-longer-support-jk-rowling.

177. **In 2020 comedian and former *America's Got Talent* TV host:** Christie D'Zurilla,
"Nick Cannon Wants 'Counsel Culture,' Not Cancel Culture, After Anti-
Semitic Remarks," *Los Angeles Times*, March 16, 2021, https://www.latimes
.com/entertainment-arts/tv/story/2021-03-16/nick-cannon-antisemitism
-apology.

178. **Loretta Ross, who teaches at Smith College:** "Calling Out vs. Calling In:
Loretta Ross Offers a Different Response to Campus Cancel Culture," Center
on Religion and Culture, posted April 12, 2021, YouTube video, 1:31:31,
https://www.youtube.com/watch?v=jKCXCpVYiww.

179. **Loretta's talk recorded at TEDx Monterey:** Loretta J. Ross, "Don't Call Peo-

ple Out—Call Them In," filmed August 2021 in Monterey, California, TED video, 14:05, https://www.ted.com/talks/loretta_j_ross_don_t_call_people _out_call_them_in/transcript.

8: Modernity's Divide

181. **In Alaska's Katmai National Park:** Mark Kaufman, "The Fat Bear Week Winner Is the Champion We All Needed," Mashable, October 5, 2021, https:// mashable.com/article/fat-bear-week-2021-champion-otis.

182. **Naomi believes we get a kind of vicarious thrill:** Yereth Rosen, "Ahead of Winter Hibernation, Alaska Celebrates Fat Bear Week," Reuters, September 28, 2021, https://www.reuters.com/lifestyle/ahead-winter-hibernation-alaska -celebrates-fat-bear-week-2021-09-28.

183. **Around the same time of Fat Bear Week 2021:** David Gilbert, "Inside the QAnon Cult That Believes JFK Is About to Return," *Vice*, November 12, 2021, https://www.vice.com/en/article/m7vaw4/qanon-jfk-dallas-protzman.

184. **By then Maureen had run out of money:** David Gilbert, "Meet the Antisemitic QAnon Leader Who Led Followers to Dallas to Meet JFK," *Vice*, November 5, 2021, https://www.vice.com/en/article/g5qpe7/qanon-dallas-jfk-michael -brian-protzman-negative48.

185. **"What drew me in was an opportunity":** Gilbert, "Inside the QAnon Cult."

185. **"We are imprisoned by our technology":** Giles Slade, *The Big Disconnect: The Story of Technology and Loneliness* (Amherst, NY: Prometheus Books, 2012).

187. **For example, Bauman described:** Ricardo de Querol, "Zygmunt Bauman: 'Social Media Are a Trap,'" *El País*, January 25, 2016, https://english.elpais.com /elpais/2016/01/19/inenglish/1453208692_424660.html.

191. **In 2013, researchers at the University of Virginia:** Matthew Hutson, "People Prefer Electric Shocks to Being Alone with Their Thoughts," *Atlantic*, July 3, 2014, https://www.theatlantic.com/health/archive/2014/07/people-prefer -electric-shocks-to-being-alone-with-their-thoughts/373936.

192. **"Most people seem to prefer":** Timothy D. Wilson et al., "Just Think: The Challenges of the Disengaged Mind," *Science* 345, no. 6192 (July 2014): 75–77, https://www.ncbi.nlm.nih.gov/pmc/articles/PMC4330241.

192. **Alan Lightman, a world-class physicist:** "In Praise of Wasting Time with MIT Professor Alan Lightman," April 14, 2019, in *Slice of MIT*, podcast, 32:56, transcript, https://alum.mit.edu/sites/default/files/2019-04/Slice_of _MIT_Podcast_Lightman_Transcript.pdf.

193. **"We're losing our ability to know":** Carrie M. King, "Alan Lightman: Outside The Book—Transcript," *Blinkist Magazine*, March 21, 2019, https://www .blinkist.com/magazine/posts/alan-lightman-outside-the-book-transcript.

193. **Psychologist Kyung Hee Kim:** Kyung Hee Kim, "The Creativity Crisis: The Decrease in Creative Thinking Scores on the Torrance Tests of Creative Thinking," *Creativity Research Journal* 23, no. 4 (2011): 285–95, https://doi.org /10.1080/10400419.2011.627805.

194. **When her study was published:** Rachael Rettner, "Not Your Imagination: Kids Today Really Are Less Creative, Study Says," *Today*, August 12, 2011, https:// www.today.com/parents/not-your-imagination-kids-today-really-are-less -creative-study-wbna44122383.

194. **It may be a coincidence:** Jean M. Twenge, "Have Smartphones Destroyed a Generation?," *Atlantic*, September 2017, https://www.theatlantic.com /magazine/archive/2017/09/has-the-smartphone-destroyed-a-generation /534198.

194. **In the decade preceding the pandemic:** Twenge, "Have Smartphones Destroyed a Generation?"

195. **One experiment published in 2018:** Melissa G. Hunt et al., "No More FOMO: Limiting Social Media Decreases Loneliness and Depression," *Journal of Social and Clinical Psychology* 37, no. 10 (2018): 751–68, https://doi.org/10.1521 /jscp.2018.37.10.751.

196. **"He was so addicted to it":** Samantha Murphy Kelly, "Their Teenage Children Died by Suicide. Now These Families Want to Hold Social Media Companies Accountable," CNN, April 19, 2022, https://www.cnn.com/2022/04/19/tech /social-media-lawsuits-teen-suicide/index.html.

196. **In 2022, one law firm filed eight lawsuits:** Malathi Nayak, "Meta Hit with Eight Suits Claiming Its Algorithms Hook Youth and Ruin Their Lives," *Spokesman-Review*, June 8, 2022, https://www.spokesman.com/stories/2022 /jun/08/meta-hit-with-eight-suits-claiming-its-algorithms-.

197. **Leaked documents from Meta show:** Georgia Wells, Jeff Horwitz, and Deepa Seetharaman, "Facebook Knows Instagram Is Toxic for Teen Girls, Company Documents Show," *Wall Street Journal*, September 14, 2021, https://www.wsj .com/articles/facebook-knows-instagram-is-toxic-for-teen-girls-company -documents-show-11631620739.

197. **"Social comparison is worse on Instagram":** Wells, Horwitz, and Seetharaman, "Facebook Knows Instagram Is Toxic."

197. **Studies have since shown there are developmental windows:** Amy Orben et al., "Windows of Developmental Sensitivity to Social Media," *Nature Communications* 13, no. 1 (2022): 1649, https://www.nature.com/articles/s41467 -022-29296-3.

197. **Emma Lembke was just twelve:** Julie Halpert, "A New Student Movement Wants You to Log Off," *New York Times*, June 15, 2022, https://www.nytimes .com/2022/06/14/style/log-off-movement-emma-lembke.html.

198. **Prominent members of the tech industry:** Anita Balakrishnan, "Facebook Should Be Regulated like a Cigarette Company, Says Salesforce CEO," CNBC, January 23, 2018, https://www.cnbc.com/2018/01/23/salesforce-ceo -marc-benioff-says-regulate-facebook-like-tobacco.html.

198. **Meanwhile, Emma still struggles:** "The 19-Year-Old Helping Gen Z Log Off," July 2, 2022, in *Offline with Jon Favreau*, Crooked Media podcast, 42:32, https://crooked.com/podcast/the-19-year-old-helping-gen-z-log-off.

198. **An influential study led by Emily K. Lindsay:** Emily K. Lindsay et al., "Mindfulness Training Reduces Loneliness and Increases Social Contact in a Randomized Controlled Trial," *Proceedings of the National Academy of Sciences* 116, no. 9 (2019): 3488–93, https://doi.org/10.1073/pnas.1813588116.

201. **Arthur C. Brooks, an author who:** Arthur C. Brooks, "How Social Distancing Could Ultimately Teach Us How to Be Less Lonely," *Washington Post*, March 20, 2020, https://www.washingtonpost.com/opinions/how-social-distancing -could-ultimately-teach-us-how-to-be-less-lonely/2020/03/20/ca459804-694e -11ea-9923-57073adce27c_story.html.

201. **"Make a house rule":** Brooks, "How Social Distancing Could Ultimately Teach Us."

202. **Rigid frameworks, as T. S. Eliot once remarked:** "When Forced to Work Within a Strict Framework, the Imagination Is Taxed to Its Utmost and Will Produce Its Richest Ideas," Quotefancy, accessed October 18, 2022, https:// quotefancy.com/quote/914665/T-S-Eliot-When-forced-to-work-within-a -strict-framework-the-imagination-is-taxed-to-its.

202. **"Love and work," Freud wrote:** "Sigmund Freud Quotes," BrainyQuote, accessed October 18, 2022, https://www.brainyquote.com/quotes/sigmund _freud_165464.

203. **Surveys have shown that approximately three in ten:** Monica Anderson, Emily A. Vogels, and Erica Turner, "The Virtues and Downsides of Online Dating," Pew Research Center, February 6, 2020, https://www.pewresearch .org/internet/2020/02/06/the-virtues-and-downsides-of-online-dating.

203. **With those who are LGBTQ:** Emily A. Vogels, "10 Facts About Americans and Online Dating," Pew Research Center, February 6, 2020, https://www .pewresearch.org/fact-tank/2020/02/06/10-facts-about-americans-and -online-dating.

203. **About 45 percent of dating app users:** Monica Anderson and Emily A. Vogels, "Young Women Often Face Sexual Harassment Online—Including on Dating Sites and Apps," Pew Research Center, March 6, 2020, https:// www.pewresearch.org/fact-tank/2020/03/06/young-women-often-face-sexual -harassment-online-including-on-dating-sites-and-apps.

204. **A survey of users of Tinder:** Mike Brown, "Is Tinder a Match for Millennials?," LendEDU, April 6, 2020, https://lendedu.com/blog/tinder-match-millennials.

204. **When writer Nancy Jo Sales:** Nancy Jo Sales, "Swipe Right for Loneliness: On the Gamification of Dating Apps," Lit Hub, June 1, 2021, https://lithub.com/swipe-right-for-loneliness-on-the-gamification-of-dating-apps.

204. **Sales noted that some people:** Sales, "Swipe Right for Loneliness."

205. **Dating apps are so addictive:** Christina Majaski, "1 in 4 People Use Dating Apps to Cheat, Says Study," AskMen, July 24, 2019, https://www.askmen.com/news/dating/1-in-4-people-use-dating-apps-to-cheat-says-study.html.

205. **Dating coach and author Jess McCann:** Caroline Colvin, "If Dating Apps Make You Feel Lonelier Than Ever, Do This," *Elite Daily*, June 17, 2020, https://www.elitedaily.com/p/if-dating-apps-make-you-feel-lonely-heres-what-experts-suggest-22882814#:~:text=one%20small%20way%20to%20begin,amount%20of%20time%20for%20swiping.

205. **The algorithms behind the apps:** James Bloodworth, "How Dating Apps Are Reshaping Our Desires for the Worse," *New Statesman*, April 27, 2021, https://www.newstatesman.com/science-tech/2021/04/how-dating-apps-are-reshaping-our-desires-worse.

205. **Black women, Asian men, and short men:** Bloodworth, "How Dating Apps Are Reshaping Our Desires."

206. **An extensive 2021 study:** Monica Anderson et al., "The State of Gig Work in 2021," Pew Research Center, December 8, 2021, https://www.pewresearch.org/internet/2021/12/08/the-state-of-gig-work-in-2021.

207. **Researchers who have studied incel:** Kayla Preston, Michael Halpin, and Finlay Maguire, "The Black Pill: New Technology and the Male Supremacy of Involuntarily Celibate Men," *Men and Masculinities* 24, no. 5 (2021): 823–41, https://doi.org/10.1177/1097184x211017954.

207. **Men espousing incel beliefs:** Preston, Halpin, and Maguire, "The Black Pill."

207. **In January 2021, a Reddit user named Ben:** Bethan Kapur, "How I Stopped Being an Incel and Started Loving Myself," *Vice*, January 4, 2021, https://www.vice.com/en/article/5dpyaa/how-to-stop-being-an-incel.

208. **The excerpts *Vice* published:** Kapur, "How I Stopped Being an Incel."

210. **Adam Lanza's young life:** Rick Rojas and Kristin Hussey, "Newly Released Documents Detail Sandy Hook Shooter's Troubled State of Mind," *New York Times*, December 10, 2018, https://www.nytimes.com/2018/12/10/nyregion/documents-sandy-hook-shooter.html.

210. **On the weekday morning he chose to die in infamy:** Josh Kovner and Dave Altimari, "Courant Exclusive: More Than 1,000 Pages of Documents Reveal

Sandy Hook Shooter Adam Lanza's Dark Descent into Depravity," *Hartford Courant*, December 9, 2018, https://www.courant.com/news/connecticut /hc-news-sandy-hook-lanza-new-documents-20181204-story.html.

211. **"There's this really consistent pathway"**: Melanie Warner, "Two Professors Found What Creates a Mass Shooter. Will Politicians Pay Attention?," *Politico*, May 27, 2022, https://www.politico.com/news/magazine/2022/05/27/stop ping-mass-shooters-q-a-00035762.

212. **In February 2018, shortly after:** Sarah Gray, "'I Was Almost a School Shooter': Man Pens Heartfelt Letter About Mental Health and Guns," *Time*, February 20, 2018, https://time.com/5167365/i-was-almost-a-school-shooter-man-pens -heartfelt-letter-about-mental-health-and-guns.

212. **In 2022, Aaron appeared on CNN:** "Man Who Said He Was 'Almost a School Shooter' Reveals What Stopped Him," CNN video, 4:48, July 9, 2022, https:// www.cnn.com/videos/us/2022/07/09/aaron-stark-mass-shooter-mindset -mental-health-advocate-brown-nr-vpx.cnn.

213. **The key, he says with great eloquence:** Aaron Stark, "I Was Almost a School Shooter: Aaron Stark: TEDxBoulder," filmed June 2018 in Boulder, CO, TED video, 7:29, https://www.ted.com/talks/aaron_stark_i_was_almost_a _school_shooter.

213. **"If you see someone who's in that spot":** Aaron Stark, "CNN Newsroom Inter-view 7/9/22," posted July 9, 2022, YouTube video, 11:07, https://www.youtube .com/watch?v=BocNShTui3I.

214. **"You have done something":**Michael Sheetz, "William Shatner Emotionally Describes Spaceflight to Jeff Bezos: 'The Most Profound Experience,'" CNBC, October 13, 2021, https://www.cnbc.com/2021/10/13/william-shatner-speech -to-jeff-bezos-after-blue-origin-launch.html.

215. **Way back in 1902:** William James, "The Varieties of Religious Experience II," Authorama, accessed October 18, 2022, http://www.authorama.com/varieties -of-religious-experience-ii-1.html.

215. **Philosophy professor Helen De Cruz:** Helen De Cruz, "The Necessity of Awe," Aeon, July 10, 2020, https://aeon.co/essays/how-awe-drives-scientists-to-make -a-leap-into-the-unknown.

215. **The boxer Muhammad Ali:** "Muhammad Ali > Quotes," Goodreads, ac-cessed January 6, 2023, https://www.goodreads.com/author/quotes/46261 .Muhammad_Ali.

215. **One study of fifteen hundred people:** Paul Piff and Dacher Keltner, "Why Do We Experience Awe?," *New York Times*, May 22, 2015, https://www.nytimes .com/2015/05/24/opinion/sunday/why-do-we-experience-awe.html.

216. **On the globe, he painted:** Jeff Lunden, "Oliver Jeffers' Out-of-This-World Art Installation Takes You Far from Earth," NPR, January 27, 2019, https://

www.npr.org/2019/01/27/689121264/oliver-jeffers-out-of-this-world-art
-installation-takes-you-far-from-earth.

216. **Jeffers said, "This is the beautiful, fragile drama":** Manoush Zomorodi, "Oliver Jeffers: An Ode to Living on Earth," NPR, May 22, 2020, https://www
.npr.org/transcripts/860144962.

217. **"Everybody in the world needs to do this":** "William Shatner Speech After Blue Origin Space Flight Transcript," Rev, October 13, 2021, https://www.rev
.com/blog/transcripts/william-shatner-speech-after-blue-origin-space-flight
-transcript.

217. **Shipments of VR headsets:** Phil Hayton, "Oculus Quest 2 Sales Jump Ahead of Xbox Series X and Series S," *PCGamesN*, June 8, 2022, https://www.pcgamesn
.com/oculus/quest-2-meta-sales-xbox-series-x-s.

218. **A small 2022 experiment:** Rhiannon Williams, "Patients Immersed in Virtual Reality During Surgery May Need Less Anesthetic," *MIT Technology Review*, September 21, 2022, https://www.technologyreview.com/2022/09/21/1059869
/patients-virtual-reality-surgery-anesthetic.

9: A Call to Connect

228. **already a global leader in arts and health:** "Arts and Health," World Health Organization, accessed January 6, 2023, https://www.who.int/initiatives/arts
-and-health.

230. **In 2016, the Montreal Museum of Fine Arts:** Alexia Jacques-Casanova, "Museum Therapy," LinkedIn, March 20, 2019, https://www.linkedin.com
/pulse/museum-therapy-alexia-jacques-casanova.

231. **The committee has more than a dozen:** "MMFA Museum Visits to Be Prescribed by Doctors," *Suburban*, October 15, 2018, https://www.thesuburban
.com/arts_and_entertainment/arts/mmfa-museum-visits-to-be-prescribed-by
-doctors/article_faf20186-cfd0-11e8-be31-a7674e5fed0e.html.

237. **The Administration for Community Living:** "Commit to Connect," Administration for Community Living, last modified December 6, 2021, https://acl
.gov/committoconnect.

237. **"up to 10 million socially-isolated adults":** Administration for Community Living, "ACL Seeks Solutions to Match People to Resources for Staying Connected and Engaged," news release, last modified October 28, 2020, https://
acl.gov/mental.

239. **"Anything you can imagine":** "Pablo Picasso Quotes," BrainyQuote, accessed October 18, 2022, https://www.brainyquote.com/quotes/pablo_picasso_107497.

239. **"Logic will get you":** "Albert Einstein Quotes," BrainyQuote, accessed October 18, 2022, https://www.brainyquote.com/quotes/albert_einstein_121643.

INDEX

Index

Index